Method in Social Science

In its second edition, *Method in Social Science* was widely praised for its penetrating analysis of central questions in social science discourse. This revised edition contains a new preface with suggestions for further readings and a bibliography. The book is intended for students and researchers familiar with social science but having little or no previous experiences of philosophical and methodological discussion, and for those who are interested in realism and method.

Andrew Sayer is Professor of Social Theory and Political Economy at Lancaster University. He has a longstanding interest in philosophical issues relating to social science, but has always combined this with research on substantive issues – primarily to do with political economy and inequality. His other books include *The New Social Division of Labor*, with R.A. Walker (Blackwell, 1992); *Realism and Social Science* (Sage, 2000); and *The Moral Significance of Class* (Cambridge University Press, 2005).

Method in Social Science
A realist approach

Revised Second Edition

Andrew Sayer

Routledge
Taylor & Francis Group

LONDON AND NEW YORK

First published in 1984 by Hutchinson

Second edition published in 1992
by Routledge

Reprinted 1999 and 2000

Revised second edition published 2010
by Routledge
2 Park Square, Milton Park, Abingdon, Oxon, OX14 4RN

Simultaneously published in the USA and Canada
by Routledge
270 Madison Avenue, New York, NY 10016

Routledge is an imprint of the Taylor & Francis Group, an informa business

British Library Cataloguing in Publication Data
A catalogue record for this book is available from the British Library

Library of Congress Cataloging in Publication Data
Sayer, R. Andrew.
Method in social science / by Andrew Sayer.—Rev. 2nd ed.
p. cm.
Includes bibliographical references and index.
1. Social sciences—Methodology.   I. Title.
H61.S353 2010
300.72—dc22
2009049685

ISBN: 978–0–415–58247–6 (hbk)
ISBN: 978–0–415–58159–2 (pbk)
ISBN: 978–0–203–85037–4 (ebk)

Contents

Preface to the revised second edition

When I was writing the first edition of *Method* back in the early eighties, it was a time of great interest in the philosophy and methodology of social science; indeed, surprising though it may seem now, it was actually a fashionable topic, and there was a steady stream of books on the subject. Where most of these were primarily critical reviews of established philosophical ideas about social science, its nature and methods, *Method* sought to be constructive and suggest how we should approach social research, instead of merely presenting a critique of others' ideas. Where others presented 'toolkits of research methods' without problematising their presuppositions or considering how we conceptualise and theorise in social research, I saw such matters as fundamental. Where other books seemed to be written for peers and potential reviewers, I wanted to write for students and researchers. As the continued use of the book after 25 years shows, the recipe seems to have worked. Apart from a few minor corrections, I have not changed the text of this edition from that of the last. Of course, much has been written on the topic since then, and so I shall use this opportunity to suggest some further reading here. But first, I want to make some general points about 'method'.

Since the previous editions there has been a growth in some quarters of scepticism about the very idea of prescribing research methods. Surely there isn't a method for doing social research? Surely how we research something will depend on the subject and what we want to find out? Surely no method can give us 'a royal road to truth'? Of course there isn't a single method. If I thought there was, I would have called the book, '*The* Method *of* Social Science'. I also use 'method' in the broad sense of 'approach'. What I argue is exactly that there are many methods or approaches, each having particular strengths and weaknesses, each appropriate for different objects and research questions, and that many research projects will require combinations of them. We also need to think about what is involved in theorising, and recognise that metaphor plays a major role in scientific theories and descriptions, that creativity is needed to find successively better metaphors, and that the interpretation of meaning in society is central to social research. But while all of these are necessary, there is no substitute for attentiveness to the object of study. Although we inevitably have to use existing ways of thinking to interpret our object, and while it usually pays to stand on the shoulders of earlier writers, attentiveness to the object and careful description, coupled with reflexivity about *how* we attend to the world, are vital. Hence not everything about method can be codified.

My colleague John Law recently published a book called *After Method*, in which he argues that the messiness of the social world is such that formal methods and theories have only limited application in many kinds of social research (Law 2004). To some extent I agree. One of the great myths of modernism is that all knowledge can be reduced to laws and that any other kind of knowledge is inferior and dispensible. This belief in formal rationality and a standardised method suitable for all subject matters reached its apogee in social science in positivism in the 1960s and has been in slow decline ever since. As critical realists have shown, that model isn't even appropriate for natural science, let alone social science, for the world is open, and qualitative change, variation and different degrees of irregularity are normal. And as Aristotle argued over two millennia ago, in addition to theoretical knowledge we also need knowledge of particulars, which generally comes from experience and practical involvement. Aristotle also warned students not to expect more precision than the subject allows. Some subjects are fuzzy and continually changing; where there are gradations there is no point in rendering them as sharp steps. We live in a world of similarities and differences, stability and change, structures, order and mess, necessity and contingency. Often our more abstract, 'thin' concepts will identify certain basic common features of particular kinds of society, but to apply them to concrete situations we are likely to need to move to more concrete, thicker concepts, and to use 'thick description'. Sometimes we will need to forge new concepts to deal with novel developments. Hence, conceptualisation, the move from abstract to concrete, and the relation of theory to empirics remain central issues in social scientific methodology.

Of course, social science, like natural science, cannot provide 'a royal road to truth'. No matter how well chosen our methods may be, our ways of thinking may still let us down. Knowledge is fallible, that is, capable of being mistaken about its object. The truth or adequacy of our ideas is a practical matter, and something that we can try to improve. To be sure, we can only know things through existing ways of seeing, and can never escape from these and get 'sideways on' to see how our ideas compare with the world. Nevertheless, in many cases, we can still register counter-evidence to our beliefs, as when our expectations fail to anticipate what happens, or when we crash into something. That the revised ideas that might be developed in response to such failures are in principle fallible too doesn't mean there can be no progress. For example, feminist social science has continually revised its claims, but this does not mean it has merely trodden water. It is precisely through continual empirical and theoretical assessment and critique that it has come to enable us to see many things that pre-feminist social science did not, and hence contributed to the development of more true or adequate accounts of society. The most simple and basic idea of realism is that the nature of the world is largely independent of an observer's ideas about it, and it is this that explains both the adequacy and fallibility of our knowledge, such as it is. Whether climate change is happening or not does not depend on my views on the matter. Neoconservatism is a social construction, shaped by the ideas of its founders, but it is not *my* construction and I seem to have failed to make any difference to it. It is whatever it is regardless of what I think, and hence my beliefs about it may be more or less true. Violence against women has clearly been influenced by ideas about women and men and what is legitimate in society at large, but it is not merely a product of an observer's view on the matter; many people do not realise how common it is. If there were no objective situation about which we could be mistaken, then we could just make up any ideas, and they would be infallible; Holocaust denial would be as good as Holocaust confirmation. Realism does not, as many imagine, involve a claim that we can achieve absolute, infallible knowledge. On the contrary, realism and fallibilism presuppose one another. Progress towards greater truth or practical adequacy is possible, but we should not expect perfection, whatever that might mean.

When research students ask me what theories and research methods they should use in interpreting their chosen topic, I generally say *use all you know* – not only the theories and methods you have learned in your subject, but what you know from your experience. Theories are selective, one-sided, highlighting particular structures and properties; that is their strength, but also their weakness. Further, not all theories relating to a particular topic are direct rivals, but may be partially complementary, so it generally pays to be open to this possibility and to compare different theories and perspectives, although we must also beware of combining ideas that contradict one another. To be sure, everyday knowledge and experience are frequently unexamined, and sometimes misleading, but while they therefore need to be treated with caution, we should beware of the kind of theoreticist elitism that dismisses them in advance as worthless and ideological. Their richness and practical versatility can make them a useful source of insights. For some topics, there may even be works of fiction and literature that provide useful insights, especially into the nature of subjective experience, though of course their appropriateness would have to be assessed in relation to the subject matter (Stones 1996).

There is one fundamental feature of the social world that *Method* and subsequent writing on critical realism – and philosophy of social science more generally – has not addressed. This concerns the model of human beings that social science either explicitly or implicitly assumes. One of the distinctive features of critical realism is that it combines two models that have often been imagined to be not merely different but incompatible – the human being as causal agent, who makes things happen, the other as 'meaning maker', who interprets the world in innumerable ways. However, although this is an improvement on approaches which assume that we have to choose between these models, it still fails to confront our nature as human animals, that is, beings who have continually to reproduce our conditions of life to survive, *and who are capable of flourishing and suffering*. We might call this, for want of a better term, a 'needs-based conception of social being' and action, viewing people not only as causal agents and as self-interpreting, meaning makers, but as needy, desiring beings (characterized by deficiency), dependent on others, having an orientation to the world of care and concern. 'Needs' here is used as a shorthand that also covers lack, wants and desire, and includes what might be termed 'culturally acquired or emergent needs' deriving from involvement in and commitment to specific cultural practices, such as the need of the religious to worship. Certainly needs and wants may sometimes be fulfilled or satiated, whether through effort or luck, and they can change, so that we can come to want and enjoy things we previously did not, but neediness in this broad sense is fundamental to us as both biological and cultural beings. Failure to acknowledge human neediness and vulnerability invites misattributions of causality or responsibility, so that, for example, discourses are treated as capable *on their own* of motivating people. Hermeneutics enables us to view people as meaning makers, but not to understand what it is about them that makes anything matter to them. People do not merely have causal powers, like other objects, or indeed understandings, but have a relation to the world of concern, in virtue of their neediness, vulnerability and dependence.

The treatment of meaning within the needs-based model goes beyond that of hermeneutic approaches in that it deals not only with signifiers and the signified, shared understandings and rule-following, but *significance* or *import*. This is what people refer to when they talk about 'what something means to them', such as what their friends mean to them or what it means to be an immigrant (Sayer 2006). In such cases, they are not merely giving a definition of those things or necessarily a thick description, but an indication of their import or significance for them, how they value them, how such things impact on their well-being or other things that they care about (Taylor 1985). Thus an ethnographic study might explain, in a matter-of-fact way, how the members of a certain group understand and act towards each other in terms of meanings primarily as conventions or shared interpretations, but give little indication of just why some things have particular import or significance for actors, that is, how they affect things they care about. To the extent that many social scientific accounts ignore this they fail to give an adequate impression of what social life is like from the inside. As I have argued elsewhere, they produce an alienated social science (Sayer 2005; 2009). This is one of the outstanding problems that philosophy and social science have to face.

Further reading

Much has been written on realism and method in social science since the second edition. Some of this literature addresses rival approaches such as post-structuralism, post-modernism and the turn to discourse, debating to what extent they are compatible with realism (e.g. López and Potter 2001; Pearce and Fauley 2008; Joseph and Roberts 2003). My own *Realism and Social Science* (Sayer 2000) deals with broader issues than *Method*, including responses to post-modernism, discussions of space, narrative and social theory, values in social science and critical social science. Theories of the relation between structure and agency have been extensively debated, with key contributions from Margaret Archer, Rob Stones and Dave Elder-Vass (Archer, 1995, 2000, and 2003; Elder-Vass 2005, 2008; Stones, 1996).

There have been many books and articles on 'using' realism in particular social sciences and research fields. In addition to Danermark *et al.*'s book on explanation (Danermark *et al.* 1997), there are collections covering several disciplines (Cruickshank 2003; Carter and New 2004), and publications on realism in relation to anthropology (Davies 2008), discourse analysis (Fairclough *et al.* 2003), economics (Lawson 1997; Fleetwood 1998) feminism (New 1998, 2003, 2005), international relations (Patomaki 2001), law (Norrie 2009), organizational studies (Fleetwood and Ackroyd 2004), political economy (Jessop 2005), psychology (Parker 1999), and sociology (New 1995). Others have written on realism in relation to more specific theories and topics, such as Marxism (Brown *et al.* 2001), concepts of nature (Benton 1993), the political theory of hegemony (Joseph 2002), 'race' (Carter 2000), quantitative methods (Morgan and Olsen 2005) and health research (Clark *et al.* 2007). This is only a small sample of a rapidly growing literature. Wherever readers are located in social science, they should be able to find discussions of critical realism that relate to their interests

At a more philosophical level, discussions continue on basic arguments of critical realism, such as objectivity and values (Collier 1994, 2003), causality (Groff 2008), new topics such as ethics (Collier 1999; Norrie 2009), and the later work of Roy Bhaskar, the main founder of critical realism. The International Association for Critical Realism and its *Journal of Critical Realism* provides a forum for many of these debates (see also Archer *et al.* 1998).

References

Archer, M.S. (1995) *Realist Social Theory: The Morphogenetic Approach*, Cambridge: Cambridge University Press.

Archer, M.S. (2000) *Being Human*, Cambridge: Cambridge University Press.

Archer, M.S. (2003) *Structure, Agency and the Internal Conversation*, Cambridge: Cambridge University Press.

Archer, M.S., Bhaskar, R., Collier, A., Lawson, T. and Norrie, A. (eds). (1998) *Critical Realism: Essential Readings*, London: Routledge.

Benton, T. (1993) *Natural Relations*, London: Verso.

Brown, A., Fleetwood, S. and Roberts, J.R. (2001) *Critical Realism and Marxism*, London: Routledge.

Carter, B. (2000) *Realism and Racism*, London: Routledge.

Carter, B. and New, C. (2004) *Making Realism Work*, London: Routledge.

Clark, M., MacIntyre, P.D. and Cruickshank, J. (2007) 'A critical realist approach to understanding and evaluating heart health programmes' *Health*, 11:4, 513–39.

Collier, A. (1994) *Critical Realism: An Introduction*, London: Verso.

Collier, A. (1999) *Being and Worth*, London: Routledge.

Collier, A. 2003 *In Defence of Objectivity*, London: Routledge.

Cruickshank, J. (ed) 2003 *Critical Realism: The Difference it Makes*, London: Routledge.

Davies, C.A. (2008) *Reflexive Ethnography*, London: Routledge.

Danermark, B., Ekström, M., Jakobsen, L. and Karlsson, J.C. (1997) *Explaining Society: Critical Realism in the Social Sciences*, London: Routledge.

Elder-Vass, D. (2005). 'Emergence and the realist account of cause', *Journal of Critical Realism*, 4, 315–38.

Elder-Vass, D. (2008) 'Searching for realism, structure and agency in actor network theory'. *British Journal of Sociology*, 59:3, 455–73.

Fairclough N., Jessop B. and Sayer, A. (2003) 'Critical realism and semiosis' in J. Joseph and J.R. Roberts (eds) *Realism Discourse and Deconstruction*, London: Routledge, pp. 23–42.

Fleetwood, S. (ed.) (1998) *Critical Realism in Economics: Development and Debate*, London: Routledge.

Fleetwood, S. and Ackroyd, S. (2004) *Critical Realist Applications in Organisation and Management Studies*, London: Routledge.

Groff, R. (ed.) (2008) *Revitalizing Causality: Realism about Causality in Philosophy and Social Science,* London: Routledge.

Jessop, B. (2005) 'Critical realism and the strategic relational approach', *New Formations*, 56, 40–53.

Joseph, J. (2002) *Hegemony: A Realist Analysis*, London: Routledge.

Joseph, J. and Roberts, J.R. (eds.) (2003) *Realism Discourse and Deconstruction*, London: Routledge.

Law, J. (2004) *After Method: Mess in Social Science Research*, London: Routledge.

Lawson, T. (1997) *Economics and Reality*, London: Routledge.

López, J. and Potter, G. (2001) *After Postmodernism: An Introduction to Critical Realism*, London: Athlone.

Morgan, J. and Olsen, W. (2005) 'Towards a critical epistemology of analytical statistics: realism in mathematical method', *Journal for the Theory of Social Behaviour*, 35:3, 255–84.

New, C. (1995) 'Sociology and the case for realism', *The Sociological Review*, 43:4, 808–27.

New, C. (1998) 'Realism, deconstruction and the feminist standpoint', *Journal for the Theory of Social Behaviour*, 28:4, 349–72.

New, C. (2003) 'Feminisms, critical realism and the linguistic turn', in Cruickshank, J. (ed.) *Critical Realism: The Difference that it Makes*, London: Routledge, pp. 57–74.

New, C. (2005) 'Sex and gender: a critical realist approach', *New Formations*, 56, 54–70.

Norrie, A. (2009) *Dialectic and Difference: Dialectical Critical Realism and the Grounds of Justice*, London: Routledge.

Parker, I. (1999) 'Against relativism in psychology, on balance', *History of the Human Sciences*, 12:4, 61–78.

Patomaki, H. (2001) *After International Relations: Critical Realism and the (Re)Construction of World Politics*, London: Routledge.

Pearce, F. and Fauley, J. (eds) (2007) *Critical Realism and the Social Sciences: Heterodox Elaborations*, Toronto: University of Toronto Press.

Sayer, A. (2000) *Realism and Social Science*, London: Sage.

Sayer, A. (2005) *The Moral Significance of Class*, Cambridge: Cambridge University Press.

Sayer, A. (2006) 'Language and significance – or the importance of import: implications for critical discourse analysis', *Journal of Language and Politics*, 5:3, 449–71.

Sayer, A. (2009) 'Understanding lay normativity', in Moog, S. and Stones, R. (eds) *Nature, Social Relations and Human Needs: Essays in Honour of Ted Benton*, London: Palgrave Macmillan, pp. 128–45.

Stones, R. (1996) *Sociological Reasoning: Towards a Post-Modern Sociology*, Macmillan.

Taylor, C. (1985) *Human Agency and Language*, Cambridge: Cambridge University Press.

Preface to the second edition

In the 1980s, the ideas of realist philosophy began to make an impact on social science. Yet the gulf between the more philosophical debates and the literature on how we should do social research remains wide, spanned by only the most rudimentary of bridges. Sadly, many social scientists can still only think of 'method' in terms of quantitative techniques, and even though these are now commonly supplemented by qualitative techniques such as participant observation and informal interviewing, the basic activity of *conceptualization* – which no one can escape – remains unexamined. Of course realism has not had a monopoly of innovations in philosophy and methodology in recent years. Particularly important has been the growing interest in language, writing and rhetoric, for these affect not merely how we re-present ideas for others but the very terms in which we think. Unfortunately these advances have been affected or infected by idealist currents which appear to rule out the possibility of any kind of empirical check on social science.

In view of this situation I believe that realism and the question of method remain very much on the agenda and that there is still far to go in developing a constructive discussion of method informed by realist philosophy. This remains the task of this second edition.

The book is intended both for students and researchers familiar with social science but having little or no previous experience of philosophical and methodological discussions and for those who are familiar with them but are interested in realism and method. These two audiences have different interests and preferences regarding style and content. The style and organization are emphatically geared towards the first group (reviewers please note!). I have therefore deliberately avoided spattering the text with name-droppings that would only alienate the first group even if they reassured the second. Issues are selected on a need-to-know basis rather than on one of fashion; philosophical doctrines are only discussed if they have had or are likely to have a major influence on the practice of social science. At the same time I feel confident that the *cognoscenti* will find the realist ideas developed here radically different from those dominant in the literature.

The two possible audiences are liable to ask different questions and raise different objections. Those likely to come from the first type of reader are anticipated and answered in the main text. Answers to probable objections from the *cognoscenti* are restricted to Notes and to Chapters 5 and 8, which provide critiques specifically directed at certain orthodox ideas. The point of this form of organization is to avoid the usual academic's habit of lapsing into writing only for specialists (including reviewers!). I should also perhaps point out that although its arguments are often philosophical, this book is primarily about method in social research, rather than about the philosophy of social science. Many fine books on the latter already exist.[1] While they offer excellent philosophical critiques they offer little constructive comment on the practice of social science. It is this imbalance that I aim to redress.

A few words about revisions for those familiar with the first edition. Second editions are an opportunity to update and another chance to get things right and this is no exception. It's common today to acknowledge that texts and the way they are interpreted can never be fully controlled by their authors, and often I have been taken aback as much by supporters' readings as by opponents'. But authors do have some responsibility for the reception of their books, so besides adding new material I have tried to correct my own errors and to block some of the misreadings apparent in reactions to the first edition.

The chief surprise to me about the reception of the first edition has been the selectivity of interest. First, for reasons I still do not fully understand, the necessary-contingent distinction introduced in Chapter 3 seems to have overshadowed much of the rest of the book. In this second edition I have tried to clarify this distinction but I remain unconvinced that it warrants the prominence within realism that some interpreters of the first edition gave it. The second kind of selectivity involves a tendency to identify realism with extraordinarily limited tendencies in social theory (e.g. particular angles on marxism) and highly restricted areas of social research (e.g. research on localities). Whatever judgements were made of this research – good or bad – seemed to have rubbed off onto perceptions of realism. Let me therefore stress that, as any scan of the literature will show, realism is a philosophy of and for the *whole* of the natural and social sciences.

Reactions from students have made it clear that a new and fuller Introduction was needed. Apart from this, the main additions concern the nature of theory and its relation to empirical research, practical knowledge, space and social theory, interpretive understanding, research design and an appendix on realism and writing. Further revisions have been made in the light of the experience of empirical research carried out in the last six years. Numerous minor changes have been made to correct and clarify arguments, to add illustrations and to improve accessibility.

Acknowledgements

The University of Sussex for sabbatical leave; the University of California, Los Angeles, Ohio State University, the universities of Copenhagen, Roskilde and Lund and the Copenhagen Business School, for their hospitality in providing me with new horizons; the many graduate students in those places and the Sussex 'Concepts, Methods and Values' students for enduring my obsession with methodology; and John Allen, Bjørn Asheim, Roy Bhaskar, Eric Clark, Kevin Cox, Simon Duncan, Steen Folke, Frank Hansen, Torsten Hägerstrand, Peter Maskell, Doreen Massey, Kevin Morgan and Dick Walker, for their support, encouragement and criticism. Finally, my love and thanks to Lizzie Sayer and Hazel Ellerby.

Introduction

The status of social science is seriously in doubt. Outsiders' attitudes towards it are often suspicious or even hostile, and social scientists themselves are deeply divided over what constitutes a proper approach to social research. The uncertainty has been heightened by increasing doubts in philosophy about traditional views of scientific objectivity and progress. Arguments about whether social science should be like natural science no longer take place on the basis of agreement about the nature and methods of the latter. However, recent developments in realist philosophy have offered new and productive perspectives in both areas that change the whole basis of discussion. In this book I shall try to explain these and show how they can resolve some of the problems that have troubled social scientists.

One of the main difficulties of the existing literature on social theory and the philosophy of the social sciences is that few *constructive* contributions have been made on the subject of method in empirical research, while texts on methods have reciprocated this lack of interest by ignoring developments at the philosophical level and in social theory. For example, much has been written on theories of knowledge, but little about their implications for empirical research. The result is that even where the philosophical critiques have been accepted in principle they have failed to make much difference in practice; indeed, the lack of work on alternative methods has actually discouraged some of the critics and their supporters from even venturing into empirical research. Meanwhile, many of the empirical researchers whose work has been under attack have been content to conclude that the debate is not really relevant to them, or else that philosophical discussions in general threaten empirical research and should therefore be avoided. To get beyond this impasse we must decide whether the critiques imply that we can continue to use the usual empirical methods of hypothesis formation and testing, the search for generalizations and so on, or whether these must be displaced or supplemented by quite different ones. One of the chief aims of this book is to answer these questions.

So much depends in social research on the initial definition of our field of study and on how we conceptualize key objects. Examples of these initial orientations include the adoption of lay categories and classifications in sociology, the equilibrium assumption in economics, the concept of the subject in psychology, concepts like 'interest group' in politics, and the selection of spatial units in human geography. All such starting points are fraught with problems which, whether noticed or not, shape the course of research long before 'methods' in the narrow sense of techniques for getting and interpreting information are chosen. Once these questions of conceptualization are settled – and frequently the answers are matters of habit rather than reflection – then the range of possible outcomes of research is often quite limited. These matters are all the more difficult in social science where our concepts are often about other concepts – those of the society that we study.

In view of this it is quite extraordinary to compare the attention given in social science courses to 'methods' in the narrow sense of statistical techniques, interviewing and survey methods and the like, with the blithe disregard of questions of how we conceptualize, theorize and abstract. ('Never mind the concepts, look at the techniques' might be the slogan.) Perhaps some would be content to dismiss these matters as questions of paradigms, social theory or intuition, not method, but it is my belief that there is method not only in empirical research but in theorizing, and that we need to reflect on it.

A second major impediment to the development of effective method in social science concerns causation. So much that has been written on methods of explanation assumes that causation is a matter of regularities in relationships between events, and that without models of regularities we are left with allegedly inferior, 'ad hoc' narratives. But social science has been singularly unsuccessful in discovering law-like regularities. One of the main achievements of recent realist philosophy has been to show that this is an inevitable consequence of an erroneous view of causation. Realism replaces the regularity model with one in which objects and social relations have causal powers which may or may not produce regularities, and which can be explained independently of them. In view of this, less weight is put on quantitative methods for discovering and assessing regularities and more on methods of establishing the qualitative nature of social objects and relations on which causal mechanisms depend. And this in turn, brings us back to the vital task of conceptualization.

Social scientists are invariably confronted with situations in which many things are going on at once and they lack the possibility, open to many natural scientists, of isolating out particular processes in experiments. Take an apparently simple social event such as a seminar. It involves far more than a discussion of some issues by a group of people: there is usually an economic relationship (the tutor is earning a living); students are also there to get a degree; their educational institution gets reproduced through the enactment of such events; relations of status, gender, age and perhaps race are confirmed or challenged in the way people talk, interrupt and defer to one another; and the participants are usually also engaged in 'self-presentation', trying to win respect or at least not to look stupid in the eyes of others. This multi-dimensionality is fairly typical of the objects of social science. The task of assessing the nature of each of the constituent processes without being able to isolate them experimentally throws a huge burden onto abstraction – the activity of identifying particular constituents and their effects. Though largely ignored or taken for granted in most texts on method I believe it to be central.

I shall therefore take a broad view of 'method' which covers the clarification of modes of explanation and understanding, the nature of abstraction, as well as the familiar subjects of research design and methods of analysis. The terrain of the discussion is therefore the overlap between method, social theory and philosophy of social science.

In view of this overlap many of the arguments have a philosophical character, involving thinking about thinking. But while I believe social scientists can learn from philosophy they should not be in awe of it, for they can also inform it. (Much damage has been done by prescriptions made by philosophers who have little or no knowledge of what social science involves.) Methodologists need to remember that although method implies guidance, research methods are the medium and outcome of research practice;[1] the educators themselves have to be educated – with frequent refresher courses. Therefore philosophy and methodology do not stand above the substantive sciences but serve, as the realist philosopher Roy Bhaskar put it, as 'underlabourer and occasional midwife' to them.[2] And social scientists should certainly not fear that philosophical thinking will subvert empirical research, though it may be heavily critical of certain kinds.

Method is also a practical matter. Methods must be appropriate to the nature of the object we study and the purpose and expectations of our inquiry, though the relationships between them are sometimes slack rather than tight. If we imagine a triangle whose corners are method, object and purpose, each corner needs to be considered in relation to the other two. For example, what do differences between the objects studied by social and natural sciences imply for the methods they use and the expectations we have of their results? Is the goal of prediction appropriate to an object such as an ideology? Can social scientific method ignore the understandings of those whom it studies? How far would an interpretive, ethnographic method be appropriate for assessing macro-economic change? To answer such questions we shall have to consider all three corners of the triangle.

Although methodology needs to be critical and not merely descriptive I intend to counter various forms of methodological imperialism. The most important kind, 'scientism', uses an absurdly restrictive view of science, usually centring around the search for regularities and hypothesis testing, to derogate or disqualify practices such as ethnography, historical narrative or explorative research, for which there are often no superior alternatives. Another kind of imperialism, formed in reaction to this is that which tries to reduce social science wholly to the interpretation of meaning. A critical methodology should not restrict social science to a narrow path that is only appropriate to a minority of studies.

The variety of possible objects of study in social science stretches beyond the scope of a single model of research. Consequently, while this book is about method it is not a recipe book, though it is intended to influence the construction of recipes for research, by suggesting ways of thinking about problems of theorizing and empirical research. Examples are therefore intended as just that – not as unique restrictive moulds to which all realist research must conform.

But what is realism? First of all it is a philosophy not a substantive social theory like that of Weber or neoclassical economics.

It may resonate more with some social theories than others (e.g. marxism more than neoclassical economics) but it cannot underwrite those with which it appears to be in harmony. Substantive questions like 'what causes inflation?' are different from philosophical questions like 'what is the nature of explanation?'

Things get more difficult when we try to define the content of realism. When confronted with a new philosophical position for the first time it is impossible to grasp much of what is distinctive and significant about it from a few terse statements of its characteristics. Particular philosophies are not simple and self-contained but exist through their opposition to a range of alternative positions. They involve loose bundles of arguments weaving tortuously across wider fields of philosophical discourse. Nevertheless, readers may prefer to have at least some signposts regarding the nature of realism, or rather my own view of it, even if their meaning is limited at this stage. Some of the following characteristic claims of realism may seem too obvious to be worth mentioning, but are included because they are in opposition to important rival philosophies. Some may seem obscure, but they provide at least some orientation to newcomers to realism. Fuller explanations will come later. The wordings represent a compromise between what would be acceptable to those familiar with philosophical discourse and what is likely to be accessible to those new to it.

1   The world exists independently of our knowledge of it.
2   Our knowledge of that world is fallible and theory-laden. Concepts of truth and falsity fail to provide a coherent view of the relationship between knowledge and its object. Nevertheless knowledge is not immune to empirical check, and its effectiveness in informing and explaining successful material practice is not mere accident.
3   Knowledge develops neither wholly continuously, as the steady accumulation of facts within a stable conceptual framework, nor wholly discontinuously, through simultaneous and universal changes in concepts.
4   There is necessity in the world; objects – whether natural or social – necessarily have particular causal powers or ways of acting and particular susceptibilities.
5   The world is differentiated and stratified, consisting not only of events, but objects, including structures, which have powers and liabilities capable of generating events. These structures

may be present even where, as in the social world and much of the natural world, they do not generate regular patterns of events.

6   Social phenomena such as actions, texts and institutions are concept-dependent. We therefore have not only to explain their production and material effects but to understand, read or interpret what they mean. Although they have to be interpreted by starting from the researcher's own frames of meaning, by and large they exist regardless of researchers' interpretations of them. A qualified version of 1 therefore still applies to the social world. In view of 4–6, the methods of social science and natural science have both differences and similarities.[3]

7   Science or the production of any other kind of knowledge is a social practice. For better or worse (not just worse) the conditions and social relations of the production of knowledge influence its content. Knowledge is also largely – though not exclusively – linguistic, and the nature of language and the way we communicate are not incidental to what is known and communicated. Awareness of these relationships is vital in evaluating knowledge.

8   Social science must be critical of its object. In order to be able to explain and understand social phenomena we have to evaluate them critically.

Amplifications of these points could fill many books but the list should provide some orientation.

No book of this kind can expect to be exhaustive in its coverage of the range of methodological issues of interest to social science or of the types of social research to which they might be relevant. As regards the latter, it is quite extraordinary how sociology has had the lion's share of attention in the literature. (Some authors give the impression that social science is reducible to sociology and sociology to the work of Durkheim, Weber and Marx!) This has produced a deafening silence on the social research practice of those in other disciplines such as economics, development studies, psychology and human geography. While I cannot address all of these I shall try to counter the usual sociological imperialism found in most books on method in social science.

Any author in this field works with implicit exemplars of particular areas of social research. Mine are somewhat different from those of existing texts; they come mostly from political economic theory and interdisciplinary studies of industry and urban and regional systems, in which researchers tend to come from geography, sociology, economics, political science and anthropology. However, no special knowledge of these is needed to understand the examples I have used and indeed many of them come from everyday arguments and events. I have deliberately avoided the philosopher's irritating habit of using trivial examples ('the tree in the quad', etc.). If a philosophical point is worth making it may as well be illustrated by an example which not only gives clarification but suggests its social and practical significance.

A few words are needed on terminology. At the centre of social science's internal crisis have been attacks on orthodox conceptions usually termed 'positivist' or 'empiricist'. So many different doctrines and practices have been identified with these terms that they have become devalued and highly ambiguous, or even purely pejorative. Those who want to continue using them increasingly find that they have to preface arguments with tiresome digressions on 'the real meaning of positivism' and these often generate more heat than what follows. I have therefore avoided using these terms for the most part. This need not prevent one from discussing some of the issues covered by them and indeed it is liberating to avoid the usual burden of unwanted associations that the terms bear. In general I have minimized the use of technical terminology. (That's what they all say, I know, but at least the intention was there!)

The word 'science' needs special comment. There is little agreement on what kinds of methods characterize science beyond the rather bland point that it is empirical, systematic, rigorous and self-critical, and that disciplines such as physics and chemistry are exemplars of it. Most users of the term obviously consider it to have strong honorific associations for few are willing to cede its use to opponents. Those who want to stand apart from the futile academic game of trying to appropriate and monopolize this descriptively vague but prized label for their own favoured approaches are liable to be accused of the heresy of not caring about science and, by implication, rigour and other virtues. While no one is likely to be against virtue, the coupling with exemplars like physics is particularly unhelpful. Not only is there little consensus on what their methods are, it is also not self-evident that they are appropriate for the study of society; indeed, that very question has been at the heart of the philosophical debates. The use of the word 'science' in this strong sense has allowed many authors to prejudge precisely what has to be argued. I therefore want to make it clear that 'science', 'natural science' and 'social science' are used in this book simply as synonyms for the disciplines that study nature and society. At the most, these subjects might be said to distinguish themselves from everyday knowledge by their self-examined and inquisitive character; but that does not say very much and proponents of the humanities may want to include themselves in this description. In other words, my lack of commitment in the use of the word 'science' does not, of course, entail any lack of commitment to the search for rigorous and effective methods of study; rather it is intended to clear away an important obstacle to their discovery.

In view of my attacks on the insulation of discussions of method from social theory and philosophy of science, readers will not expect me to plunge immediately into a discussion of particular methods or techniques. In Chapter 1 we look at knowledge in context, situating social scientific knowledge in relation to other kinds and to practice. Any theory of knowledge is handicapped from the start if it ignores this context for it is likely to ignore how the internal structure and practices of science are shaped by this position. And it is a particularly important consideration for studies of society, for everyday knowledge is both part of their object and a rival source of explanations. A discussion of the nature of the relation between subject and object in social and natural science then provides a basis for an introduction to the necessarily interpretive and critical character of social science.

Having looked at the context of knowledge, Chapter 2 examines some dominant views of its status and reliability. The time when science was thought to involve the steady accumulation of objective knowledge through a neutral medium of observation has long since gone. In its place there has been a crisis of confidence in which relativism and doubts about the possibility of empirical evaluation and scientific progress have been rife. We begin from the point at which most popular discussions confront the problem – the nature of facts, observation and theory and the relationship between them. To make any progress on this, and in order to say anything sensible about method, particular attention has to be paid to the meaning of 'theory' (woefully underexamined in the philosophical and methodological literature), and to the linguistic and practical character of knowledge. Traditionally doubts about objectivity and the status of scientific knowledge have involved arguments about the nature of truth and how it might be established. In our case we shall approach these matters differently, attempting to counter the neglect of the linguistic and practical character of knowledge, arguing that the concept of truth (and falsity) is incoherent, and that knowledge needs to be evaluated in terms of 'practical adequacy'. The chapter ends with an assessment of the problem of relativism and the resolution of inter-theory disputes.

This prepares the ground for a more focused discussion of method in the ensuring chapters. In these we move continually between the three points of our triangle of method, nature of the object and purpose of study. Following our emphasis on the activity of conceptualization and theorizing we begin in Chapter 3 at the most 'primitive' level with an important but under-analysed aspect of it – abstraction and the relation between abstract and concrete research. We then consider the nature of social relations and structures and how abstraction can illuminate them. We then clarify the nature of generalization, with which abstraction is commonly confused. The chapter ends with a discussion of the realist concept of causation in social science and its implications for methods of causal analysis.

Chapter 4 considers method in relation to ontology or the nature and structure of the social and natural world: first, in so far as it is 'stratified' so that certain objects, such as institutions, have powers emergent from, or irreducible to, their constituents; second, in so far as it consists of 'open systems' in which regularities in events are at best approximate and transitory. The implications of these characteristics for the possibility of discovering laws and for explanation and prediction in social science are then assessed. Further implications of ontological matters for method are then examined: 'rational abstraction' and the need to make abstractions sensitive to the structure of their objects; the relationship of theory and empirical research to the discovery of necessity in the world; and the consequences and dangers of the abstraction from space and time in social science.

Chapter 5 is a digression from the main argument of the book. It is included for those readers who are familiar with more orthodox positions in philosophy and methodology and who may require answers to certain objections which these raise before proceeding any further. Others may wish to 'fast forward' to Chapter 6. The main issues concern a connected set of problems in mainstream philosophy of science, many of them particularly associated with the work of Karl Popper, who has been particularly influential in social science: induction, atomistic ontology, causation, necessity, essentialism, logic and deductivism.

In Chapter 6 we turn to quantitative methods. As before, and in contrast to the usual treatment in texts on method, these are evaluated in relation to their appropriateness to the nature of the object of study, the scope for quantification and the implications of open systems for modelling. The discussion then opens out into a critical assessment of the use of models themselves and the role of assumptions. Lastly I examine the resonances between the use of quantitative positions and particular views of society as atomistic and views of method which misguidedly focus on the search for regularity and neglect conceptualization and interpretive understanding.

The evaluation, or verification and falsification, of social scientific accounts and theories is the subject of Chapter 7. In accordance with our emphasis on the diversity of appropriate methods, we argue that evaluation is a complex and differentiated business, varying according to different objects of study and types of claim. Chapter 8 is a second digression for readers familiar with orthodox philosophy of science, presenting a critique of Popperian views of falsification.

In Chapter 9, we return to problems of explanation in social science. Explanations are shown to be characteristically incomplete and approximate and to vary according to the relationships of our triangle of method, object of study and purpose of research. Yet researchers often over-extend particular approaches, for example in expecting too much of generalization. I therefore discuss the limits and interrelations between key types of research, and try to illuminate them by comparing the capabilities of different kinds of research design. The chapter concludes by returning to the wider context of knowledge with which we began: ultimately our judgements about problems of explanation depend in part on whether we accept or try to resist the critical and emancipatory role of social science.

Finally, in the Appendix, I comment on some implications of recent interest in the fact that scientific knowledge is usually presented in the form of *texts*. Arguably, the rhetoric we use and the form in which we present knowledge are not neutral carriers of meaning but influence the content. Ways in which this can happen are illustrated briefly. Contrary to many commentators, I argue that while these concerns do indeed require further attention, they need not threaten realism.

1 Knowledge in context

We feel that even when all possible scientific questions have been answered, the problems of life remain completely untouched.
(Wittgenstein, 1922, 6.52)[1]

'Method' suggests a carefully considered way of approaching the world so that we may understand it better. To make judgements about method it helps considerably if we have some idea of the nature of the relationship between ourselves and that which we seek to understand. Yet it is at this fundamental level that many arguments about method go wrong, for they fail to consider knowledge in its context.

How does social science relate to everyday knowledge in society and to natural science? Does it merely mystify or reproduce the former? Should it emulate the latter? Some of those who have attacked social science for the alleged triviality of its findings and for lacking relevance to practical matters have argued that this is due to its failure to use the 'proven' methods of natural science. Others have argued that triviality is precisely the result of using such methods. There is disagreement about whether it should adopt a 'disinterested' stance with respect to practice or be actively involved in the process of social development. Some see social science as a natural science of society which can be applied through social engineering. Others see their role as having more in common with a therapist than an engineer, their aim being the development of greater self-understanding. Still others consider the role of social science to be the critique of society.

In this chapter, I shall examine in abstract terms[2] the context in which knowledge, especially social science, develops and how it relates to practice and to its objects. This, I hope, will provide a basis upon which the above problems can be discussed in this and later chapters. Some of the questions posed here might seem strangely broad, even for philosophical discussions, and superficially some of the answers may appear obvious. But if such points are ignored or taken for granted, we may fail to notice how they challenge some of the underlying assumptions of social science's practice. Indeed, their significance goes beyond academia to everyday life, for they suggest that in certain ways society systematically misunderstands itself.

One of the most extraordinary features of the literature on the methodology and philosophy of science is the extent to which it ignores practice and the way in which knowledge is involved in what scientists and lay people *do*. If, as is the custom of this literature, we reduce practice to knowledge, knowledge to science, and science to observation and contemplation, then it is small wonder that it should prove difficult to assess the relation between the social and natural sciences and their objects. Although there is far to go in working out the implications of the practical context of knowledge, I wish at least to set out on this road.[3]

Some misconceptions about knowledge

I shall start by combating the following (interrelated) misconceptions:

1   that knowledge is gained purely through contemplation or observation of the world;
2   that what we know can be reduced to what we can say;
3   that knowledge can be safely regarded as a *thing* or *product*, which can be evaluated independently of any consideration of its production and use in social activity;
4   that science can simply be *assumed* to be the highest form of knowledge and that other types are dispensable or displaceable by science.

1 and 2 are highly interrelated and together constitute the 'intellectualist fallacy' or 'prejudice'. All four misconceptions help to make the relationship between social science and society problematic.

Against 1, I shall argue that knowledge is primarily gained through activity both in attempting to change our environment (through labour or work) and through interaction with other people, using shared resources, in particular a common language.[4] Although the development of knowledge may be furthered through passive contemplation of the world, it always presupposes the existence of these two contexts, which provide a kind of feedback or test for our ideas and a language in which and with which to think. Individuals cannot develop knowledge independently of a society in which they can learn to think and act. The nearest approximation to the unsocialized individual in human experience is the 'wolf-child' who, having largely been brought up outside human society, is often scarcely able to walk on two legs, let alone speak or perform the simplest tasks of reasoning.

In so far as people and their ideas are included among our objects of knowledge, the relationship of knowledge to practice may be interactive rather than passive and purely reflective. It is particularly clear with self-reflection that in thinking *about* ourselves, we can change our 'object'. Under certain conditions, social science can have a similar effect on its object. Moreover, the search for truth, the attempt to rid social knowledge of illusion, puts reflective, examined knowledge into a critical relationship with false beliefs and their effects in society. In this sense the role of social science and perhaps also the humanities may be critical, therapeutic and even emancipatory. For example, arguments about the meaning of masculinity and femininity, about the nature of economic recession or about international politics don't take place outside society as competing external descriptions: they are part of the social process itself. I will develop these points shortly.

Another aspect of the contemplative view of knowledge is the assumption that the only function of knowledge and language is 'propositional'[5] (to make propositions about the world) or 'referential'. What is overlooked in this view is that knowledge concerns not only 'what is the case' or 'knowing-that' but 'know-how', that is knowing *how to do something*, whether it be physical behaviour or communicating successfully with others.

Misconception 2, the second component of the intellectualist fallacy, follows this closely. It concerns the tendency to pedestal spoken or written forms of knowledge and to imagine that these are the only ways in which meaning can be communicated and knowledge can be 'carried' and applied. With this goes a tendency to derogate those types of practical knowledge which do not require much linguistic competence, but which nevertheless involve practical skills. Much of everyday knowledge takes this practical form: a young child learns a great deal before it acquires a language; we have many skills which we are aware of and yet cannot describe verbally and also many of which we are usually unaware. Not all social behaviour is acquired and mediated linguistically, even in the form of talk internalized in our heads. Much of what we do does not proceed on the basis of a model of 'rational choice' but involves a learned accommodation to familiar circumstances which, as Bourdieu puts it,

[is] . . . neither the outcome of the explicit aiming at consciously pursued goals, nor the result of some mechanical determination by external causes . . . [but] . . . guided by a practical sense, by what we may call a feel for the game.[6]

Social scientific knowledge is primarily propositional or referential, rather than practical, and this should immediately provide some clues as to why it seems unable, except very indirectly, to help us decide how to live. No doubt the common fear of the alleged danger of 'value intrusion' in social science also inhibits its practical application.

There are also material circumstances which reinforce this intellectualist prejudice. Academics generally occupy a place in the social division of labour in which the development of knowledge in propositional forms, in a contemplative relationship to the world, has unusual primacy. Within this restricted but privileged context, the activities of speaking and writing are elevated above those of making and doing, as if it were possible to live on propositional knowledge and linguistic communication alone. Not surprisingly, as we shall see, social scientists, philosophers or intellectuals frequently project these characteristics onto society as their object of study, underestimating the extent to which social behaviour is guided by a vague and unexamined practical consciousness.[7] Social scientists may examine it but the results of that examination should not be confused with the original and projected back onto it, or divorced from its practical setting. We shall have more to say about these problems in Chapter 3. Despite the extent of the freedom of academics to reflect upon almost anything, the restricted horizons of their place in the social division of labour encourage a blind spot where practical and tacit skills are concerned. The slanting of our educational system towards a one-sided emphasis of an intellectualist and linguistic view of intelligence and skill is partly attributable to this.

Having written this, in a *book* I can obviously only combat this prejudice from within!

Misconception 3 concerns the common tendency to think of knowledge as a product or thing which exists outside of us, which we can 'possess' and which is stored in finished form in our heads or in libraries. We tend not to think in terms of *knowing*, which is in the process of becoming, 'in solution', as consciousness, but as a thing already 'precipitated'.[8] Despite the work involved in developing and sharing knowledge, this active side (perhaps again as a result of the intellectualist prejudice) tends to be overlooked. As such, it is an instance of the common tendency to *reify* the social world; that is, to turn active, conscious social relationships and processes into things which exist independently of us so that we think of them in terms of 'having' rather than 'being'.[9] Although, for the sake of accessibility, I have used the reified noun-form 'knowledge' in preference to the unreified but unfamiliar and ambiguous 'knowing', I shall try to counteract the misconceptions which it can encourage.

To combat this static view it is imperative to consider the *production* of knowledge as a *social activity*.[10] To develop 'knowledge' we need raw materials and tools on which and with which we can work.[11] These are linguistic, conceptual and cultural as well as material. In trying to understand the world, we use existing knowledge and skills, drawn from whatever cultural resources are available, to work upon other 'raw' materials – knowledge in the form of data, pre-existing arguments, information or whatever. It is only by this activity, this process, that knowledge is reproduced or transformed: it is never created out of nothing. To paraphrase Bhaskar, knowledge as a product, a resource, a skill, in *all* its various forms, is 'both the ever-present condition and continually reproduced outcome of human agency'.[12] Science is not a thing but a social activity.

The fourth common misconception about knowledge concerns *scientism*.[13] Despite the fact that philosophy is generally taken to allow no limitations on what it can question, there is a striking tendency in Anglo-American philosophy of science and social science simply to assume that science is the highest form of knowledge, to which all should aspire. Again, this resonates with and reinforces the intellectualist prejudice. A large number of texts on the philosophy of science take this as their point of departure and immediately pass on to the description or prescription of its internal procedures. But this unquestioning attitude towards the status of science and how it relates to other kinds of knowledge can prejudice the whole discussion of the internal questions of procedures of empirical study, modes of inference, models of explanation and testing etc.

I shall argue that different types of knowledge are appropriate to different functions and contexts; for example, engineering for the task of making nature move to our designs, ethics to the harmonization of the conduct of people in society. But these contexts are not mutually exclusive but overlapping. Scientific practice embraces several types of knowledge, including some which are generally excluded as non-science or even anti-science by scientism. For example, many philosophers who have adopted this stance of 'scientism' have treated ethical decisions as a-rational, purely emotive and not part of science, which by contrast deals purely with matters of fact, with rational and objective questions of 'what is the case'. Yet science is also a specialized type of social activity and as such it requires rules governing what is proper and improper conduct; without *ethical* principles such as those concerning honesty of reporting and refusal of illogical argument, science could not exist. In other words, scientific knowledge presupposes among its very foundations a kind of knowledge which 'scientism' has sought to deny, exclude or derogate.[14] We will return to other excluded but overlapping forms of knowledge shortly.

Having discussed some of the different kinds of knowledge, let us now look at the context in which it develops and see what effect it has.

Knowledge, work and communicative interaction

Knowledge is developed and used in two main types of context – work (or 'labour') and communicative interaction.[15] These contexts are highly related but neither is wholly reducible to the other. By 'work' or 'labour', I mean any kind of human activity which is intended to transform, modify, move or manipulate any part of nature, whether it be virgin nature or nature that has already been extensively modified; that is, whether it be mining, transport, making and using machines, or putting letters in envelopes. All of these activities involve the manipulation of matter for human purposes.

Human labour, unlike the behaviour of animals, is conscious; the worker has some conception of the goal, the end product of the labour.[16] Even where the labour has become thoroughly habitual, this goal can be recovered. We can not only monitor the progress of our material works; we can record and reflect upon our monitorings, discuss them with others and generate new methods, goals or projects to work on. The process of 'knowing' in this context derives a certain kind of check through feedback from the results of the work – not just through observing the world passively as if it were external to us, in order to see if our knowledge 'mirrors' it successfully – but from the results of material *activity* as one of nature's forces, operating within nature. Natural science itself is by no means just a matter of observation and conceptualization; its practitioners spend most of their time *intervening* in nature, doing things to it, trying to make experiments work.[17] In monitoring and checking the practical knowledge that we use in work, what is at issue is the success or failure of this *transformation* – this active 'objectification' of knowledge – rather than a passive 'mirroring' or 'representation' of the world. This, in turn, should affect how we evaluate or test knowledge: 'The question whether objective truth can be attributed to human thinking is not a question of theory but a *practical* question. In practice man must prove the truth, i.e. the reality and power . . . of his thinking.'[18]

Given that human life depends on it, work, as the transformation of nature for human purposes, gets surprisingly little attention in philosophy and even in social science. This might be an instance of the academics' projection of their own way of life on to the lives of those they study. It is not only films and popular fiction that tend to neglect the means by which people earn their living. Many social theories pay great attention to how society is organized and how it coheres, without considering how people (re)produce their means of life. Yet work is the most transformative relationship between people and nature. It is both a material process and a conscious one: it cannot be reduced either to pure physical behaviour or passive contemplation.[19] It is a 'missing link' that bridges the gap between knowledge and the world – a gap which has been widened both by the intellectualist prejudice and the real separations of work and 'living' of capitalism.

Labour is also central to an understanding of human development or 'self-change'. In changing our social and natural milieux we change the forces and conditions which shape the character of society and its people. As new kinds of work and social relations develop, people develop new needs. In other words, human beings have a capacity for 'self change', for making their own history, though as Marx noted: 'they do not make it just as they please, they do not make it under circumstances chosen by themselves, but under circumstances directly encountered, given and transmitted from the past'.[20] In other words, history not only happens to people but is made by them, consciously or unconsciously. Any conception of society – whether lay or scientific – which treats people as passive objects of history and mere carriers of knowledge, rather than agents or producers, is doomed to misrepresent both its object and itself.

The second basic context of knowledge is 'communicative interaction'. By this I mean any kind of interaction between people which involves the sharing or transmission of meaning. It is by no means limited to spoken or written communications, but includes many kinds of activity which presuppose understanding the meaning of signs, conventions, concepts, pictures, rules and actions. Even where the communication is linguistic, there is often an important non-verbal dimension. An obvious example is in job interviews, where both interviewer and interviewee draw upon a wide range of social skills of interpretation, self-presentation and 'impression-management'[21] in addition to those involved in speaking.

Paradoxically, while it has been common to ignore knowledge which is not expressed in language, until recently social scientists and methodologists have taken the linguistic character of their own knowledge for granted, as if language were nothing more than a transparent and unproblematic medium. On reflection it seems extraordinary that methodology should treat the ability to use language effectively as irrelevant to our ability to understand and explain the world. The attention normally given to technical methods of analysis is in gross disproportion to the consideration given to the language in which we characterize the world. Language therefore needs to be put in its place, elevated from its present position of neglect, though not abstracted from its context.[22]

First of all, language has effects of its own, which go beyond those intended by users. The possible meanings that spring from the interaction between the play of associations among the various components of language and contexts depend in part upon the structure of language. We are accustomed to thinking of language as something which we, as users, speak with and through. But there is a sense in which the reverse applies too; I am not the sole author of this book: the structure of language and narrative forms, such as those of academic texts, of which I am only partially aware, speak through me. At one level we might say that this is analogous to any act of production, such as the construction of a house, for the nature of the materials, as well as the work of the builder, determine the properties of the result. But the effects of language are not fixed like those of bricks and steel. New interpretations are always possible; they can never be foreclosed.

Secondly, language cannot exist for an isolated individual who has never been socialized, for language is both a medium and product of social interaction.[23] Propositional knowledge is constructed and expressed in terms of the concepts available in a language and we seek *intersubjective* confirmation of the propositions through communicative interaction. In scientific communities this kind of checking is highly formalized in order to strive for rigour of thought.

Thirdly, language also has an expressive function. Although the expression of feelings may seem particularly personal or individual, it is nevertheless done in the terms available in one's language and hence has a social dimension.

Fourthly, much of our knowledge and our uses of language concern neither making propositions about the world nor expressing our feelings but rather have a directly social function through providing the means by which we question, command, argue, confer respect or distribute contempt, establish relationships and generally conduct our business in society.[24] In no case can knowledge or language be treated as if they existed outside the social context. Even if our interest (like many philosophers') is primarily in the truth or falsity of knowledge 'regardless of its social origins' it must be remembered that judgements of truth or falsity require *intersubjective* appraisal.

For analytical and expositional convenience, I have dealt with these two contexts of knowledge of labour and communicative interaction separately. This gives us only a very provisional, crude outline, for the two are in fact interdependent. The development of human labour from merely animal behaviour requires the simultaneous development of a high level of communicative interaction through which people can acquire and develop the 'instrumental' knowledge which they use in labour.

Systems of meaning are *negotiated* by people in the course of social interaction.[25] As such these systems have a *conventional* character – they become conventions according to which actions of individuals can be related; the systems of meaning related to money are a good example. However, not just any conventions will do; those which can inform *successful* labour and interaction which we need to undertake to survive will be preferred, while those which (it is intersubjectively agreed) cannot inform successful projects will be winnowed out. It is because nature and its material processes (including human activity) have particular structures and properties which exist independently of our understanding of them, that not just any understanding will serve as a basis for activity.[26] Through intersubjectively monitoring our interventions in nature we try to develop our language and knowledge in accordance with those activities which seem practically possible. The presence of power and domination in the social determination of meaning modifies this situation only slightly, for the powerful are bounded by the realm of the possible too. I will return to and develop these points more fully later.

Although human labour and communicative interaction are highly interdependent, we cannot collapse one into the other.[27] At the limit, even though communication can be hard work (!), it cannot be reduced wholly to the material transformation of the world. Even though the interpretation of meaning and the most passive forms of contemplation involve material processes in the brain, meaning is not reducible to them. Even if you could observe the chemical and physical processes at work in someone's brain as they spoke, you would still need to know the meaning of what they said in order to be able to understand them. Conversely, work as the transformation of matter cannot be wholly reduced to the sharing or interpretation of meaning.

Once again, misconceptions about the context of knowledge can distort social scientists' views of both their object of study and their own activity. An approach called 'radical behaviourism' provides a good example: its proponents insist that the meanings people attach to their actions and to other objects play no part in determining what they do. Knowledge is therefore divorced from practice. This, of course, raises the question of the radical behaviourists' view of their own activity – have their ideas nothing to do with their actions? This is an extreme case whose absurdity is clear enough, and usually the misconceptions are less obvious. Nevertheless, it is certainly not unusual for social scientists to ignore many of the meanings people attach to situations, although few would insist on doing so as a matter of principle. In discussions of philosophy and methodology few accept radical behaviourism, but in actual social scientific practice something approaching it is common, particularly in the work of those who see their task as the search for law-like empirical regularities equivalent to those found in some of the natural sciences. It is therefore important to explore the misconceptions further.

The relationship between subject and object

This account of 'knowledge in context' can be developed and further clarified by examining the relationship between 'subject' and 'object'. In most discussions of this, the term 'subject' (or sometimes 'knowing-subject') refers to the observer or investigator or simply 'thinker', while the 'object' is defined as the thing being studied. I want to make two qualifications or additions to these definitions. First, as before, I do not want to restrict the meaning of 'subjects' to scientists, on the grounds that I want to bring out similarities and connections between scientific and other kinds of knowledge at this stage. Second, I want to include the older meaning of 'subject', as a creative agent who brings about change. The point of this modification is to avoid restricting the conception of the relationship to a passive, contemplative mode from the start.

I will begin by introducing and criticizing some naïve conceptions of the relationship and then go on to develop alternative conceptions as they apply to natural and social science. This will lead into a discussion of the differences and similarities of natural and social science and of the contrasting approaches to them, and finally bring us back to the problem of how social science relates to everyday knowledge and practice.

Behind most views on this topic lies a conceptual framework which includes the following series of dualisms or dichotomies:

people	–	nature
individual	–	society
subjective	–	objective
thought	–	action
mental	–	material
mind	–	body
knowledge	–	practice
beliefs	–	facts
expressive function of language	–	referential/propositional function of language

This framework of oppositions is deeply embedded in our culture; indeed it is difficult to think outside it. It is not only implicit in common-sense thinking but explicit in much of British and American literature on philosophy and social science. Nevertheless, although these dualisms are 'second nature' to us and probably look quite harmless, I shall argue that every one of them is beset with misconceptions which generate problems in our understanding of the world and of ourselves. The dualisms do not operate singly but in parallel, providing mutual reinforcement, so that in the vertical dimension of the diagram, meanings or associations 'leak' from one term to the next.

I have already alluded to some of the problems generated by this framework, but I have hardly begun to draw out the implications. These include the following:

1 Work and activity are excluded and banished to a kind of limbo, so that people are separated from society and their own activity, making it difficult for us to understand how thought actually relates to and functions in nature and society. This implies not only an inadequate theory of knowledge (epistemology) but an alienated view of ourselves.

2 The framework is also alienating because the exclusion of social relations and *inter*subjectivity tends to reduce society to nothing more than a group or loose aggregate of individuals. At the same time it obscures the social function of language.

Indeed, the omission of intersubjectivity, as the context in which language is (re)produced, makes language in general difficult to comprehend.

These points can be substantiated in the course of a critique of models of the subject–object relationship.

The simplest model fits comfortably within this conceptual framework (Figure 1), where S, the subject, observes and records information about O, the object. On the basis of our earlier arguments we can amend this so that the relationship includes activity, particularly labour.

S ———————————————————————— O

Figure 1   Subject and object: 1

It was also argued that the subject must have a language in which to think about the object.[28] Given the social nature of language, the subject–object relationship in Figure 1 must presuppose the existence of social relations, or 'subject–subject relations'[29] within some language community. Usually the language community is internally differentiated, embracing specialist sub-groups with some of their own linguistic and conceptual resources, be they those of physics, economics, farming, cooking, computer programing or whatever. As this social context is not incidental but indispensable to the subject–object relationship, we shall modify the diagram accordingly, assuming for the time being, for the sake of simplicity, that O consists only of non-social objects (Figure 2).

Figure 2 echoes the points made earlier about work and communicative interaction as interdependent contexts of knowledge, for it shows that subjects (whether laypersons, specialists, academics or whatever) stand in a double relationship – to their object and to other subjects. Subjects cannot gain propositional knowledge of their objects or acquire practical knowledge of how to manipulate them without using the cognitive and conceptual resources of particular communities. In other words (to put it crudely), in order to understand the world we must simultaneously understand one another. In everyday life, in so far as common sense is characteristically unexamined, we tend not to notice this social aspect and imagine that we can know objects in an unmediated fashion. In common sense, we think *with* our beliefs and concepts but not about them.[30]

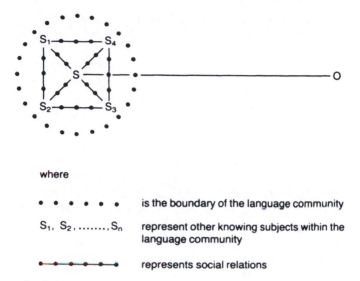

where

• • • • • •   is the boundary of the language community

$S_1, S_2, ..., S_n$ represent other knowing subjects within the
language community

●—●—●—●—●   represents social relations

Figure 2   Subject and object: 2

The other (interdependent) relationship in which the subject
stands – to the object – is also widely misunderstood in that it
is frequently conceived of as merely contemplative rather than
practical. It is therefore not a question of knowledge developing
autonomously first and then (perhaps) being applied in a practical
context later: knowledge and practice are tied from the start. (But
again, note how the common-sense set of dualisms makes it difficult to see this.) Even 'pure' science is also a set of practices.

The importance and interdependence of these two dimensions
of knowledge can be readily appreciated by recalling experiences
of learning a new skill or science. For instance, in mineralogy, it
can take weeks to begin to understand the concepts and to learn
how to look at the images under the microscope so that we see
particular minerals rather than pretty kaleidoscope patterns. And
we achieve this not just by looking but by *doing* things with the
minerals and microscope. For a while we may feel lost because the
two dimensions do not 'connect up'; in using the instruments and
materials we seem only to be 'going through the motions' without
knowing why, while using the concepts feels like merely 'mouthing'
or 'parroting' without understanding them. Later, connecting up
the two dimensions becomes 'second nature' and we are then
tempted to *forget* the dual relationship in which we stand as

subjects so that we may imagine that we have acquired a 'stock of knowledge' without either material work or communicative interaction.

If we broaden the meaning of 'practice' to include both these dimensions, it can be seen that the nature of the practice both determines and is determined by the kind of subject and object which it links. For example, a cook and a nutritionist, or an accountant and an economist have certain interests in common, yet they are different kinds of 'subject' with differently defined objects, the differences being determined by their *practices*, in terms of the types of conceptual tools they use and material actions and social relations in which they engage. Yet it is still common to compare knowledge in different communities and at different points in history in abstraction from these practical contexts as if they were merely different modes of contemplating the world.

Although these two aspects of practice are interdependent, they are, as noted above, qualitatively different. In Figure 2, the crucial aspect of the social relations between subjects is the sharing of meaning. In the case of knowledge of non-social objects the relationship between S and O is not itself social. Even though it requires the application of concepts and a language which can only be gained in a social context, the object itself does not include concepts or meanings.[31] Non-social phenomena are impervious to the meanings we attach to them. Although one could say that such objects are 'socially-*defined*', they are not socially-produced. Definition and production are utterly different, though some of the literature which has stressed the idea of 'the social construction of reality' tends to forget this, as if when we abandoned the flat earth theory for a spherical earth theory, the earth itself changed shape![32] 'Subjects', however, interact on the basis of shared understandings which can be changed. Nature can be altered but through work and not merely by changing systems of meaning: non-social objects such as atoms do not act on the basis of shared understandings and so are not susceptible to change in them. This may seem all very obvious, but it is surprising how often change on the left side of the diagram (conceptual change) is confused with change on the right. On the other hand, given that it is only via the left side that we can make sense of the right, perhaps it isn't so surprising!

What does the relationship look like where the object is society? (Note, once again, that I do not at this stage want to restrict the discussion to '*scientific study*'.) In so far as this object includes other subjects and their interaction, then the relationship should have some features in common with that between the subjects on the left side, so that the diagram becomes symmetrical (Figure 3).

For expositional clarity, the diagram shows two separate language communities, which might represent situations such as those found in history or the study of other cultures. It is, of course, more common for S and O^s to be in the same language community or society. Given that even anthropological or historical investigation requires the establishment of conceptual connections between the two communities, the separation in the diagram should perhaps be regarded as an analytical device rather than a widely applicable substantive description. In practice, there is usually a partial identity of subject and object,[33] so that we are often already familiar with the meaning of the social phenomena in our 'object'. Nevertheless, even where the identity is full rather than partial, it is possible for the subject S to characterize Os' knowledge as wrong or incomplete, and vice versa. Given the equivalence of the horizontal subject–object relationship in Figure 3 to those within language communities, social knowledge, including social science, is sometimes said to stand in a 'dialogic' relationship with its object, or in a subject–subject relation rather than a subject–object relation. As we shall see, this relationship is widely misunderstood and needs careful analysis, but before embarking

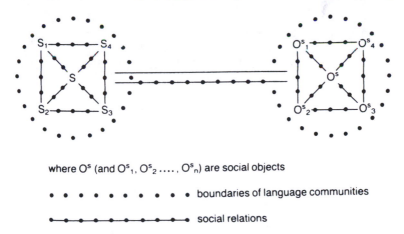

where O^s (and O$^s_1$, O$^s_2$ ...., O^s_n) are social objects

• • • • • • • • • • boundaries of language communities

●━●━●━●━●━●━●━● social relations

Figure 3 Subject and object: 3

on this, there still remain some further modifications to be made to the diagram.

Understanding social phenomena is by no means *just* a question of understanding concepts in society and the meanings of practices.[34] In the study of the British economy, for example, we need to know not just what, say, 'monetarism' or 'inflation accounting' mean to those who have claimed to put them into practice; we also need to know under what conditions, to what extent and with what effects they have been used. Social phenomena have a crucial material dimension and are closely associated everywhere to relationships with nature, both in its virgin and its artificially transformed states. Knowledge of society, whether scientific or lay, should therefore always include reference to this material side, although it tends to be overlooked in some 'interpretive' approaches to sociology and anthropology (Figure 4).

It will be noted that the lines relating the communities to nature correspond to the horizontal subject–object relations in Figure 2. As such these involve a material, practical relationship. However, the situation in social *science* is more complex for two reasons: 1 the unavailability of experiments makes it more

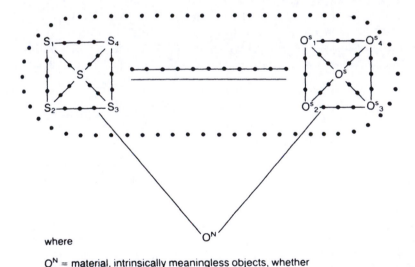

where

O^N = material, intrinsically meaningless objects, whether natural or artificial

(other symbols as before)

Figure 4   Subject and object: 4

difficult to use such material interventions for scientific purposes;[35]
2 social phenomena can be changed *intrinsically* by learning and
adjusting to the subject's understanding. It is not just that social
experiments may be deemed undesirable, it is also that social
phenomena are likely to be irreversibly changed by them in a
way which does not happen with non-social phenomena, which
learn nothing from being manipulated. In the desire to know
society *as it is*, rather than as it might be when modified by
responding to our investigations under uncontrolled conditions,
it has widely been assumed that social science should try to
neutralize such interactive effects. As we shall see, this position
is being increasingly challenged – with important implications for
the role of social science in society. But for now, it can at least
be noted that characteristic 1 does not automatically reduce social
science's relationship with its object to a purely contemplative one,
precisely because of 2.

Some implications of subject–object relations

In some ways the above account may seem too obvious to warrant such laborious treatment. Yet the implications, particularly
of Figures 3 and 4, are profoundly at odds with the dominant
conceptual framework of oppositions of 'subjective and objective', 'thought and action', etc., in which we are accustomed
to think (see above p. 25). Failure to grasp these implications
underlies some of the most common misunderstandings of social
science, but unfortunately the failure is as common in social
science itself as it is in natural science and everyday knowledge. Given their extent, it is necessary to proceed rather slowly
and carefully in examining what is implied by these last two
diagrams.

The first point concerns the 'intrinsically-meaningful' or 'concept-
dependent' nature of social phenomena.[36] What does this mean?
It obviously denies the (tempting) assumption that meanings are
merely descriptions which are only externally applied to social
phenomena, as they are to non-social objects. The correct point
that ideas and meanings are not the same as material objects lends
some support to the 'mental–material' and 'subjective–objective'
dualisms. Yet this type of thinking also makes it difficult to see
how the material structure of society – its institutions, social

relations and artefacts – are dependent on social meanings in various ways.

The most obvious candidates for intrinsically meaningful social phenomena are the ideas, beliefs, concepts and knowledge held by people in society. As part of the object – as well as the subject – of knowledge, their meaning must be understood. There is no equivalent of this where non-social phenomena are concerned. As will be shown, this distinction (embodied in the contrast between Figures 2 and 3) constitutes an absolutely fundamental difference between social science, the humanities and everyday social knowledge on the one hand and informal and scientific knowledge on the other. In studying a fascist society we must interpret what fascism means in it, for its members. The same goes for social 'objects' such as status, politics, nationality and gender, to name but a few: but it does not apply to objects such as atoms, cells, black holes or rock formations.

As we have seen, the point that these ideas and meanings are not only *in* society but *about* society tempts us back into the common-sense framework – back into the separation of knowledge, language and meaning from the world of objects. Against this, the crucial point to remember is that social phenomena are *concept-dependent*. Unlike natural (i.e. non-social objects) they are not impervious to the meanings ascribed to them. What the practices, institutions, rules, roles or relationships *are* depends on what they mean in society to its members. In one of the most influential discussions of the constitutive role of meaning in society, the philosopher Peter Winch has argued that the essential feature of social institutions is that individuals have a practical knowledge of more or less tacit constitutive rules concerning not only what can and cannot be done but *how* things should be done.[37] Nevertheless, the influence of the common-sense oppositions or dualisms mentioned above is such that this argument tends to produce bafflement or resistance, so I will illustrate it with several examples.

Money, and the institutions and practices associated with it, are extremely important in our society ('money makes the world go round!'). A necessary condition of the use of money is that users should have some understanding of what the act of exchanging little metal discs and specially printed pieces of paper for commodities means or 'stands for'. The users must have some concept of money and also of related phenomena such as rights of ownership, exchange, etc. Hence these social phenomena are 'concept-dependent'.

Likewise, for conversations, interviews, seminars or debates to take place, the participants must have a practical knowledge of the rules concerning what is supposed to happen in such situations.

A third and rather well-worn example of concept-dependent practices is that of voting and holding elections. A necessary condition for the holding of elections is that people must have some understanding of what elections, voting, ballot papers, candidates, democracy and so on mean. If we forced uncomprehending individuals to mark crosses beside names on ballot papers, it would not count as a proper election. Finally, given the symmetry of Figure 3 we can treat social science itself as an example of an intrinsically meaningful practice.

In all these cases and a host of others we can distinguish between the physical '*behaviour*' and the meaning of the '*actions*' involved in the practices. In the case of using money, we could observe the physical behaviour of handing over the little metal discs until the cows came home and we could use every statistical technique in the book to process our observational data, yet if we didn't know the meanings on which the use of money is dependent in the society under study, we would still not have any idea of what was actually happening, or what kind of 'action' it was. Accordingly, Winch and others have argued that this kind of understanding requires not the amassing of empirical data but a conceptual or philosophical analysis of the action and the rules implicit in it.[38] 'Mere' physical behaviour such as blinking, walking, sleeping or swallowing has no intrinsic meaning, although in exceptional circumstances some of these can acquire a certain social significance – for example, the disapproving cough. Many actions are conventionally associated with physical behaviour, but some are not; examples of the latter case are remaining silent under interrogation or deciding not to vote.

Sometimes the same behaviour can, in different contexts, constitute different meaningful actions. The physical behaviour of different political groups in demonstrations may be very similar, yet the meaning of their actions could be utterly different. I may raise my hand in a meeting, but whether this constitutes voting, asking to speak or bidding in an auction depends on the context and what the other 'social actors' take it to mean.

Note that by 'constitutive meanings' or 'concepts in society' I most emphatically do *not* mean simply the subjective beliefs, opinions or attitudes of individuals. This conflation follows readily from the conceptual framework of dualisms discussed earlier. Those trapped within it tend to react to the above arguments by assuming that constitutive meanings in society are nothing more than the subjective beliefs of individuals which can be ascertained through questionnaires or interviews and then treated as untroublesome objective facts about those individuals. Meaning, on this common-sense account, is reduced to either 'private', subjective 'feelings' or opinions – expressions of 'inner states' – or references to *things*. What is missing in this conceptual framework is any recognition of the properties of language mentioned earlier. Nor has it any concept of meaning as being *for* a subject, *for* a person, or of utterances and actions meaning something *to* someone.[39] Moreover, and related to this, there is a lack of recognition of the *inter*subjective context of language: to speak or write is to enter into a social relationship.[40] As was explained in our earlier remarks about the contexts of knowledge, even our most personal feelings or opinions can only be constructed and communicated (and hence have any chance of becoming constitutive or having any impression or influence on others) within intersubjectively-understood (though often non-verbal) terms. Although they do not realize it, those who would reduce the interpretation of meaning to an opinion (or belief) data-gathering exercise can only make sense of their data by already presupposing knowledge of the meanings of the vocabulary in which they are constructed. It is not merely that beliefs are shaped by others, but that they are *constructed* in terms of intersubjectively-available meanings.

Likewise social practice does not consist in the collisions of individuals acting out their private beliefs, using language only as a set of labels for their feelings (expressive function) or for the states of the outside world (propositional function). As has been argued, language has a social function through which actions are co-ordinated (or opposed) and people communicate with one another.

Beliefs and opinions are not the only phenomena which are borne by individuals and yet are socially constituted. Roles and personal identities also generally cannot be determined unilaterally by individuals (or even by groups sometimes). You cannot simply become an employed person by believing and declaring yourself to be one. Whether you can become one depends on (among other things) what other people are prepared to take you as and on what they themselves have become (e.g. whether they control access to the means of production). Intersubjectivity is therefore an essential category for understanding not only how scientists and others gain knowledge of the social world (the epistemological relation) but also how societies themselves cohere and function.

Material arrangements are also important in the determination and confirmation of the meaning of practices within societies. Consider the example of the concepts 'public' and 'private'. Although their meanings have certainly not been static, they have informed actions in our society for centuries and have in turn been objectified in its material organization, most obviously and simply in the enclosed and locked spaces which are interpreted as confirming the conceptual distinctions on which the actions producing the material arrangements depend.

Sometimes material objects which do not depend at all for their existence upon our conception of them may nevertheless be ascribed a concept-dependent (symbolic) function in society. Obvious examples are gold and diamonds. Manufactured objects such as gold coins or fast cars are constructed out of intrinsically meaningless objects, but signify certain concepts in their design, use and function. The fast car not only objectifies technical knowledge but also acts as a bearer of macho social imagery. Male owners of such objects assume that others will respond in ways which confirm their self-image, though, of course, they may inadvertently prompt a debunking. The point to be made here is that although, in one sense, material objects are intrinsically meaning*less*, their use and functioning in society is concept-dependent. Conversely, although systems of meanings and beliefs are not themselves material, they usually require some material mode of objectification if they are to communicate and function socially in a stable manner. In other words, practices, material constructions and systems of meanings are *reciprocally confirming*.[41]

Given this 'reciprocal confirmation', we usually find that changes in meanings and practices go hand in hand. The struggle of feminists and anti-racists to erase the negative *meanings* associated with women and blacks cannot be effective purely at the level of semantic battles. It must also involve the dislocation of those material arrangements which objectively restrict them (e.g. access to paid work) and those which as a matter of convention are interpreted by sexists and racists as reciprocally confirming these negative meanings. Understanding concepts in society and how they change therefore requires an understanding of the material practices associated with them and the way in which they are contested. As Bourdieu puts it, unquestioning use of everyday categories for things such as occupations or ethnic groups amounts to 'settling on paper issues that are not settled in reality, where they are the stake of ongoing struggle'.[42]

A common reaction to these claims is to concede them but then assume that they are only relevant for understanding small-scale features of the social world, e.g. the way in which interpersonal relations are reproduced. While it is true that most social scientists who have made this process of reciprocal confirmation of meaning and practice their specialism have concentrated on micro-phenomena, large-scale phenomena such as the reproduction of status systems, forms of political organization, nationalism and religious systems are no less concept-dependent.[43] Raymond Williams's studies of shifts in social concepts and practices such as 'democracy', 'individualism', 'art', 'culture' and 'industry', in *Culture and Society* illustrate this point.[44] (The fact that many social scientists don't consider this as social science is indicative of the 'scientism' and widespread ignorance of the significance of constitutive meanings.)

There is, of course, another kind of dependence between the realms of ideas and matter, which derives from the fact that people are themselves material, animal and part of nature such that they are subject to certain of its causal laws and conditions. *Whichever* system of meanings societies adopt, they must satisfy certain basic material needs in order to survive. This might be called a materialist principle but it is not the kind in which satisfaction of material needs must chronologically precede communication, culture, etc., for even the most basic and desperately needed material requirements are simultaneously interpreted in terms of some kind of system of meanings.[45]

So nothing I have said about the reciprocal relationship between the construction of meaning and constructions and use of material environments is incompatible with the 'materialist principle' thus qualified. Unfortunately, 'vulgar materialists' often forget the former relationship while students of the construction of meaning ('vulgar symbolic interactionists'?) often forget the latter. Social beings live neither on bread alone nor on ideas and symbols alone.

Systems of domination invariably exploit both types of dependence. They are maintained not only through the appropriation, control and allocation of essential material requirements by the dominant class, race or gender, but also through the reproduction of particular systems of meanings which support them.[46] The relevant constitutive meanings (e.g. concerning what it is to be a boss, master-race, untouchable, husband or wife) are certainly not neutral or indifferent to their associated practices and different groups have very different or even contradictory material stakes in their reproduction or transformation.

I hope that the arguments and examples of the last few pages have demonstrated that the initially apparently obvious claims about subject–object relations and the context of knowledge have implications which go beyond the conduct of social science to social practice in general.

Verstehen

Having discussed what the 'concept-dependence of social phenomena' means, I will now look more closely at the *kind* of understanding involved. It is emphasized that the understanding referred to here is common to *all* the relationships shown in Figure 3: it is not unique to social science, and the relationship between S and O^s (subject and social object). Any member of a society achieves this understanding in everyday life; indeed it is precisely because it is universal that it is often not noticed.

The discipline or science concerned with the interpretation of meaning is called '*hermeneutics*'. Using this term we can say that the study of natural objects (Figure 2) only involves a 'single hermeneutic' ($S_1, S_2 \ldots, S_n$) while the study of ideas and concept-dependent social phenomena involves a 'double hermeneutic'.[47]

It is sometimes said of someone that they 'read' a social situation well or badly. This is a revealing description, for the understanding to which we refer, sometimes termed '*verstehen*', is rather like that used in and obtained from reading a book.[48] We do not understand a book (any more than we come to understand a foreign language) by observing and analysing the shape of words or their frequency of occurrence, but by interpreting their meaning. *To* this reading, we always bring interpretive skills and some kind of pre-understanding (though not necessarily a correct one) of what the text might be about. In other words there is an interpenetration and engagement of the 'frames of meaning' of the reader and the text. We cannot approach the text with an empty mind in the hope of understanding it in an unmediated fashion, for our own frame of meaning is an indispensable tool or resource for understanding.[49]

However, the role of meaning in social interaction in everyday life is usually different from that in a discourse, such as a text or an argument, in that many of the successive elements of the interactions in the former do not relate to one another in a logical and conceptually consistent way. For example, in a confrontation between two nations, although conflict requires communicative interaction, responses are unlikely to succeed one another logically, as if they were governed merely by the force of the better argument; they are more likely to be determined by relative economic strength, membership of power blocs, or contingencies such as unanticipated consequences of political changes within each country. Particularly where actors state their intentions fairly formally, we should be wary of assuming that what appears to be coherent on paper will be possible in practice; political manifestos provide a good illustration of the danger! The analogy with reading a text is useful for distinguishing the situation from that of natural science, but only up to a point. The 'text' of actual social processes is usually highly disjointed and often contradictory, and whereas it is not generally necessary to know how a book was produced in order to understand it, little sense can be made of social interactions like international conflicts without exploring the production of particular actions.[50]

As Figure 4 showed, hermeneutics is not the only kind of understanding used in social science or everyday social practice. Yet it is certainly the most widely misunderstood. I shall therefore attempt to counter some of the misconceptions and objections.[51]

Perhaps the most common misunderstanding runs like this: 'Social science has to concern itself with the subjective as well as the objective, with people's opinions and feelings as well as their material states and circumstances. Understanding why people act as they do requires that we examine this subjective side and for this we need to "empathize" with them, by asking ourselves what we would have done in their circumstances.' Note again how the subjective–objective dualism is asserted and intersubjective meanings are collapsed back into subjective, essentially private, opinions and feelings. Once this adulterated account of the hermeneutic element of social knowledge has been taken as authoritative, it is open to certain typical objections. One is that while empathy may be a useful source of hunches or hypotheses about why actions occur it is not a privileged source and what matters is not where such explanatory hypotheses come from but how they stand up to test. As one critic put it: 'Empathy, understanding and the like may help the researcher, but it enters into the system of statements as little as does a good cup of coffee which helped the researcher do his work.'[52] The absurdity of this 'cup-of-coffee-theory-of-understanding' is illustrated by one of the most famous critics of *verstehen*, Abel, who gave as an example the problem of explaining why the marriage rate changes from year to year in a certain community.[53] *Verstehen* is presented as the use of empathy to understand the motives of actors and hence as a source of hypotheses explaining their actions. Once it is reduced to this role, *verstehen* can easily be relegated to a dispensable status. But the absurdity derives from the fact that simply by already knowing what marriage is – as an intrinsically meaningful social phenomenon – Abel unwittingly presupposes *verstehen*, not as empathy but as the understanding of constitutive meanings, just as any person presupposes it in social action. Indeed, without *verstehen*, Abel would not be a social actor.

Note also that this implies that *verstehen is universal*: it is not a special technique or procedure but is common to all knowledge, both of nature (where it is restricted to a single hermeneutic, as in Figure 2) and of society (where it is situated in a double hermeneutic, as in Figures 3 and 4). However, this is not to deny that it is used differently according to context. The intellectual's interpretation of meaning is (or should be!) rigorous and self-aware, thinking, as noted earlier, *about* beliefs and concepts as well as *with* them. By contrast, a very much less examined kind of interpretive understanding is used in everyday, practical contexts, where people are rarely aware that their actions presuppose it. It is exactly this unawareness which explains the above misunderstanding of *verstehen* by unreflective social scientists. In everyday practice, however, it must be admitted that too much self-consciousness of the processes by which people achieve mutual understanding can actually interfere with the successful execution of the most mundane social acts, such as holding a conversation. So, although *verstehen* is common to knowledge in any context, it does not take the same form in each.

Another common misconception about *verstehen* is the assumption that understanding implies agreement.[54] Once this is accepted, it is, of course, difficult to make sense of conflict and disagreement in society. However, to say that social actions and communication take place on the basis of common understandings in society is not to suggest that every member agrees with all the concepts and associated practices of their society. In fact, the more completely we come to understand the practices and conventions of say, *apartheid*, the more strongly we may disagree with them.[55] Moreover, to suggest that concepts and actions in society may be understood and 'shared', is not to imply that they become established by some democratic process. On the contrary, they pre-exist each member of society, and are largely imposed upon them through the process of socialization.

Different groups have very different cognitive, linguistic and material resources with which to set up new reciprocally-confirming circles of meanings and practices. Even in supposedly liberal, open and self-critical institutions such as universities, the definitions of what is to count as education are predominantly imposed and only open to negotiation in a marginal, piecemeal, fashion and then on unequal terms. While social organization would break down if every practice and convention were *simultaneously* 'up for grabs', this, of course, cannot serve as a legitimation of the undemocratic nature of the reproduction and transformation of actual existing societies.

A related objection is that many social relations and practices are dependent on (among other things) *mis*-understandings rather than understanding. This is true, but the important point is that both misunderstanding and understanding concern meaning, and that whether the meanings are delusions or correct they can be constitutive of social phenomena and therefore cannot be ignored in studying society.

Nowhere in the foregoing account has it been suggested that people understand themselves or others or their circumstances perfectly and truthfully, or that the concepts in which they think are adequate or coherent. In fact, as Gellner[56] argues, the force of many concepts in society derives from their ambiguity, hypocrisy, deceptiveness and their effect in reinforcing power structures. Political discourse is particularly rich in examples such as the concept of 'the national interest', or the use of the first-person plural in exhortations made in divided institutions or societies – 'we are all going to have to tighten our belts'. (As Brecht once said, 'You and I are not we'). In so far as people's actions are guided by such ideas, illusions and falsehoods may therefore be 'constitutive' of practice. So, for example, a study of east–west relations in the cold war would have to look at not only the material resources of either side, but also at the complex of understanding, misunderstanding, bluff, double standards (e.g. over human rights) and deliberate misrepresentations of the enemy for 'internal consumption'.

So far, we have explored the common ground between social science and everyday knowledge and practice and have introduced some differences between social and natural science. This can now serve as a foundation for considering the question of the social scientist's conscious relationship to society – in particular, whether it should be critical or disinterested.

Critical theory[57] and the relationship between subject and object

When we reflect upon our beliefs and the concepts we use, we often change them in the process: we notice and try to resolve inconsistencies and so we come to understand ourselves and the world in a new way or discover new 'levels' of meaning. And so it is with science; indeed, science is redundant if it fails to go beyond a common-sense understanding of the world. Since social science includes common sense among its objects, it cannot avoid a critical relationship with it, for in seeking to understand popular consciousness, *as it is*, in examining what is normally unexamined, we cannot help but become aware of its illusions. As Ricoeur puts it, the 'restoration of meaning' inevitably slides into the 'reduction of illusion'.[58] Moreover, the effects of actions which are informed by false ideas will often differ from those which actors expect them to have. If we are to represent such situations adequately, we must attempt both to report those ideas, as they are held, authentically, *and* show in what respects they are false. (Note that to criticize an idea as false is not to deny that it is held or that it has consequences.) Therefore, *in order to understand and explain social phenomena, we cannot avoid evaluating and criticizing societies' own self-understanding.*

For example, any attempt to explain the present economic recession would have to make a critical evaluation of the (formal and informal) theories which have not only described but informed the actions of politicians, institutions and other individuals. Likewise an account of South African society would not be explanatorily adequate if the constitutive meanings concerning racial superiority and inferiority that inform and are objectified by *apartheid* were not criticized as false, although, of course, it would have to be acknowledged (it is true that) they are held.

The structure of the argument is important here. I am not saying that social scientists should criticize things simply because they may happen to disapprove of them. Rather, the point is that the explanation of social phenomena entails that we critically evaluate them. Moreover, criticism cannot reasonably be limited to false ideas, abstracted from the practical contexts in which they are constitutive, but must extend to critical evaluation of their associated practices and the material structures which they produce and which in turn help to sustain those practices.[59] When we say hoarding money is irrational or wrong we do not mean that only the idea of it is wrong: we mean the practice is wrong. Likewise, it is not just the *ideas* (of racial differences, etc.) behind *apartheid* in the abstract that are wrong, but the actual practices (enforcement of pass laws, etc.) and material structures (segregated and materially deprived townships, etc.) which reciprocally-confirm, legitimate and are legitimated by those ideas. Many advocates of a value-free, 'disinterested' stance in social science fear that permitting such evaluations will lead us to produce a distorted picture of the facts about what exists. Yet it would be factually incorrect to say that the architects of *apartheid* were factually correct in their beliefs about race. We can't simply refuse to make *any* evaluation, negative or positive, because unless we decide whether the actors' own explanations of their actions are right, we cannot decide what explanation to choose ourselves. Consider a further example: suppose that in a study of domestic labour, we find that a husband says he does 6 hours' housework per week while his wife says he only does 2 hours. They cannot both be correct: we have to decide, and in so doing judge who is mistaken. Note that to judge what they said as mistaken, is not to deny that they said it; on the contrary we should report what they said as it may be important for explaining their behaviour.

It is therefore important to recognize that this critical element in understanding society cannot be avoided, even by those who believe social science should be value-free and 'disinterested'. For example, an economist who supports the value-freedom doctrine cannot avoid evaluating *some* economic behaviour as rational or misguided in trying to explain economic events such as recessions. Characteristically, though, the work of such researchers shows a *restricted* form of criticism in which only the actions ('policies') of a somewhat arbitrarily limited group ('decision-makers') are considered open to evaluation. This restriction would seem to derive from several mutually-reinforcing, unaware assumptions: that practices and relationships *not* deriving from such 'policies' are not concept-dependent and hence are not open to evaluation – as if only those parts of the social world produced by 'policies' are socially-constructed; that meaning is external to social practice, with the exception of policy, which anyway is seen as impinging on society from above; and that given this separation of meaning from practice, and policy from other actions, judgements of the former can be made without passing over into judgements of the latter. According to this incoherent view, evaluative statements about forms of social organization under capitalism are excluded as having nothing to do with 'science', but evaluations of this or that government policy are quite acceptable!

A further reason for resistance to the idea that social science must be critical of its object derives from an assumption that its subject–object relations are no different from those of natural science, i.e. like Figure 2. As non-social objects are not concept-dependent, it makes no sense to criticize them. *Intrinsically*, atomic reactions are neither good nor bad, rational nor irrational, although we may say they are good or bad *for* us, in relation to our own schemes. The idea of saying 'it's the world that's wrong, not our theories' is certainly ridiculous with regard to knowledge of nature, but if the above discussion is correct it may be reasonable when talking about socially produced phenomena.

So the radical nature of this proposal that social science must stand in a critical as well as an explanatory and interpretive relationship to its object and to common-sense knowledge should not be underestimated. It means more than merely a different way of 'doing social science': it implies a different view of the social role of this type of knowledge and for 'intellectuals'. It means that social science should not be seen as developing a stock of knowledge about an object which is external to us, but should develop a critical self-awareness in people as subjects and indeed assist in their emancipation. It does this first by remembering that its 'object' includes subjects, that the social world is socially produced and hence only one of many possible human constructions. It encourages emancipation and self-development by denying the reified, nature-like quality of the appearances of social life and by bringing to light formerly unrecognized constraints on human action. In capitalist societies, with their extraordinarily extended economic relations between anonymous people, the results of people's actions – their own products – take on 'nature-like' qualities in the sense that they react back on us as *blind forces* to which we must submit. Triumphs of human creativity, such as computers, can, if constructed and applied in certain ways, enslave people in their work. The language of economic 'booms', 'slumps', 'depressions', 'rising and falling markets' is significant. Although all of these events are the outcomes of human agency, they confront us rather like changes in the weather, floods or earthquakes – as external (natural) 'facts' that we must simply face up to. Whereas a large part of our social knowledge including much of social science takes for granted and reinforces this understandable reification of human action, critical theory challenges it as *real but nevertheless false*.

These features of our society go some way towards explaining (though not excusing!) the ignorance among many social scientists of the concept-dependent and socially-produced character of their objects of study. Consequently, they underestimate the problems of interpreting and conceptualizing the meaning of social phenomena and restrict their recognition of methodological problems to other operations such as sampling and the testing of hypotheses about quantitative relations. 'Radical behaviourists' project this conception (equivalent to Figure 1) of the subject–object relation on to the social interactions they study, so that people are assumed to relate to one another on the basis of physical stimulus and response, unmediated by *verstehen*.[60] In practice, these behaviourist conceptions may be reciprocally confirmed by actions which deny people their status as subjects; for example, electro-convulsive 'therapy' for 'disturbed' people, imprisonment for those with political grievances. The falsity of this position does not prevent it being practised, although this can never be done completely; any thoroughgoing realization of the behaviourist reduction of meaningful action to intrinsically-meaningless behaviour would make communication and hence social life impossible.

On the view developed here, if the term 'science' refers to a particularly examined knowledge, it cannot be merely an extension of common sense, as many people imagine; in many respects it will be its rival. Common sense tends to naturalize social phenomena and to assume that what is, must be. A social science which builds uncritically on common sense, and reproduces these errors, may, at a superficial level, appear to produce correct results. On the other hand, from the standpoint of common sense, which takes its knowledge to be self-evident and beyond challenge, the knowledge produced by critical theories such as marxism will appear to be false because it *conflicts* with what it judges to be the case ('an affront to common sense!'). Yet such theories aim not just to present an alternative or to reduce the illusions inherent in social understanding, but to represent and explain what actually exists as authentically as possible. It is only if it is recognized that part of 'the facts' about human existence is that it depends considerably on societies' self-understanding, that it is socially produced, albeit only partly in intended ways, and that changes in this self-understanding are coupled with changes in society's objective form,[61] that it becomes possible to see how knowledge can simultaneously be not only explanatory and descriptive but also evaluative, critical and emancipatory.

Conclusions

Instead of taking the nature and context of social scientific knowledge for granted and rushing into an account of its internal procedures, I have tried to look at this and other kinds of knowledge in context, in the belief that doing so will reveal something about its role and what are generally registered as its internal problems.[62] One of the main themes has been the relationship between knowledge and practice, in particular that between social science and its object of study. Through the idea of 'reciprocal confirmation', the interdependence of knowledge and practice has been stressed. Knowledge – whether adequate or not – never develops in a vacuum but is always embedded in social practices and we can more fully understand the former if we know the latter.

If this is true, then it ought to be applicable, reflexively, to our own subject matter. In other words, different conceptions of the relationship between subject and object should derive from or be closely associated with particular kinds of practical situation. By looking at this question, we can further illuminate the strengths and limitations of critical theory and the position of 'intellectuals' and scientists *vis-à-vis* everyday practice and practical knowledge.

Now I realize that at several moments in the discussion of sub-ject–object relations it may not have been clear whether it was the relationship between the 'investigator' and his or her social object of study or the relationship between 'ordinary' people in society that was being examined. Partly, the ambiguity was intentional, for it demonstrates some of the similarities between the two sets of relationships and serves as a reminder that the investigators do not exist outside their object and that the 'ordinary' people are 'subjects' too. Indeed, to be consistent, any discussion of knowl-edge must avoid asserting a particular characteristic of people as subjects (or investigators or students) only to deny it to them in their perceived role as objects, and vice versa. In other words, where there are similarities between the two relationships it ought to be possible to project the characteristics of one on to the other. Hence the symmetry of Figures 3 and 4 (pages 27 and 28).

Yet we have also noted some significant *differences* in types of knowledge and their contexts. The most important is between the practical knowledge involved in knowing how to do something and propositional knowledge of facts about the world. Later in the book we will discuss further differences within social science and look at their aims and the contexts in which they can be successful. One of the main arguments will be that social science is not simple and monistic but differentiated in its aims, methods and types of object. This chapter has paved the way for this argument by making similar points about knowledge in general. It has deliberately resisted the usual strategy of taking 'science' as given and out of context and of prescribing a single model for its internal procedures. Despite the consequent unusual breadth of the discussion, I have tried to show how they relate to quite concrete practices in social science and society.

2 Theory, observation and practical adequacy

Any serious consideration of method in social science quickly runs into basic issues such as the relation between theory and empirical observation and how we conceptualize phenomena. In turn, any reflection on these matters raises still more fundamental problems of objectivity, of the status of our knowledge. Traditionally, texts and courses on social scientific method have given these matters a wide berth, but since these more philosophical issues frequently come up in the evaluation of substantive work – in some disciplines more than others – this a dubious strategy. I therefore make no apology for addressing these issues. They are more than a prelude to a discussion of method, for they address its most crucial moment – how we conceptualize.

The present doubts about objectivity and the status of scientific knowledge followed a period of relative confidence and certainty, in which science was predominantly seen as the steady accretion of objective knowledge through the unproblematic medium of observation or 'experience'. On this 'naïve objectivist' view, the facts 'spoke for themselves', and only needed to be 'collected' as 'data'. In so far as theory had a role it was in the subsequent stages of ordering, explaining and perhaps predicting the facts.

Naïve objectivism continues to thrive in common-sense thinking and isn't quite dead yet in science. A politician recently insisted that a strongly contested economic doctrine – monetarism – was not 'mere theory', but 'fact', while another called for 'theory' to be abandoned and for 'a return to the facts'. And one still hears scientists saying that Darwin's theory of evolution is 'just a theory' and 'not fact'.

The contrast of fact and theory is being invoked here as if it were indisputable. Yet in considering such applications of the distinction, especially the last, we begin to doubt the distinction

itself and indeed in philosophy it has been comprehensively challenged: theory is increasingly recognized as affecting observation
itself, so that the latter is said to be 'theory-laden'. The idea that
knowledge is based upon experience then becomes at least highly
ambiguous and a number of fundamental problems begin to come
into focus: if empirical observation is theory-laden, can it provide
an independent test of theory? If the world can be understood only
through particular ways of seeing, can we still talk of 'truth' and
'objectivity'? The shattering of the innocent belief in the possibility of unproblematic theory-neutral observation has driven some
scientists to the opposite extreme of 'radical relativism', in which
truth is purely relative to one's theory, 'paradigm', 'problematic'
or 'world-view' and for which no independent tests exist. It is
not uncommon to find such scientists saying 'it all depends on
your paradigm' or that 'such-and-such a concept is employed not
because it is claimed to be "true", but because it is "useful"'.
In some quarters, the overthrow of the notion of theory-neutral
observation has undermined researchers' confidence in any kind
of empirical research and has driven them into theoretical and
philosophical introspection.[1] But then there are others who react
to the seemingly endless theoretical disputes by casting doubt on
the value of theory itself. So confusion reigns. Is there a way out
of these problems?

   If we are to find answers, it is vital not only to consider
some matters of epistemology (the theory of knowledge), but
to examine the nature of theory and observation in more depth.
En route I will also examine the nature of sense and reference,
the distinction between the conceptual and the empirical, and the
relationship between meaning and context. This will assist the
ensuing discussions of truth and relativism, and the development
of knowledge.

Knowledge and object

'We can improve our conceptual scheme, our philosophy, bit by
bit while continuing to depend on it for support; but we cannot
detach ourselves from it and compare it objectively with an
unconceptualized reality. Hence it is meaningless, I suggest, to
inquire into the absolute correctness of a conceptual scheme as
a mirror of reality' (Neurath, quoted in Quine, 1961).[2]

The invocation of 'facts' in popular discourse plays upon a hidden ambiguity, between 'facts' as states or properties of the world itself, and 'facts' as 'factual statements' putatively made about those states. A factual statement like 'the Earth is spherical' is not the same as the thing to which it refers. One is a 'thought object', the other is a 'real object', something which exists regardless of whether we happen to know it. We can of course only think about the real object in terms of a thought object; as Neurath reminds us we cannot get outside language or knowledge to see how it compares with the object. The illusion of the appeal to facts in popular discourse involves collapsing statements into their referents, thought objects into real objects. It thereby appears to appeal to the facts themselves, the way the world is, in an unmediated fashion, but it is actually an appeal to a particular way of talking about the world in some conceptual system, and therefore may be contested. Consequently, facts as factual statements do not have the authority generally claimed for them.

To avoid such dangerous confusions, we therefore need a distinction between thought objects and real objects, in which not only theoretical statements but empirical or observational statements are both included within the realm of thought objects. In other words, instead of

Thought Objects – *Real Objects*

theory – fact

we need:

Thought Objects – *Real Objects*

theory ⎫
⎪
⎬ – facts as things
empirical ⎪   or states of the
observational ⎪   world
factual knowledge ⎭

The items listed on the left-hand side may attempt to refer to those on the right-hand side but they are qualitatively different from them. We can now see that theoretical and factual knowledge have something in common, and that the popular contrast between the allegedly speculative and unrealistic character of theory and the allegedly undeniable reality of 'facts' loses much of its force.

But we cannot rest content with this second model. Three further modifications need to be made which resist diagrammatic representation. First, though cognitive processes are not reducible to material structures, they are set within them, and are constrained and enabled by them. These material structures and processes include the brain itself. This is often treated by non-psychologists as *tabula rasa*, a view which of course renders unintelligible such phenomena as the dramatic effects on behaviour of brain tumours.[3] That knowledge is linguistic to a significant degree does not mean that it does not also have a physical side.

Secondly, practice, as we noted in the last chapter, is a link between knowledge and the world, though it does not abolish the radical difference between them just noted or provide knowledge with absolute guarantees of truth. But there *is* a crucial difference – usually overlooked in discussions of the status of knowledge – between the relationship between thought and the objects to which it refers, and the relationship between practice and its objects. As Charles Taylor puts it:

We can draw a neat line between my *picture* of an object and that object, but not between my *dealing* with the object and that object. It may make sense to ask one to focus on what one *believes* about something, say a football, even in the absence of that thing; but when it comes to *playing* football, the corresponding suggestion would be absurd. The actions involved in the game cannot be done without the object; they include the object.[4]

In light of this we should perhaps think of knowledge not so much as a representation of the world, as a means for doing things in it. Hence, to continue the last chapter's emphasis on practice, science itself is practical as well as cognitive and many activities normally considered to be purely cognitive, often involve material processes of searching, making contact, separating out, dividing, combining, activating, manipulating.

A third modification to our diagram is needed to take account of the nature of the objects which social science studies, which may include conceptual and concept-dependent phenomena. Here the real objects under investigation include thought objects, though not necessarily ones familiar to the investigator. The double hermeneutic – the need for the interpenetration of the frames of reference of observer and observed, for mediation of their respective understandings – blurs our distinction between thought object and real object. Nevertheless, the thought objects of those who are being studied are not, except in self-reflection, the same as those of the investigator, and it is misleading to imagine otherwise. *Although social phenomena cannot exist independently of actors or subjects, they usually do exist independently of the particular individual who is studying them.* Social scientists and historians produce interpretations of objects, but do not generally produce the objects themselves. Thus, properly qualified, the thought object/real object distinction still applies to social science.[5]

These criticisms of popular lay and academic conceptions of the relationship between knowledge and its objects resolve some problems such as the confusion between statements and what they refer to, and they provide a framework which brings other fundamental problems of relativism and the nature of truth into clearer relief. But as I indicated earlier it is helpful first to look more closely at the nature of theory, observation, and concepts such as sense and reference, which also illuminate the nature of language and its relation to the world. If we do not do this, subsequent discussions are liable to be subverted by inconsistent usages of these terms.

'Theory'

Rather than start with a formal, prescriptive definition of theory, it is worth first reflecting upon the range of uses of this highly 'elastic' term in science and everyday life. Common-sense conceptions of theory are complex and presuppose a set of significant contrasts:

	⎧ –	fact or reality
theory	⎨ –	practice
	⎩ –	common sense
idealized, hypothetical	–	actual
speculative	–	certain
opinion, value, belief	–	fact
subjective	–	objective

Once again, many of these contrasts are wrongly drawn, but as they appear in more 'respectable', 'scientific' uses, they cannot be ignored.[6] Again also, the associations of these terms 'leak' from one to another in the vertical dimension. For example, once theory has been opposed to what actually happens in practice, it only takes a little bit of sloppy thinking to align the theoretical with the impractical. Indeed, several more or less pejorative uses of 'theory' are available and are fully exploited by those who seek to preserve the status quo which common sense upholds. (Note how the terms 'academic' and 'intellectual' can be added to the left-hand side of the table, where they can also be given these negative associations.)

It is fairly common for theorists to counter with 'there's nothing so practical as a good theory', but a more radical reaction attempts to reverse the pejorative loading, pedestalling theory and derogating common sense and writing 'sic' when quoting people who innocently (or not so innocently) talk of 'the facts'.[7]

But what are theories? In (social) science, the following senses are particularly important:

1   Theory as an *ordering-framework* (or as Milton Friedman puts it, as a 'filing-system'),[8] which permits observational data to be used for predicting and explaining empirical events.
2   Theory as *conceptualization*, in which 'to theorize' means to prescribe a particular way of conceptualizing something.
3   Theory is also often used interchangeably with 'hypothesis' or 'explanation'.

The differences between 1 and 2 are subtle but important, as will be seen shortly. Provisionally, theory in 1 can be thought of as a way of ordering relationship between observations (or data) whose meaning is taken as unproblematic. In 2 this ordering function is secondary and the conceptualization of objects, both in their observable and unobservable properties, primary. The popularity of these alternative uses varies across the social sciences. 1 is perhaps the more common in disciplines with a high degree of orthodoxy, such as economics, where many of the ordering frameworks have been cast in mathematical form, and perhaps so too is 3 as 'hypothesis'. This is also the model which has been most frequently assumed in books on methodology and how to do empirical research. In some places it has become institutionalized in the form of standard expectations of research (particularly that of junior members of the academic community, such as PhD students) and those who reject these criteria are likely to incur disapproval. 2 is more common in subjects characterized by fundamental divisions and considerable philosophical and methodological introspection such as sociology.

In the next section the notion of 'theory-laden' observation will be examined more closely.[9] I shall argue that theory and observation are implicitly mischaracterized by the ordering framework model and that the idea of theory as an examined conceptualization of some object is more appropriate.[10]

The conceptual mediation of perception

Our senses of sight, hearing, touch, taste and smell are so taken for granted in everyday life that it is tempting to assume that they connect us to the world in a simple, straightforward manner: hence the common-sense faith in the neutrality of observation. Yet, as some wag remarked, 'there is more to seeing than meets the eye'. Research on perception has shown it to be complex, but basically consisting of three parts.[11] I will use visual perception as an example, but equivalent processes exist for the other senses.

There is first the object of perception, the material substance which emits or reflects energy in some form, such as that which we call 'light'. Second, there are mechanisms – retinal cells in the case of sight – which are sensitive to this energy. When activated these transmit minute electric currents to the brain, which give us sensations. Third, if and only if these sensations are conceptualized in some way is it possible for us to identify particular objects of perception. What we therefore claim to be able to perceive is the outcome of a complex set of factors; not just the nature of the object, but the condition of the physical mechanisms which are sensitive to certain types of energy (e.g. the condition of our eyes) and the type of concepts we have for making sense of the 'sense data'.[12]

For the purposes of this discussion, it is the third part which is most significant. Our visual (and other sensory) fields are 'conceptually-saturated'.

New born infants and patients blind from birth recovering from surgery to restore their sight are doubtless the only human creatures with unconceptualised visual fields. We no longer remember what it was like to have one. . . . Certainly any expression in language of a visual experience, however primitive and ill-defined, is already conceptually-tainted (Even, for example: 'I see yellow').[13]

In the case of the formerly blind, it can take not seconds but weeks and months for patients to *learn* how to perceive and how to form systems of concepts through which they can interpret their visual sense-data.

The psychology of perception literature further demonstrates the key role of *practice* in learning processes. Perception and learning are greatly assisted by the active manipulation and exploration of the world, by interaction with objects, including other people. Learning is significantly retarded where this is not possible and subjects are restricted to using only their cognitive faculties, merely contemplating the world. As we indicated in the previous chapter, many philosophers have tended to ignore this latter dimension, and have consequently obfuscated the relationship between knowledge and the world and questions of the status, truth or reliability of knowledge.

Aside from their neglect of the practical dimension, philosophers and scientists have interpreted the implications of this research regarding the cognitive side in different ways. There is one quite common interpretation which supports the ordering-framework view of theory and which I want to contest. This assumes an equivalence between 'data', in the sense in which the word is ordinarily used in social science, and 'sense-data', in the sense in which it is used in the study of perception. It then appears that 'data' such as survey results or statistics are untainted by concepts or theories and only *subsequently* interpreted, explained or predicted using some theoretical or conceptual 'framework'. This is clearly utterly contrary to the results of the perception research for it smuggles in the notion of theory- or concept-neutral (yet intelligible) observation. The data we 'gather'[14] in science are *already* (pre-)conceptualized. We may have 'sensations' without concepts, but we have no perception without concepts. Social scientists who treat 'data' literally as 'given things' (often those who feel most confident about the objectivity of their knowledge and the 'hardness' of their facts) therefore unknowingly take on board and reproduce the interpretations implicit in the data: they think *with* these hidden concepts but not *about* them. As Pratt puts it, 'Our system of concepts imposes categories, divides experience into discrete items between which relationships become possible. So far from labelling pre-discriminated entities, our concepts make their discrimination possible'.[15] However, Pratt's correction itself needs qualification, for concepts do not usually discriminate on their own, without the assistance of material discriminations and interventions made in practice.

Precisely because we are accustomed to thinking in terms of a particular set of concepts, we rarely recognize their influence. In this respect, an analogous discussion by the art historian E. H. Gombrich[16] is instructive. Gombrich examines the role of 'schemata', which we might take as equivalent to concepts, in the work of artists by comparing two paintings of the same landscape in the English Lake District, one done by a Chinese artist, one by a European. Both paintings were intended as 'faithful representations' but to European eyes the former's looks like a Chinese landscape.

Given the 'conceptually-saturated' character of observation, it is difficult to distinguish between what is observable and what is unobservable. Can we really claim to be able to observe the earth orbiting the sun? Can we really *see* that a landscape is glaciated or that a person is bored?[17] What a layperson and a biologist claim to be able to see under a microscope will differ considerably, not just in the sense that they see the same shapes but interpret them differently (which would fit with the 'ordering framework' view of theory), but because they have learned to see or 'discriminate' different patterns in the first place. The distinction between the observable and the unobservable is therefore not simply a function of the physical receptivity of our sense organs: it is also strongly influenced by the extent to which we take for granted and hence forget the concepts involved in perception. This somewhat arbitrary contrast between areas of experience whose concepts are unnoticed (e.g. common sense) and areas where they are still noticed then often supports a popular but questionable distinction between 'factual' and 'theoretical' knowledge.[18]

There are many examples in the history of science of concepts which were initially regarded as speculative and 'theoretical', later becoming so familiar and unquestioned that they are treated as observable. Instead of being interpreted tentatively, as ways of understanding objects, they are taken as descriptions of observable characteristics of the objects themselves. Many scientific concepts formerly regarded as 'theoretical', in the sense of speculative aids to understanding, have passed into common sense, where ignorance of the conceptually-mediated nature of experience allows them to acquire the status of 'fact' and to be used for dogmatically rejecting other, still conspicuous, 'theoretical' concepts. The idea that the earth went round the sun could, of course, easily be refuted by reference to the 'observable facts'. Not surprisingly, in inter-theoretical disputes, one often finds one side protesting that what the other side (presumably sincerely) claims to be able to observe is really just a 'theoretical hypothesis'. In learning a new body of theory, whether it be marxism or neoclassical economics or pluralist theories of politics, we usually eventually come to find that the new concepts enable us to see new objects or aspects of objects and not merely offer a different interpretation of everyday observations. The point to be made here, then, is that some of the accepted criteria for distinguishing the observable from the unobservable, and hence observation statements from theoretical statements, lack foundation. Both have in common the feature of being conceptually mediated. In view of the universality of theory-ladenness, the popular alignment of the distinction between empirical and theoretical knowledge with the observable and the unobservable must therefore be judged dubious.

Further, if theory means little more than a system of concepts theory-ladenness cannot be regarded as a question of degree.[19] In appealing to observable facts we are not appealing to a 'less theory-laden' kind of experience but rather an area of experience about which we feel more confident, but which is no less conceptually-saturated for that. The tendency to imagine that it is is probably derived from and supports the reservation in everyday ways of speaking of the word 'concept' for esoteric ideas.

In view of the demise of the distinction between theoretical and observation languages, it makes no sense to talk, as social scientists often do, of the need for a 'middle ground' between theory and empirics.[20] What they are typically searching for is a middle ground between something different, between highly abstract and often esoteric concepts, like alienation or ontological security, and everyday concepts, like work satisfaction. Bridges or middle ground are indeed often needed, but they are no less theoretical and observable than that which they attempt to join.

Despite these arguments, it is surprising how limited the understanding of the theory-laden character of observation has been and how often naïve objectivism is replaced by a model which retains the neutrality of observation but merely gives theory, as an ordering framework, a more prominent role. For example, many scientists, both physical and social, will stress how observations are not made in a vacuum but are guided and shaped by prior questions, problems, hypotheses, conjectures or theories. This view tends to be justified by a certain reading of the early work of the philosopher Karl Popper.[21] The problem with it is that it can easily lapse into a 'two-stage' model in which hypotheses are first advanced and ordering frameworks designed and *then* filled out with and tested by 'data' whose meaning is taken as unproblematic. In other words, in assuming that theory only makes conjectures (etc.) about relationships (especially regularities) between variables, it has been possible for many authors to pay lip-service to the idea that observation is theory-laden, while continuing to treat it as theory-neutral in practice. Clearly, this view supports the ordering-framework or 'filing system' conception of theory.

As this misunderstanding of 'theory-ladenness' is quite common, it may help to examine the role of concepts more closely. Once again the work of Gombrich is useful. According to Gombrich, the individual elements of schemata do not uniquely provide a way of seeing particular objects, but in terms of contrasts and similarities with other elements.[22] He compares the 'progress of learning, of adjusting through trial and error' . . , 'to the game of "Twenty Questions" where we guess the identity of an object through inclusion or exclusion among the network of classes'. This is helpful provided that it is remembered that we do not see the object first and then fit it into our schemata or conceptual system: just as the players know absolutely nothing about the object until they try out questions such as 'animal, vegetable, mineral or abstract?' we do not perceive objects without some schemata, however basic the contrasts or relationships they can discern. Nevertheless, we must note the limitations of this analogy, for once again it ignores practice; our schemata are very much developed through acting upon a differentiated world which does not respond neutrally to different actions.

As with the schemata of the artist, the terms of our language do not refer to objects (whether material or abstract) independently of other terms, but by making contrasts with others – by differentiation. A particular term takes on meaning only through its relationship to others: 'night' and 'day' cannot be understood independently of one another or of certain other terms. The systems of oppositions or dualisms that I have used earlier (subjective–objective, theory–fact, etc.) can be taken as examples of how meaning is constituted through the '*play of difference*' among the units of the language.[23] Where we have to make a conscious effort to 'conceptualize' or 'theorize' something, we (re)construct and modify these patterns of differences by which we grasp the differentiation of the world.

It is sometimes assumed that we have only one or at least very few theories in terms of which we can observe. This implies that theories are monolithic and procrustean and hence unresponsive to the world. It certainly does not rest easily with the idea of the possibility of subtly changing the 'play of differences'. On this view, as we shall see, theoretical change is an all-or-nothing affair and it seems scarcely possible for experience to contradict theory for the only available criteria for judging the theory are those internal to it. Yet on any definition, we have many rather than few theories and we certainly have a very large number of concepts and schemata. As the 'Twenty Questions' analogy suggests, understanding requires the use of a range of schemata or concepts, drawn from a large repertoire. The number of possible combinations of these is by no means unlimited, because there are logical restrictions on the relationships between concepts,[24] but it allows considerable flexibility and a certain amount of cross-checking of observation or reflection under one group of concepts by another. Under concept A we may expect an object to have property x and not y, but it may be possible to determine which it has by an independent concept B.

Sense and reference and the conceptual and the empirical

I now want to argue that the 'ordering-framework' conception of theory is supported by suspect distinctions between 'sense and reference' and 'the conceptual' and 'the empirical'. The former distinction was first introduced in philosophy only to be challenged later. Although non-philosophers are generally unaware of the distinction by name, something approximating to it is implicit in the ordering-framework model. Consider Figure 5 which concerns the meaning of the word 'child' (the similarity to Figure 2 (p. 25) should be clear). It is tempting to distinguish between the *reference* of the word 'child' (i.e. the object to which it refers) and its *sense*, which derives from the set of connections or 'sense-relations' that tie it to other words.[25] These 'sense-relations' may be of different types, e.g. synonymy, heteronymy (opposite meaning). It then appears reasonable to say that the sense-relations represent the contribution of language, as if this were separable from the act of reference, and conversely as if the latter were possible independently of language, by simply pointing at the object. This separation then resonates with the separation of observation (apparently leading to reference) from interpretation (apparently yielding sense).

Yet closer examination shows sense and reference to be *inter-dependent* rather than separable. If reference by pointing is to work, we must know not only what pointing means but what aspect of the object is being referred to and how we are supposed to observe it. So, to be successful, the act of reference must

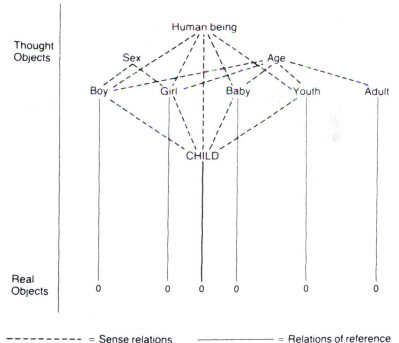

Figure 5 Sense and reference

simultaneously invoke or construct sense-relations.[26] Conversely, the 'play of difference' constituted among sense-relations in conceptual systems is reciprocally confirmed by reference to, and by action within, the material world. And to say that two words are synonymous is to say (at least) that they have a common reference.

This relationship is again echoed in the more widely known distinction between the *conceptual* and the *empirical*. Examples of 'conceptual questions' might include the meaning of actions associated with witchcraft, the meaning of an ideology or the meaning of a scientific concept. Examples of empirical questions might concern the distribution of support for a political party or levels of investment in different industries. It should by now be clear that: 1 answers to empirical questions presuppose answers to questions about the scientific (and other) concepts used in identifying their objects; 2 that in the case of concept-dependent social objects empirical knowledge presupposes understanding the constitutive concepts; and 3 that any kind of question about concepts must take account of the (empirical) circumstances in which they are used. This is not to suppose, however, that *every change* in our empirical beliefs about X's produces a change in the meaning of the term 'X'.[27]

Now it is common to argue that a theory can be evaluated in two different and apparently separate ways: in terms of its internal, conceptual consistency, and of its empirical adequacy. However, because of the interdependence of sense and reference and the conceptual and the empirical, they cannot be treated as entirely separate. The empirical success of a theory is affected by how the networks of sense-relations are constructed and how the resultant expectations and actions relate to the actual structure of the world, though our judgements about the latter will always be made *through* practical relations and conceptualizations. And looking at it from the other direction, the *coherence* of any system of concepts which attempts to enable reference to, and action within, the world cannot be judged independently of its empirical reference and the results of social practice. For example, whether it is conceptually inconsistent to describe an individual as both a capitalist and a proletarian depends on what we take to be the possible nature of a person, means of production, etc.

In such cases we find that conceptual inconsistencies are grounded in practical inconsistencies. Consider another example. Marxism has been criticized for supposing that a post-capitalist society could involve a free association of workers, in which workers had more freedom than under capitalism, *and* a centrally-planned economy. But as Lenin and others acknowledged, the latter implies that workers submit completely to central discipline – the despotism of an economy run as 'one big factory'. What is involved here is not merely a problem of inconsistencies between ideas, but fundamental contradictions or incompatibilities between different social structures and practices, in this case ones which the history of socialist experiments with comprehensive central planning have exposed only too clearly.

As before, these examples are intended as reminders of the practical context of knowledge and as counters to the intellectualist fallacies noted in Chapter 1. But let me make the points more explicit.

First, we develop and use concepts not only through and for observing and representing the world but for acting in it, for work and communicative interaction; for making and doing as well as speaking, writing, listening and reading, for running organizations and working in them, for programming computers, cooking meals, teaching children, sorting mail, and so on. Nor do we need to be aware of the names of concepts to have them.[28] Conceptual systems concern not only what we (think we can) observe, but what we can do and how we do it. Again, it may be wise to avoid thinking of knowledge as attempting to 'represent' or 'mirror' the world like a photograph.[29] A better analogy may be that of a map or recipe or instruction manual, which provides means by which we can do things in the world or *cope* with events.[30]

Second, concept and schemata should not be abstracted from their use by people in the course of their business, as if they could exist in a vacuum. They are not fixed but can be developed, extended or allowed to atrophy, and they can be used with differing degrees of skill.[31] Good artists can use the most highly developed, richly differentiated schemata so skilfully that they enable us to see things in a new way, while poor ones use them clumsily and produce results that are either unintelligible or clichéd. The equivalent is true for the use of concepts in science and everyday practice.

Third, communication, through the construction and interpretation of the 'play of differences' among linguistic expressions, has a material side to it. We have already illustrated how

meaning is reciprocally confirmed by reference to and construction of material arrangements by the example of the concepts
of 'public' and 'private'. Successful communication, including
the establishment and negotiation of concepts, depends to some
degree on particular temporal sequences of actions, both linguistic
and non-linguistic, and spatial, material settings: in other words
meaning is context-dependent. In extreme cases, such as marriage
ceremonies, meaning is very rigidly confirmed by formalized
actions in particular spatio-temporal settings. Even in cases of
acts which are fairly flexible in their use, success depends on
improvised contextualization; philosophical discussions can be
held in a variety of circumstances, but if I were to say to a
stranger in the street, 'meaning is context-dependent', I would
be thought mad, though it's the sort of thing which would be
expected in a philosophical seminar.[32] So making sense of events
requires that we 'contextualize' them in some way.

Understanding of social phenomena requires a double contextualization owing to its situation in a 'double hermeneutic' (see
Chapter 1). When we encounter unfamiliar events, this may
prove difficult, requiring us to 'scramble' through our repertoire
of familiar contexts to find one in which the event 'makes sense'.
These contextualizations are present not only in carefully considered analyses but in the simplest, most 'primitive' and immediate
descriptions, including photographic representations. Arguments
often concern the selection of appropriate contextualizations:
should the conflict in Northern Ireland be construed as class-based
or religion-based, or by some other means? This process is perhaps
most obvious in the reporting of news, which by definition mainly
concerns the unfamiliar and the abnormal, deriving its interest
from the contrast with normality and routine.[33] Journalists have
repertoires of contextualizations which, despite their common
belief to the contrary, are often quite specialized and different
from those used by their readers. In the worst cases journalism
appears to consist of clichéd contextualizations in search of news
which can be adapted to them: the bank holiday beach violence,
the 'wildcat' strikers and their wives urging them to go back,
the 'human interest' story, the 'fanatical' nature of supporters
of left-wing policies, and so on.[34]

There are some events, however, which are so novel as to lie
out of reach of even these elastic contextualizations. In the early
days of the urban riots of summer 1981 in Britain, most papers

rapidly chopped and changed their contextualizations as they encountered unfamiliar combinations of events – not only black but white rioters, not only young, single working-class looters but 'middle-class' married ones with cars. . . . Often the papers could only arrive at 'conclusive', settled contextualizations by forgetting certain aspects which they had earlier reported. But then this phenomenon of forgetting what had previously been identified through 'low-order' schemata, e.g. those involved in identifying which social groups were involved, because they do not fit easily with 'higher order', more comprehensive schemata (say, about 'class struggle' or 'race riots') is very common outside journalism too. Even in natural science, there have been many cases of anomalous evidence ('observations conflicting with theory') being ignored in preference to disturbing familiar theories, the latter being claimed to be 'tried and tested' despite the fact that they are also being protected from test by such decisions. Although there is no context-free, theory-free factual base towards which we can retrace our steps in cases of disagreement, it is reasonable to try to settle the issue by retreating to those concepts and empirical evidence (remembering that the two are interdependent) where there is no disagreement and then attempting to check the consistency of the disputed concepts and empirical evidence with these.

Contextualizing events involves finding familiar patterns of associations, but the process of making inferences from the latter is fraught with difficulties. The dangers are clear in cases where associations which are accidental or 'contingent' (neither necessary nor impossible) are treated as if they were necessary properties of objects. For example, bad housing may be associated with occupation by members of racial minorities and racist thinking may treat this contingent – and hence changeable – relation as a *necessary*, essential characteristic of such people by virtue of their race. In unexamined thinking, sets of associations can inadvertently 'leak' from one object or context to fix upon another.

These processes are particularly clear in 'moral panics' where certain individuals, groups or institutions ('folk devils') suddenly come to be seen as symbols of everything that society fears.[35] Generally these fears are extremely ill-defined. They find common expressions in concern over perceived decline of moral values, the disintegration of idealized institutions such as the nuclear family, the loss of ideals and the rise of 'anarchy' and disrespect for authority and property. During a moral panic these normally diffuse associations are projected and focused on to a particular group, providing a temporary outlet for these pent-up fears. Similar processes occur in periods of euphoria – for example, following a victory in war.

A useful way of comprehending this 'leakage of meaning' (and one which I have already borrowed) has been developed by Douglas, who characterizes the conceptual and practical distinctions of everyday life in terms of rules according to which people structure their experience, actions and institutions.

Sets of rules are metaphorically connected with another, allow meaning to leak from one context to another along the formal similarities that they show. The barriers between finite provinces of meaning are always sapped either by the violent flooding through of social concerns or by the subtle economy which uses the same rule structure in each province.[36]

These changes in systems of meaning are clearly tied to changes in practice in society: they are not merely external descriptions. They can also be crude and somewhat irrational. Social science which neglects the importance of conceptualization is prone to insert the misconceptions of unexamined common sense into its ordering frameworks. It can even reinforce false consciousness by elevating contingent and historically specific associations to the status of natural laws and then feeding them back into common-sense thinking bearing the stamp of 'science'.[37] Throughout the history of social science, for example, contingent gender relations such as those of the nuclear family have been naturalized, hence legitimating patriarchal social structures. *A crucial role of social science must be to monitor and restructure the casual patterns of associations or sense-relations of unexamined knowledge, so that differences between necessary and contingent relations, and between warranted and unwarranted associations, are understood.*

This is certainly not to argue that shifts or 'leakage' in meaning do not occur in social science, indeed they may be encouraged in order to produce conceptual innovation. Metaphors and analogies play an important but often misunderstood role in the process of conceptual development in social science. Sometimes the displacement of a concept to a new object of reference leaves the concept relatively intact, but in more interesting cases the displacement changes the meaning of the 'root' concept. For example, redescribing war as 'state-sanctioned violence' can alter our general concept of violence, leading us to look at more conventionally denoted instances of violence (e.g. 'terrorism') in a different light.

It is common to underestimate the extent to which our conceptual systems are constructed through metaphor. In an expression such as 'the miners are the shock-troops of the labour movement' the metaphor is obvious because of an unfamiliar displacement of words from their home usage. But some such 'live' metaphors may become so familiar and widely used that we forget the displacement. The previous two sentences also contain several 'dead' metaphors.[38] New concepts can only be developed from pre-existing ones. We generally try to explain the unfamiliar by reference to the familiar. It is therefore not surprising that closer examination of our vocabulary shows it to be rich in metaphor and understandable that we rarely coin new terms which are not related to existing ones in some way. Sometimes older metaphors may become conspicuous once again (e.g. electric 'current') but may nevertheless be retained if they are untroublesome or refer to a different aspect of an object from that denoted by more modern terms. These modern terms will themselves often be metaphorical; metaphors are not a pre-scientific residue which is gradually being removed. The most advanced no less than the most ancient scientific vocabulary is loaded with metaphor.[39] In social science, 'inflation', 'co-operative game', 'free rider', 'supply chain', 'careeral organization', and the like are no less metaphorical than Adam Smith's 'invisible hand'. Contrary to the usual view of the development of science, progress consists partly in improving and extending our ability to *picture* the world.

Some scientists and philosophers have disregarded the role of metaphors and 'picture-carrying expressions'[40] and have represented scientific language as a combination of sets of empirical terms, each of which is (mistakenly) taken to be capable of referring, on its own, to its object (like the individual cards of a card-index system) plus logical formulae which relate these atomistic observational terms together (like the rules by which the cards are placed in a particular order). The logical relations may in some cases be written as mathematical formulae. These enable the use of one set of data for calculating another set. Mathematical models in subjects such as economics, demography and geography have this form; they are primarily *calculating devices*. Indeed, the economist Friedman has described 'theory' as a blend of two elements: 'a body of substantive hypotheses designed to abstract essential features of a complex reality' and a 'language' consisting of a set of tautologies which serves as a 'filing system'.[41]

While it is true that logical relationships between sets of statements are important constituents of theories, this ordering-framework view of theory fails to appreciate: 1 the theory laden character of observation, and, related to this, the fact that many theoretical terms don't merely order 'data' like a filing system but make claims about the nature of the world; 2 the interdependence of sense and reference; and 3 the indispensable 'picture-carrying', metaphorical nature of 'language'. Indeed, if this view of theory were plausible, science would never encounter conceptual problems, that is, problems of meaning. The only difficulty would be in finding a logical structure which would allow 'calculations of unknowns' to be made. Certainly, elaborate mathematical 'theories' have been devised in many sciences, and, as many have complained, they are often developed and discussed in abstraction from any reference to the real world. When they are used to explain, predict (or calculate) something in the real world then the widespread ignorance of 1, 2 and 3 tends to allow their proponents to imagine that unproblematic observations can simply be 'plugged in' to the equations and that the real business of empirical science only begins once this has been done.[42]

This is not to say that other scientists sharing the same view of theory as Friedman have not often discussed the role of metaphor and analogy in the development of science, but they have restricted the meaning of these terms in a way which does not challenge the ordering-framework view of theory.. For example, some human geographers have suggested using mathematical models of the spread of diseases as an 'analogue model' of the spread of social phenomena such as technological innovations, riots, or minority social groups.[43] Here, an existing ordering-framework theory is applied to novel situations. It is clear that there are disanalogies involved in such comparisons – riots, racial minorities and innovations are very different kinds of things from diseases – but this hasn't unduly worried the advocates of this 'diffusion theory'. Their approach only encourages them to think about the quantitative dimensions of their 'filing system' (the choice of appropriate mathematical formulae) and not about the meaning of the concepts involved in the observational statements which are 'plugged into' their formulae.[44]

Truth and practical adequacy

On the basis of the foregoing exploration of the nature of theory and observation, we can now confront some fundamental doubts about the objectivity of our knowledge, in particular whether the impossibility of theory-neutral observation leaves theory and knowledge in general without any external check, whether disputes between competing theories are resolvable and whether the development of knowledge takes place discontinuously and possibly a-rationally.

We have seen that naïve objectivism's innocent faith in observation and 'the facts' derives either from a belief that observation gives an unproblematic access to the world, or worse, from a confusion between factual statements and their referents, between knowledge and what it is about.[45] Its dogmatic character – which is perhaps most evident in the language of populist politicians – derives in turn from ignorance of the latter distinction and of the necessity of a vocabulary or conceptual system by means of which claims can be made about the world. Statements have to be intersubjectively negotiated, in order first to be established as intelligible and second as true or false. Unawareness of this is all the more serious in social science where the existence of a double hermeneutic requires a *conscious* or examined interpretation of concepts and beliefs in society, whether they be true or false. But note that given the unavoidability of the theory-laden character of observation and the hermeneutic relationship, it is inconsistent to criticize naïve objectivists (or 'empiricists') for lacking theory and a hermeneutic aspect in their analyses. What they *can* be criticized for is their ignorance of these dimensions and hence the unexamined and dogmatic character of their knowledge.

Given the double hermeneutic of social science, the problems concerning the status and reliability of its knowledge go beyond the simple relationship between thought and material objects to that between the thought objects of the investigator and the concepts and beliefs of the society under study. However, the importance of the material dimensions of society makes the following discussion of the relationship between thought and the material world relevant.

Thought objects and their material referents are utterly different, and yet we can consider the latter only via the former. Now there are two common responses to this dilemma, both involving fundamental challenges to the way we think about knowledge.

1   How do we know that there is a real world existing independently of us if its existence can only be postulated in thought? How do we know that we are not dreaming, that our 'real objects' are but figments of our imagination? (idealism)
2   If there are real objects, how can their relationship to thought objects be discovered? What justification, other than reference to the internal criteria of particular systems of thought or theories, can be given for saying that some statements are true or that they 'correspond' to or 'represent' their objects? (relativism)

Although these are fundamental questions, I realize that some readers may feel impatient with 1 or even be irritated by it, with its associations of the idle and apparently affected doubt of philosophers about the existence of 'this table', etc. I sympathize with the impatience but I will try to give an answer as it may help to deal with more 'bread and butter' issues such as scientific testing later on.

Advice is sometimes given that we should doubt everything, but it is impossible to doubt everything simultaneously. In order to call into question one area of knowledge we must at least temporarily use some other area as an anchorpoint and a tool.[46] We can only answer scepticism by checking whether it is compatible with – or better, presupposed by – knowledge about which both believers and sceptics feel most confident. To refuse any such appeal to provisional common ground would be to render thought and communication impossible. Arguments about 1 and 2 can only be useful if the disputants try to be consistent: that is, they must accept that they must not presuppose something which their conclusions deny. But herein lies the problem of total, 'sham' scepticism. It is very easy, but quite useless, to affect doubt about anything without considering whether such doubts are consistent with other beliefs and practices. If everything were a dream, nothing could be. If we were to relabel all our experience 'dreaming' we would merely have to think of new labels for the old distinction between dreaming and 'waking experience'.[47]

Like any other belief, the ideas contained in this argument against idealism are themselves fallible, but the common experience of being taken by surprise by what we see gives us reasonable grounds for supposing that the world is not our own invention, even though the *concept* 'world' undoubtedly is. Whenever we open our eyes, the objects before us are not thereby pre-determined, although the way they are seen is certainly conceptually (and physiologically) mediated. Like naïve objectivism, idealism collapses thought and its objects together, only the direction of the reduction is different.[48]

The questions under 2 are more worthy of attention and have caused plenty of problems in debates in social science. We have already argued that the practical dimension of the relationship between thought and the world must be kept in mind. Perhaps the main problem concerns how something as immaterial as a concept or statement or equation can be said to be 'true of', 'correspond to' or 'represent' something material. If you think about this, the normally hidden metaphorical nature of terms such as 'correspondence' becomes apparent.[49] But then, as has already been shown, much of our language is unavoidably metaphorical and given the impossibility of apprehending the relationship between thought and the world directly, the difficulty in describing it is hardly surprising.

Strictly speaking, then, we can never justifiably claim to have discovered the *absolute* truth about matters of fact, or to have established some absolute foundation for our knowledge ('foundationalism'). Our knowledge must be admitted to be *fallible*. Realists need not see this as a threatening statement, because paradoxically, the common experience of making empirical errors, of mistaking the nature of the world, supports rather than undermines realism. For it is precisely because the world does not yield to just any kind of expectation that we believe it exists independently of us and is not simply a figment of our imagination. If there were no cases of our statements being confounded, if wishful thinking worked, there would be no reason for being a realist, and we could say that truth was purely relative to our conceptual scheme.

However we must beware of some common non-sequiturs here which have appeared in social science from time to time: first from the fact that knowledge and the material world are different kinds of thing it does *not* follow that there can be no relationship between them; and second, the admission that all knowledge is fallible does not mean all knowledge is equally fallible.[50] This latter point is especially important for defending social science against the irrationalism and relativism which often followed the demise of naïve objectivism.

We must also beware of a further confused argument which goes: 1 Absolute foundations for knowledge cannot be found. 2 Realist philosophy cannot provide them. 3 Therefore realism can be dismissed, and there is no need to provide a better alternative. Realists *accept* 2, but believe it is inconsistent to reject a philosophy for failing to meet a criterion which neither realism nor its critics accept. Nor is it reasonable to dismiss it without proposing a superior alternative. Wishful thinking, thoroughgoing conventionalism or 'anything goes', patently do not work: not every method works, not every convention can be upheld without absurdity.

Yet the rejection of foundationalism clearly does have major implications. In particular it calls into question received notions about the nature of 'truth'. If '*absolute* truth' about matters of fact is neither knowable empirically nor intelligible as a concept, and the nature of the relationship between knowledge and its object can only be known indirectly, what does this leave of the concept of truth? (Note: I am leaving aside the question of 'analytic truths', that is, statements which are true by definition, and also questions of what is morally desirable.) The question ought to be a disturbing one as the idea of truth has a vital role in society. It is quite understandable that people should be wary of letting go of such a concept, but some accommodation must be made between notions of fallibility and truth.

Attempts at qualifying the concept have come from two directions – that concerned with the intersubjective nature of decisions about the status of knowledge and that concerned with practice. In the former case, truth has been treated as *nothing more* than a matter of consensus. All that can be said about so-called true statements on this view is that they have been defined and accepted as such by convention. Not surprisingly, the implication that truth is whatever people choose to make it has been widely resisted. For while the common-sense concept of (absolute) truth presupposes more about the relationship of knowledge to the world than can be justified, this alternative 'conventionalist' view suggests less than can be justified. As noted in the previous chapter, although this intersubjective and conventional dimension exists, not just any conventions will do: they must be usable in practice. As part of their argument, conventionalists sometimes appeal to the arbitrary nature of the relationships between words and objects: why should some say 'children' and others 'Kinder' or 'enfants'? While the choice of individual words does seem arbitrary (except in rare onomatopoeic cases), the sense-relations of words attempt to grasp the determinate properties of objects and hence are not freely choosable. Once we have chosen to call something 'water', we don't freely choose to describe it as 'emotional' or 'punctual' rather than as 'clear', 'murky', 'hot' etc. Once objects have 'arbitrarily' been given names, the conventions governing how terms are combined to make meaningful discourse are far from arbitrary.[51] The conventions are revisable, but wherever language concerns material phenomena, it is likely to have considerable stability. Conversely, the success of languages in informing practices suggests that the structures of the world to which they refer have some permanence. Equally, *failures* of knowledge to inform successful practice suggest that structures are what they are regardless of what we think about them.

This brings us to the second type of qualification to the concept of truth – concerning practice.

Here, it may help to replace (or if you prefer, modify) the concept of truth with that of 'practical adequacy'.[52] To be practically adequate, knowledge must generate expectations about the world and about the results of our actions which are actually realized. (It must also, as conventionalists have insisted, be intersubjectively intelligible and acceptable in the case of linguistically expressed knowledge.) The practical adequacy of different parts of our knowledge will vary according to context. The differences in success of different sets of beliefs in the same practical context and of the same beliefs in different contexts suggests that the world is structured and differentiated. The error of conventionalism is to ignore practice and the structure of the world. By default, the apparently fickle, haphazard character of knowledge and truth as matters of convention which can be changed at (the collective) will is projected on to the object of knowledge which then assumes a structureless, entirely malleable character. Not only is knowledge apparently whatever we care to make it, the world is too. Such beliefs belong strictly to what has been called 'nocturnal philosophy', for in the 'diurnal philosophy' of their own practice, professed idealists are as realist as anyone else; they do not generally try to leave rooms through the ceiling rather than the door, nor do they dismiss words such as 'Danger: 240 volts' as having no reference or material significance.

The reason that the 'convention' 1 that we cannot walk on water is preferred to the convention 2 that we can, is because the expectations arising from 1, but not 2, are realized. They are realized because of the nature of the associated material interventions (trying to walk on water) and of their material contexts. In other words, although the nature of objects and processes (including human behaviour) does not uniquely determine the content of human knowledge, it does determine their cognitive and practical possibilities for us.[53] It is not thanks to our knowledge that walking on water doesn't work, but rather that the nature of water makes 1 more practically adequate than 2. The fact that 1 is nevertheless still, in principle, fallible, needn't alter our preference for it over 2.[54]

Why not simply say then, as some (social) scientists do, that knowledge should be judged as more or less 'useful' rather than as true or false. This position is called 'instrumentalism' and it is usually countered by the reply that useful knowledge is only useful because it's true! As it stands, this kind of argument can easily go round in circles, but the important point about the reply is that it is trying to say that the usefulness is not accidental but due to the nature of the objects of knowledge. One might say it is useful because it 'corresponds' to the structure of the world but we have already dealt with the limitations of such a description. Knowledge is useful where it is 'practically-adequate' to the world.

While there are similarities between realist and instrumentalist criteria the realist criteria are more demanding; characteristically instrumentalists only worry about the outputs (usually predictions) of their theory, not the inputs (assumptions, categories), and hence instrumentalists are wholly undisturbed by the possibility of getting the right answers for the wrong reasons, or by the possibility of the model not working on another occasion.[55] Realists could only accept this as a provisional solution: we should also try to find inputs to our theories which are practically adequate, which work in other contexts, which are consistent with other knowledge and practices; our theories should explain the situation under study by giving an account of what produced it and not merely a way of 'deriving' or calculating the results; and finally, unless it concerns unique objects, we should expect the theory to be robust.

Close to instrumentalism is the view that our theories do not tell us how the world is, and that all we can say is that things behave *as if* our models of them were true. At one level this seems similar to our realist position, for it recognizes the difference between knowledge and its object and the problems of how the relationship between them might be characterized. To say that something behaves as if our theory of it were true is similar to saying that it is not inconsistent with our theory. But in two respects it is objectionable. First it forgets that there is still something more that we can say about the relationship, namely that it is the structure of the world, rather than our theories about it that make practices possible or impossible. Second, the 'as if' rationale is frequently *disingenuous* in so far as it obscures the difference between theories which we know to be convenient fictions (i.e. know to be wrong in certain respects but nevertheless serviceable for some purposes) and theories which for the time being have not been bettered (i.e. whose limitations have not yet been discovered). It is significant, for example, that economists are often more charitable to attempts to theorize economic behaviour 'as if' it involved perfect competition, than they are to attempts to understand it 'as if' it did not involve a spaceless world of perfect knowledge, large numbers of buyers and sellers, etc. As Österberg notes, the appeal to the 'as if' rationale is usually more a function of the desire to protect a particular favourite mode of abstraction from criticism, than a defence of an abstraction found to be safe.[56]

In conclusion, we must acknowledge that it is not easy to find good substitutes for terms like 'truth' and 'falsity' or 'representation' and 'correspondence', but if they are to be continued to be used, we must keep in mind the shortcomings of superficial interpretations which ignore the crucial distinction and radical difference between thought objects and real objects,[57] and the practical context of knowledge.

Relativism, inter-theory disputes and discontinuities in the development of knowledge

Some readers may have been surprised that the above points should have been laboured so much, but it is necessary in some quarters where a highly relativistic conception of knowledge has gained ground. This relativist view presents knowledge as divided into discrete, monolithic and mutually unintelligible or contradictory systems of thought. It is supposed that each system is immune to criticisms from outside, for it will disallow or neutralize them by refusing the critics' criteria of what counts as knowledge. Appeals to evidence as a way of settling disputes will not work because it can be interpreted in ways which are so different as to be incommensurable. Indeed, in an inversion of naïve objectivism, theory is taken to be effectively observation-neutral. Members of different systems will only talk past one another and disagreements will always be based on mutual misunderstanding. Under the influence of these ideas, it is not uncommon to find social scientists prefacing their work with defensive remarks like 'as a "—ist", I believe such and such', as if you just 'paid your money and took your choice' of one or other of a range of mutually exclusive options.

The 'systems of thought' involved have been variously dubbed 'paradigms', 'problematics' or 'world views'. These terms are notoriously ill-defined. While they generally seem to denote extensive bodies of thought, the same scepticism about the possibility of meaningful dialogue and effective external criticism is sometimes to be found in comments on disputes between quite specific theories. At whatever scale, I shall argue that this scepticism is grossly exaggerated.

A related set of ideas concerns the historical succession of such systems of thought and derives from Thomas Kuhn's influential book *The Structure of Scientific Revolutions*. Here I do not wish to discuss Kuhn's original ideas so much as the popularized (and often adulterated) versions common in social science.[58] These stress the discontinuities or scientific revolutions which punctuate longer periods of gradual development and mark the overthrow of one paradigm and its replacement by another. The overthrow of the Newtonian paradigm by the Einsteinian paradigm is perhaps the most famous example. Instead of a gradual transmutation of knowledge (i.e. change with continuity), change takes place by replacement. This is exemplified by one of the most influential elements of the relativistic account, the gestalt switch analogy, with its familiar illustrations of ducks that can be seen as rabbits and the vase that can be seen as a pair of inward-looking faces, for it is only possible to see one or other image at a time and change between them is instantaneous. Supposedly, the process of change during a scientific revolution is more like a gestalt switch or mystical conversion experience than a matter of rational persuasion by means of arguments and evidence.[59]

Perhaps the most basic deficiency of these views is the drastic underestimation of the number of schemata and concepts we use or the implication that they are all tightly welded together by relations of logical entailment into a monolithic block. It then appears that there can be no shades of difference of meaning, only either total conformity (within paradigms) or total incompatibility (between paradigms). The extent of redundancy and unresolved tensions within theories is underestimated, as are the areas of overlap between them on which there is agreement or indifference. Having exaggerated the unity of major theories it then appears that any falsification of a part must be fatal to the whole. To borrow an analogy from Ernest Gellner, this makes theories seem like lone entrepreneurs, staking their all on the success of a single product, rather than like diversified corporations, able to cope with inevitable failures and to survive by modifying parts of their internal operations.[60] Often an illusion of incommensurability is produced by reducing the description of the competing systems of thought to those terms which are unique to them, ignoring the wealth of usually more mundane concepts which they share and to which appeal can be made in trying to resolve disputes. Furthermore, what is often not noticed is that for two sets of ideas to be in contradiction they must also have certain terms in *common*, over which they can contradict one another, and they must be mutually intelligible.

The ideas that observation which is theory-*laden* must therefore be theory-*determined* and that theories are observation-neutral can easily be refuted. Consider the example of finding out how much money a person has. To do this, I must be in command of a number of concepts, concerning money in its various forms, persons, the operation of counting and so on. But knowing these would not, of course, answer my question. I would still have to go and look, observing in a way which was unavoidably theory-laden but not theory-determined. So although we can only think within particular conceptual systems, these are internally differentiated and what we can think *of* is not necessarily already contained within these systems.[61] Moreover, precisely because *many* theories are implicated in any observation, measurement or test, there need be no circularity in which the theory being assessed so governs what we observe that nothing can refute it. Instead, 'the theories or expectations which lead us to inquire about the measured [need not be] the theories and principles used in its measurement'.[62]

As regards the alleged neutrality of theory with respect to observation, the conventions of such theories would be free of any constraints regarding practical adequacy and all thinking could be wishful thinking, for in being immune to challenges from any possible observations they would be unable to make any firm commitments about any real objects. Those who support such a position (and there are some!) often defend it by reference to the non-sequitur that the radical difference between knowledge or 'discourse' and material objects rules out the possibility of a relationship of practical adequacy between them. Yet they usually carry on talking about much the same kinds of objects and events as do those who believe in the possibility of judgements of practical adequacy. If they were to be consistent, there would be nothing to stop these idealists talking about absurdities such as the amount of Saturday in their dinners. The fact that they do not shows that, despite their philosophical beliefs, their discourse is influenced by similar constraints of practical adequacy, although they fail to acknowledge it.[63] Such are the consequences of ignoring practice and reducing the relationship of subject and object to one of reflection. As regards the analogy with gestalt switches, some have argued that it is inappropriate in that scientists who have changed paradigm cannot change back again as one can with images. But there is a more important yet less widely recognized problem with the analogy: namely that for it to be possible to switch from seeing, say, a duck to seeing a rabbit, or vice versa, we must *already* know what each looks like.[64] Likewise, the intelligibility of 'new' concepts requires some prior acquaintance with similar concepts, perhaps from different contexts. The usual interpretation of the gestalt switch overlooks this and therefore underestimates the continuities spanning so-called scientific revolutions.

As Campbell argues, the net effect of all these relativist misconceptions is to generate the impression, evident in Kuhn's work,

> that all of physical knowing is tied up in one single integrated theory, one single equation, and that the 'facts' against which this theory is checked are all laden with, and only with, this one encompassing theory. When this master-theory is changed, then it is supposed that *all* of the 'facts' [or theory-laden observations] change simultaneously.[65]

I now want to argue that despite their diametrically opposed conclusions, naïve objectivism, conventionalism and relativism share the same basic structure of misconceptions and that the ordering-framework view of theory is implicated in them. Although the philosophical proponents of conventionalism and relativism add many qualifications, they fail to alter this structure.

In naïve objectivism, words refer to objects unproblematically and independently of one another, as if they could be simple 'glued' to their referents, one by one. Observation is taken to be theory-neutral and the role of theory, if any, is to provide a way of ordering data. Change in knowledge can then only be comprehended as growth – as a process of accumulation in which new terms are added without altering the meaning of the old. But this view is patently false: meanings do change and there are at least some discontinuities and displacements. What I have called relativism and conventionalism respond to this situation largely by reversing the signs, as it were. Instead of being glued to objects, terms and their concepts are glued together into a solid structure and they lack any constraints in terms of their reference. Instead of theory-neutral observation, we have observation-neutral theory: instead of truth as a simple 'mirroring' of reality, it becomes purely a matter of convention. Change in knowledge can then only be an all-or-nothing affair, the replacement of one rigid structure by another.

In a similar vein, Shapere attacks the common conception of 'meaning' in the rival positions:

> Two expressions or sets of expressions must [on these views] either have precisely the same meaning or else must be utterly and completely different. If theories are not meaning-invariant over the history of their development and incorporation into wider and deeper theories, then these successive theories (paradigms) cannot *really* be compared at all,

despite apparent similarities which must therefore be dismissed as irrelevant and superficial. If the concept of the history of science as a process
of 'development-by-accumulation' is incorrect, the only alternative is that
it must be a completely noncumulative process of replacement. There
is never any middle ground. . . . But this relativism, and the doctrines
which eventuate in it, is not the result of an investigation of actual
science and its history; rather, it is the purely logical consequence of
a narrow preconception of what 'meaning' is.[66]

Indeed, the ordering-framework view of theory encourages us
to overlook the extent to which theorizing is concerned with
meaning, with negotiating modifications simultaneously in the
sense and reference of terms. It can only work with pre-existing
materials; it cannot take up another *completely* different set,
for innovations cannot be *completely* novel if they are to be
understood; bridge-heads must be established, again with existing
materials.

If theories are instead thought of as more or less distinctive
localities within a continuous conceptual map, which is continually
and unevenly evolving, both continuity and novelty and disconti-
nuity can be recognized in the development of knowledge.[67] Some
localities may be distant and poorly connected to others, but new
links may be established. If we are to avoid the opposite poles of
relativism and naïve objectivism, the hermeneutic character of the
development of knowledge and the interdependence of sense and
reference must be understood. Reference is not a simple matter
of 'gluing' a term to an object but a practical achievement arrived
at through a partly trial-and-error process of experimentation
with available conceptual resources. Moreover, meaning variance
need not render communication and criticism impossible. In fact,
communication between parties who differ, at least partially, in
their experience and/or interpretation of meaning is a normal state
of affairs; indeed, there is only any point in communication if this
is the case.[68] Admittedly communication is unlikely to be possible
where experience, language and meaning differ totally, but at the
other extreme of total identity, it is redundant! Communication
with others whose frames of meaning differ in some respects from
our own is an ordinary achievement of day-to-day life. Certainly,
the differences in frames of meaning necessitating resolution in
social science are likely to involve more abstruse matters, not
only in communicating with other researchers but in interpreting
meaning in society, particularly in the study of other cultures,

past or present. Certainly, also, inter-theory disputes often do involve criticism based on misunderstanding or alternatively are hidden by spurious consensus; but while their resolution can be extremely difficult and drawn out, it is defeatist to interpret it as impossible.

This defeatism can produce either dogmatism: 'don't bother to criticize my paradigm from outside it, because I know *a priori* that you will have misunderstood it', or an ineffectual eclecticism, 'all theories or paradigms have something useful to contribute.' Taken to its logical conclusion, this latter, apparently open-minded and liberal view becomes empty-headed and conservative in that it makes light of the fact that opposing theories are likely to contain at least some contradictory claims, some of which may be fundamental. It can therefore neutralize the key role of criticism in the development of knowledge. At the extreme, such a view could, for example, see the origin of profit *both* in surplus value and in the 'marginal efficiency of capital', or see Britain as both a class society and as classless. Also the naïve objectivist and relativist positions can even be surreptitiously *combined* by using the eclecticism of the latter to protect the former from criticism: 'this is my paradigm and I will pay lip-service to the idea that other paradigms may have their uses too, provided that I am left to get on with my own'. Most disastrously for relativism, it is self-refuting, for if every possible system of thought is to be treated as equally true (or untrue) and beyond challenge, then anti-relativism must be too.

But is there a more reasonable, limited form of eclecticism? It can sometimes be enlightening to look at an old subject in a completely different way, borrowing concepts from other theories. This may improve the existing system, and even if it doesn't it may help to throw the strengths of the latter into greater relief. (We can sometimes learn a lot in this way from reading lousy books.)

Marxism is often thought of as a particularly distinct body of knowledge, but its internal diversity as well as its continuities with other knowledge are frequently underestimated. Like any other system of thought it was forged out of pre-existing theoretical traditions (e.g. Scottish political economy, Hegelianism) and has subsequently been interpreted from a wide range of standpoints as shown by the endless succession of 'readings' and attempts to assimilate marxism to other traditions. The relationship between such theoretical systems and others has a hermeneutic character and involves a process of exchange in which, for example, sociology has learnt from marxism and marxism is learning from feminist theory.

There are cases, however, where incommensurable, *though non-contradictory*, theories appear, at least in some contexts, to have equal practical adequacy, e.g. acupuncture and western medicine, or methods of agriculture informed by theistic beliefs and methods informed by science. Yet it would probably sound strange to say that two or more very unlike theories could be 'equally true'. Truth is generally thought of as singular, and the idea of multiple truths an abomination. (This latter idea *is* absurd where knowledge is confused with its object so that differences in beliefs are taken as indicating multiple realities. This view is also dangerous in that it evades critical evaluation – 'my critics are in fact talking about different realities'.)

We have already questioned the assumption of a single, privileged relationship of perfect truth or correspondence between thought and the world. Although, with hindsight, we may want to say that the flat earth theory was definitely 'false', it did have a certain degree of practical adequacy, the limits of which were discovered through such practices as voyages of exploration. And the first makers of steam engines succeeded in getting their desired results with a theory which took heat to be a substance which flowed between things.[69] In other words, the absolute quality of the term 'false', like that of 'true', and hence also 'falsification', 'refutation' or 'confirmation', needs to be moderated to avoid giving the impression that to hold such false beliefs is necessarily to know nothing and hence to be able to do nothing.[70]

To acknowledge that a theory 'works' or has some practical adequacy in a particular context is not to suppose that every one of its constituent elements is 'true' or practically adequate. The achievements of ancient astronomers in predicting the movements of the stars are still impressive and yet, from a modern standpoint, they had not the slightest idea of what stars were.[71] But in the contexts in which they made practical use of their 'science', this ignorance and hence uneven quality of their knowledge did not really matter. Not all beliefs which we hold as relevant to particular contexts actually make a difference to our actions and their results; some may be redundant for practical purposes, although they may be important for making sense of what happens. Others may be satisfactory as a description but not as an explanation and equally some may enable us to do the right thing for the wrong reasons. Once again, to echo our earlier explanation of the 'usefulness' of particular ideas, it is the structured, differentiated and uneven nature of the world that gives rise to these cognitive possibilities of unevenly developed yet practically adequate knowledge.

Given that material processes are distinct from our beliefs about them, it shouldn't be surprising to find cases where two or more radically different and indeed incommensurable sets of beliefs have equal practical adequacy. (We often in fact hold inconsistent beliefs even within what appear to be unified belief-systems.) Inconsistency of sense does not necessarily guarantee the total practical inadequacy of the mutually inconsistent beliefs. Conversely, having a perfectly internally consistent and coherent set of beliefs does not guarantee their practical adequacy either. Nevertheless, particularly in examined knowledge such as science we try to eliminate such inconsistencies or contradictions because we are not content merely with knowing what works; we want a coherent understanding of what it is about the world which enables certain practices and expectations to be successful.

In social science, this kind of judgement is made not only within the 'scientific' community concerning its own concepts but also with respect to those of the society under study. And the fact that we may conclude that the beliefs of certain groups in society are founded on illusion does not necessarily mean that they have no effects and no practical adequacy at least in the sense of being 'liveable'.[72]

'Theorizing' and the development of knowledge

Having discussed the inadequacies of the naïve objectivist and relativist interpretations of the process by which knowledge develops, it is now time to spell out more clearly the nature of the alternative. I would suggest that for analytical purposes the process can be broken down into the following components:

1   The most simple type of change involves the discovery of further instances of objects which are deemed to be already satisfactorily conceptualized.

2 A more interesting kind of change, involving development rather than mere growth, can occur when the displacement of an existing concept to a new situation actually changes its meaning.

3 Change may follow discovery of the failure of expectations generated by existing knowledge. This is usually referred to as a 'disagreement with the facts', but as has been argued such an expression is misleading as it blurs the distinction between facts and statements about them and supports an often questionable distinction between 'observational' and 'theoretical' statements. Discoveries of practical inadequacy can identify problems concerning either what we think of as 'observational statements' or what we think of as 'theoretical' claims and assumptions. Barring mistakes in the use of concepts and associated techniques, and leaving aside the far from uncommon practice of turning a blind eye to anomalies, the appropriate response is to change some part of our conceptual system, whether 'observational' or 'theoretical'.

4 Changes in the structure of conceptual systems and hence in meanings can be precipitated not only by empirical, practical anomalies but by discovery of inconsistencies or omissions in the system through theoretical reflection. The inconsistencies may be of a quantitative kind – in terms of equations which don't work out – or of a conceptual kind where two or more concepts refer to the same object but seem to be impossible to reconcile in terms of their 'picture-carrying' content, their associations and expectations. As would be expected, this kind of change is most common in highly examined types of knowledge such as science. In contrast, as Barnes puts it, 'In everyday language, contradiction which does not get in the way of function is tolerated . . . [It is] not taken as contradiction at all because it is taken in context.'[73] The stimulus to eliminate contradictions is strongest where they support or indicate incompatible sets of activities. Nevertheless theoretical reflection may anticipate the actual occurrence of such problems just as they can sometimes anticipate and stimulate empirical discoveries of type 1.

5 While examples of the above types of change can be found in social knowledge, some important additional characteristics arise from the fact that it is part of its own object. As was indicated in Chapter 1, change in social scientific knowledge

can prompt change in its object and vice versa. Given this relationship and the possibility of beliefs having self-fulfilling effects, the existence of 'false' beliefs *in* the object of study becomes a problem for social science which is not rigorously critical.

It is important to recognize the *difficulty* of producing effective conceptual change. Neurath compared the development of knowledge with the task of trying to rebuild a boat, plank by plank, while on the high seas.[74] Moreover, while we can only forge new concepts out of old ones, some of the latter may be part of the problem we are trying to escape. To abandon too much is to destroy our ability to think and to find ourselves struggling to do what used to be straightforward. In times of scientific crisis, the situation of the scientist can be like that of an artist who wants to break out of the hackneyed conventions of contemporary art but has to use these if the results are to be recognized as art. There is therefore an inevitable inertia restraining innovation.

When faced with an anomaly, of whatever kind, the usual response is to minimize the extent of change in our conceptual system and our techniques. Yet some may require fundamental reformulations of basic concepts (e.g. concerning the meaning of causation, time and space) which change the sense of major parts of the system (although this does not always make much difference to practice).

Whether extensive or minor, these changes involve reconstructions of the networks of sense-relations linking and forming concepts, rather like changing the wiring of a complex but faulty circuit. These alterations require us to 'explicate' problematic concepts; that is, give concise definitions to important but vaguely understood terms through re-working their relations with other terms in the network. As Quine puts it, 'Any word worth explicating has some contexts which, as wholes, are clear and precise enough to be useful; and the purpose of explication is to preserve the usage of these favoured contexts while sharpening the usage of other contexts.'[75]

I would suggest that much of what is called 'theorizing' involves primarily this process of 'normative explication'. It is particularly evident in many of the most difficult and persistent theoretical debates in social science, such as those concerning concepts of 'value' in economics, 'class', 'civil society', the (capitalist) 'state', the 'urban', the distinctions between the 'political' and the 'economic', or the 'biological' and the 'social', and so on. This is exactly what I have been trying to do with the word 'theory' itself. It has been difficult, 1 to identify the problems with existing uses, 2 to stop using problematic senses and hence, 3 to know which sense-relations to alter and which to leave intact. These are characteristic problems of theorizing. Not surprisingly, many attempts at normative explication lead into 'culs-de-sac'.[76] Some of these may be quite long, and while they may heighten awareness of a particular aspect of a major thinker's work and of society itself they quite often also produce a kind of 'collective amnesia' about other aspects. In marxist scholarship, for example, swings towards structuralist or determinists and humanist 'readings' have alternated in the post-war period, each started by 'rediscoveries' of aspects of marxism which had been filtered out by the previous school of interpreters. This is, of course, a caricature, and there have been some resolutions of oppositions and not merely swings between them. Similar swings, rediscoveries and developments also occur in the continual shifts in the dominant values of popular culture, for example, between permissive and authoritarian approaches to the rearing of young children.

There are also cases where there are so many competing explications of particularly difficult concepts that it becomes uncertain whether we are still talking about the same thing. So many sense-relations may be brought into question and suspended that the term loses its meaning; possible examples are 'ideology', 'class', 'value' (in economics), and 'urban'.

Despite appearances, the process of normative explication or theorizing is not to be dismissed as 'merely semantic' or 'academic', for it concerns the way in which we 'carve up' or differentiate the world in thought. As we argue in the next chapter, the crucial aspect of this differentiation is the specification of the powers and ways of acting of objects, be they natural or social, for this affects the success of our practical interventions within the differentiations of the world. Conversely, as we have seen, developments in material events and practice can prompt modifications to our conceptual schemes. The splitting of the atom is an obvious natural science example, the shifts in the concept of the family with the rise and fall of the nuclear family is a social example. Theorizing, on this view, has a particularly direct social significance where it is concerned with the explication of ideas associated with practices in which powerful interests are at stake. For example, the explication of terms which are ill-defined but carry a heavy affective load, like 'democracy', may be of considerable use in uncovering the confusions sustained by their common reduction to slogans.[77]

Most political struggles include, as an integral part, a 'contestation of meaning'. Conflicts concerning race are not only about access to material resources and opportunities; they are also concerned with identity – in the case of the black consciousness movement, with what it is to be black. Those involved are attempting to change the ways in which their identities are reciprocally confirmed by everyday actions and habits of thought. In other words, theorizing and the contestation of meaning are analogous, and precisely because of the partial identity of subject and object in social knowledge, the former may have a direct effect on the latter, although in most cases it is small.

Conclusions

In this chapter I have begun to outline the relations between theory and observation. Any conclusions on this matter depend on how we understand theory and perception and the relationship between knowledge and its object. The 'imprint' of the interdependent relations between subjects and subject and object introduced in Chapter 1 has appeared in the discussions of sense and reference, the conceptual and the empirical, practical adequacy and the process of development of knowledge. Naïve objectivism and relativism (and conventionalism) are contrasting but complementary consequences of failure to grasp this interdependence.

In examining these issues, we have been drawn into a wider discussion of epistemology, or the theory of knowledge. The world can only be understood in terms of available conceptual resources, but the latter do not determine the structure of the world itself. And despite our entrapment within our conceptual systems, it is still possible to differentiate between more and less practically-adequate beliefs about the material world. Observation is neither theory-neutral nor theory-determined, but theory-laden. Truth is neither absolute nor purely conventional and relative, but a matter of practical adequacy. Differences in meaning need not render inter-theory or inter-paradigm communication and criticism impossible. Knowledge changes neither wholly continuously and cumulatively nor by comprehensive replacements of one monolithic paradigm by another. Theory does not order given observations or data but negotiates their conceptualization, even as observations.

There is more to be said about theory than this, but further specification must await the development of some other themes, to be introduced in the next chapter, regarding method and the particular properties of our objects of study.

3 Theory and method I: abstraction, structure and cause

Having completed the general discussion of the nature of theory and social scientific knowledge I now want to introduce some key concepts of the realist philosophy of science which concern the more immediate problems of method in social research. In this chapter I shall deal primarily with qualitative methods of analysis, leaving quantitative methods to Chapter 6. Now, little can be said about method without taking into account the nature of the things which the methods are to be used to study; for example, decisions regarding causal and structural analysis will depend on judgements about the nature of causation and structures. It will therefore be necessary to switch back and forth between these two aspects in the course of this chapter. I shall mention some of their practical implications as I go through the methods, but inevitably others will not become clear until later, when the whole structure of the realist approach has been set out.

Although much of the realist approach is unorthodox, I will only permit myself a few digressions at this stage to answer possible objections. Replies to the main criticisms likely to come from orthodox philosophy of science are contained in Chapter 5.

We begin at the most 'primitive' level with an important but under-analysed way of conceptualizing objects – *abstraction* – and proceed to one of its specialized forms – structural analysis. This requires an examination of the nature of *relations* and *structures*. In the course of this discussion a fundamental distinction between *abstract* and *concrete* research is introduced. We then pause to look at the perennial problem of the relationship between *structure and agency*; namely are social processes to be accounted for by social structures, such as class structures, of which individuals are merely bearers, or by the conscious activity of individuals and groups, or is there some other solution to the problem? The next section deals with *generalization* and here it is shown that despite its familiarity to social scientists, its limitations are rarely fully appreciated. The chapter ends with an extended examination of *causation* in society and how it can be analysed.

Abstraction and structural analysis

To be practically-adequate, knowledge must grasp the differentiations of the world; we need a way of individuating objects, and of characterizing their attributes and relationships. To be adequate for a specific purpose it must 'abstract' from particular conditions, excluding those which have no significant effect in order to focus on those which do. Even where we are interested in wholes we must select and abstract their constituents.

In many accounts of science abstraction is assumed to be so obviously necessary that little is said about how it should be done. It is a powerful tool and hence also a dangerous one if carelessly used. Once we have become accustomed to a particular 'mode of abstraction' it is often hard to dislodge, even where it generates problems in research and applications. In contrast to some accounts,[1] I therefore want to emphasize the importance of trying to keep in mind what we abstract *from*. Thus, before using a production function for representing the combination of capital and labour, economists should assess whether the abstraction from the rigidity of capital and from the actual organization and sequencing of work matters, whether it makes a significant difference. Similarly, in using the metaphor of 'reproduction' for describing social processes, sociologists need to consider the costs of ignoring their open-ended nature and their dependency on skilled actors. Often the abstractions will indeed prove safe, but simply using them out of habit or because they seem redolent of 'science' is hardly a recipe for rigour.

Secondly it is advisable to seek (non-contradictory!) ways of combining different types of abstraction instead of using just one. It will be recalled from the previous chapter's discussion of perception that the skilled observer is one who can use many schemata and knows their limitations and the extent to which they are compatible. This is not an argument for eclecticism for the eclectic uses abstractions without appreciating their limitations and incompatibilities.

In popular usage, the adjective 'abstract' often means 'vague' or 'removed from reality'. The sense in which the term is used here is different; an abstract concept, or an abstraction, isolates in thought a *one-sided* or partial aspect of an object.[2] What we abstract *from* are the many other aspects which together constitute *concrete* objects such as people, economics, nations, institutions, activities and so on. In this sense an abstract concept can be precise rather than vague; there is nothing vague about abstractions such as 'temperature', 'valency', 'gender', 'income elasticity of demand', or 'the circuit of money capital'. And the things to which these abstractions refer need be no less real than those referred to by more concrete concepts. Hence the abstract and the concrete should not be aligned with the distinction between thought and reality.

The concept of 'concrete objects' does not merely concern 'whatever exists' but draws attention to the fact that objects are usually constituted by a combination of diverse elements or forces.[3] As a concrete entity, a particular person, institution or whatever combines influences and properties from a wide range of sources, each of which (e.g. physique, personality, intelligence, attitudes, etc.) might be isolated in thought by means of abstraction, as a first step towards conceptualizing their combined effect.

In other words, the understanding of concrete events or objects involves a double movement: concrete → abstract, abstract → concrete. At the outset our concepts of concrete objects are likely to be superficial or chaotic. In order to understand their diverse determinations we must first abstract them systematically. When each of the abstracted aspects has been examined it is possible to combine the abstractions so as to form concepts which grasp the concreteness of their objects.

Before proceeding it should be noted that not all concrete objects are empirically observable, nor are all abstract aspects of objects unobservable. Concept-dependent phenomena apart, they exist regardless of whether anyone happens to be able to observe or otherwise know them. Abstractions need not be seen as 'idealizations', nor are they merely heuristic devices for ordering observations. As concepts, abstractions are obviously different from the material objects to which they may refer, but this applies to empirical observations and concrete concepts no less than to abstractions: all of them can refer to real objects.

In the previous chapter I tried to soften the distinction between the 'theoretical' and the 'empirical' by drawing attention to their shared conceptual content and I argued that it had no parallels with the distinctions between the mental and the real, or the unobservable and the observable. I now want to dissociate the abstract–concrete distinction from such parallels too. This can be summarized thus:

$$
\begin{bmatrix} \text{theoretical} \\ | \\ \text{empirical} \end{bmatrix} \not\equiv \begin{bmatrix} \text{mental} \\ | \\ \text{real} \end{bmatrix} \not\equiv \begin{bmatrix} \text{unobservable} \\ | \\ \text{observable} \end{bmatrix} \not\equiv \begin{bmatrix} \text{abstract} \\ | \\ \text{concrete} \end{bmatrix}
$$

where $\not\equiv$ means 'not equivalent to'.

Neither objects nor their relations are given to us transparently; their identification is an achievement and must be worked for. Some attributes and powers appear to be necessary features of what objects are (e.g. having a respiratory system in the case of animals or use values in the case of an economy), while others appear to be incidental. Abstractions should distinguish incidental from essential characteristics. They should neither divide the indivisible nor lump together the divisible and the heterogeneous. Much of the business of 'theorizing' involves adjusting our abstractions of objects and relationships so that these dangers are avoided and their practical adequacy increased.

In making abstractions it is helpful to distinguish relations of different types. The term 'relation' is a very flexible one but there are some significant contrasts implicit in its various uses.[4] A simple distinction can be made between '*substantial*' relations of connection and interaction and '*formal*' relations of similarity or dissimilarity. Houses are connected by roads and electricity cables, individuals may interact directly, but they may also bear a purely formal relation, lacking any interaction, as objects having similar characteristics. Clearly, things which are connected need not be similar and vice versa.[5] As will be shown later, although this is a very simple distinction, many approaches in social science have difficulty in recognizing relations of connection.[6]

Another useful distinction can be made between *external*, or *contingent relations* and *internal* or *necessary relations*.[7] The relation between yourself and a lump of earth is external in the sense that either object can exist without the other. It is neither necessary nor impossible that they stand in any particular relation; in other words it is contingent. (Note that this sense of contingent is quite different from that common in everyday uses where 'contingent upon' means 'dependent upon'.) Although a relation may be contingent it may still have significant effects; thus people may break up lumps of earth or be buried beneath them – but the nature of each object does not necessarily depend on its standing in such a relation. By contrast, the relation between a master and a slave is internal or necessary, in that what the object is is dependent on its relation to the other; a person cannot be a slave without a master and vice versa. Another example is the relation of landlord and tenant; the existence of one necessarily presupposes the other.

In using the necessary/contingent or internal/external relation distinction several important qualifications need to be noted.

First, even if the internal relation is made part of the definition of either of the objects, as it might be in the case of landlord and tenant or husband and wife, it does not boil down to a tautology, as some have imagined. As a tenant, for example, it is not thanks to a tautology that you pay rent to a landlord but thanks to your involvement in a material social relation, and although each part of the relation cannot exist as such without the other, there is no problem in identifying them separately.

Secondly, although internally related phenomena are interdependent in a strong sense, this does not mean that they cannot change, just that change in one part is tied to change in the other. The changes that have occurred in the relations between husbands and wives are a good example.

Thirdly, the necessary/contingent distinction has nothing to do with importance or interest – either kind of relation may be insignificant or important; the relationship between British governments and North Sea oil is contingent in the sense that each could exist without the other, but the effect of North Sea oil revenues on the position of British governments is of considerable importance. The external relationship between the British government and my musical preferences is contingent and insignificant. Similarly, not all the necessary conditions of existence of people are of much interest to social science, for instance their need to breathe.

Asymmetric internal relations can also be distinguished in which one object in a relation can exist without the other, but not vice versa. The relations of money and banking systems, state and council housing are examples. Even when symmetric, internal relations are not always harmonious or evenly balanced – on the contrary, many instances combine mutual dependence with one-sided domination.

These distinctions are helpful for clarifying different concepts of class. The marxist concept of class hinges upon internal relations, in the case of capitalist society, primarily the relation between wage-labour and capital. In many sociological, official and popular versions, class is defined in terms of a number of shared attributes (income, education, status, attitudes, etc.) and individuals are 'classified' according to their correspondence with these definitions. The relations between such classes are therefore contingent. These two concepts of class must be clearly distinguished as they relate to quite different aspects of society, but they are not necessarily mutually exclusive. A considerable blurring of the differences between externally related classes need not imply a weakening of the internally related divisions conceptualized by marxism. Conversely, the removal of the capital/wage-labour relation in a revolution might not automatically eliminate all the differences identified by the sociological concept, and divisions based on other internally related practices, such as those concerning gender and intellectual and subaltern labour, might persist without much change.

Many actions which we casually regard as capable of existing in isolation are in fact embedded in internal relations. For example, attitudes and actions associated with 'respect' and 'contempt' each presuppose reciprocal relations between people and sets of rules regarding acceptable behaviour.[8] In so far as many actions are context-dependent they involve internal relations, though perhaps asymmetric ones in many cases. To sit an exam or answer a question is to presuppose other prior and expected actions, events and surroundings, often in particular spatio-temporal sequences. They are invariably rule-governed. In the absence of their particular contexts they do not count as actions of these sorts; to say that a practice is concept-dependent is to acknowledge that it is internally related (again perhaps asymmetrically) to particular concepts. One of the most common errors in social science is the reproduction of common sense's characteristic unawareness of the internally related nature of human action.

In any real situation there is usually a complex combination of these types of relation. The structure of a system of interest can be discovered by asking simple questions about such relations: What does the existence of this object (in this form) presuppose? Can it exist on its own as such? If not what else must be present? What is it *about* the object that makes it do such and such? These questions may seem simple to the point of banality, but the answers are often complex and many errors of conceptualization and abstraction stem from evasions of them.[9] Let us consider three examples, starting with an artificially simple one, concerning the relations between two people, Jones and Smith. They may be employer and employee respectively, and in this respect they are internally related, although in others, such as religion, attitudes or recreational activities, they may be contingently related. In other words, *unless we make it clear what aspect of Jones and Smith we are considering, the attempt to distinguish internal from external relations, or necessary from contingent conditions, of certain attributes or practices is liable to result in confusion.*[10]

A more complex example which demonstrates the need for clear definition in assessing the nature of relations concerns the question of whether capitalism and patriarchy are interdependent. At the level of the most basic relation of capitalism – the capital/wage-labour relation – it is contingent whether capitalists or workers are male or female. At this level capital is 'sex-blind'. However, in their *concrete* forms, instances of the relation may be affected by gender, and less basic structures of particular capitalist societies, such as the British welfare state, may include practices determined by and reproductive of gender which 'interlock' patriarchal and capitalist structures. So even though in virtually every instance, capitalist social relations are gendered in some way, and even though patriarchy and capitalism take advantage of one another (though they can also cause problems for one another), we can argue that the relation between patriarchy and capital is contingent.[11] For not only has patriarchy existed without capitalism but there seems to be nothing about class relations, exchange-value, production for profit, etc., which would make them dependent on the survival of patriarchy. Provided due care is taken in abstraction in deciding which *aspects* of the phenomena are being considered, illumination rather than confusion should result.[12]

A third example illustrates the importance of asking qualitative questions about the nature of our objects. This concerns the explanation of why some industries are more strike-prone than others. Many social scientists would tackle this by proceeding quickly to a statistical analysis in order to evaluate possible independent variables such as union membership, size of establishment, gender composition, etc. But interesting though the results might be, this line of inquiry ignores our simple qualitative questions: e.g. What does strike activity presuppose? What is it *about* the size of establishments which affects propensity to strike? Is it just size *per se* in terms of numbers employed, or the nature of social relations and forms of management control associated with different sizes? Often, researchers stop short of such questions as if the revelation of statistical relationships were sufficient to explain things. Alternatively, they may be tempted to treat the answers to the questions as further 'independent variables' and run additional statistical tests, but whatever the results we will still need to arrive at a conclusion in answer to the qualitative questions. In turn, answering them again requires considerable attention to how we abstract and what we abstract from.

Abstraction is particularly important for the identification of *structures*.[13] These can be defined as sets of internally related objects or practices. The landlord–tenant relation itself presupposes the existence of private property, rent, the production of an economic surplus and so on; together they form a structure (see Figure 6). Contrary to a common assumption, structures include not only big social objects such as the international division of labour but small ones at the interpersonal and personal levels (e.g. conceptual structures) and still smaller non-social ones at the neurological level and beyond.

Within social structures there are particular 'positions' associated with certain roles. It is particularly important to distinguish the occupant of a position from the position itself. One of the most pervasive illusions of everyday thinking derives from the attribution of the properties of the position, be they good or bad, to the individual or institution occupying it. Whatever effects result, it is assumed that particular *people* must be responsible;

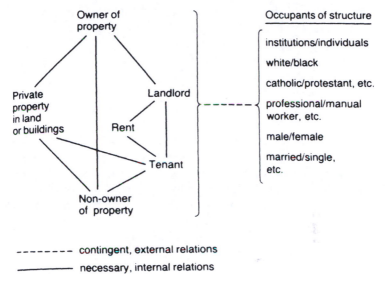

```
-------- contingent, external relations
———————— necessary, internal relations
```

Figure 6 Structure

there is little appreciation that the structure of social relations, together with their associated resources, constraints or rules, may determine what happens, even though these structures only exist where people reproduce them. In such circumstances it is futile to expect problems to be resolved by the discovery of a guilty persons and their replacement by a different individual. We may question individuals in a structure in the hope of finding someone to blame or credit for certain outcomes without ever finding one where 'the buck stops here'. As André Gorz writes:

> The predefined obligations inherent in [the bureaucrats'] function[s] relieve them of all personal responsibility and decision and enable them to meet the protest with the disarming reply: 'We haven't chosen to do this. We're only enforcing orders.' Whose orders? Whose regulations? One could go back indefinitely up the hierarchy and it would still be impossible to find anyone else to say, 'Mine'.[14]

Gorz is not attacking the evasion of individual responsibility but its non-existence in such cases. Failure to recognize the existence of internal relations and structures can also be seen in the example of responses to criticism of the police. This is sometimes expressed and interpreted in terms of the presence of 'bad apples' in the force, that is, as criticism of particular members of the police. Even when criticism is explicitly directed against the structures of positions, rules and powers which make up the institution of the police, it is sometimes – perhaps deliberately – misconstrued as being directed against individuals.

The reduction of structures to the individuals who compose them is also responsible for the illusion that high social mobility implies the abolition of social classes. Moreover, the invisibility of structure to common-sense thinking leads to an underestimation of the *interdependence* of positions and what is called the 'fallacy of composition'.[15] This is the assumption that, in all cases, what is possible for an individual must be possible for all individuals simultaneously. For example, it is often imagined that in capitalist economies, because individual firms may be made 'more competitive', all firms might simultaneously become more competitive without any thereby becoming less competitive, as if economic competition were a race in which all could win first prize simultaneously. Similarly, in the hope of reducing youth unemployment many 'experts' have advised young people to get better qualifications and improve their interview technique, but those who do this can only improve their chances of getting a job by worsening the chances of other individuals: it does not increase the number of jobs available, that is, the number of positions within the structure.

Although not every kind of individual, group or institution can occupy any structural position, there is usually a certain latitude. For example, landlords and tenants can each have a variety of characteristics, some of them constituted through other internal relations. Structures can therefore be said to be 'invariant under certain transformations',[16] that is, they can continue to exist while their constituents undergo changes in attributes which are not relevant to their reproduction. The landlord–tenant structure can survive a continual turnover of members during which their age, sex, race, religion, politics, occupations, etc. may change.

People and institutions themselves invariably exist within several social structures. You may not only be renting property but attending college and taking exams, and the latter, of course, presuppose educational structures. While it may be true that large numbers of students in a housing market may have a significant effect on the availability of rented accommodation, other types of individuals besides students could have this effect and hence the coexistence of students and rented housing is still contingent. (Note again that to say that the coexistence of two or more objects is contingent is not to deny that they may affect each other in some way.)

The complex articulation and mutual reinforcement of structures typical of social life creates some of social science's most difficult problems. Since we cannot isolate them one by one in experiments we are always prone to attribute to one structure what is due to another. This is especially so: (a) because we usually need to rely on actors' accounts which may confuse the effects of different structures, (b) because actions are informed by such understandings and have real effects in reproducing (perhaps inadvertently) those structures, and (c) because social structures are concept-dependent – often on systematically-confused concepts. In relation to (a) and (b), a male trade unionist might blame capitalism rather than patriarchy for women's weak position in the labour market, and reproduce the problem through his own actions. In relation to (c), studies of skill classifications in industry have shown many of them to reflect the gender of the typical worker rather than any intrinsic difference in skill requirements. That a typist may be classified as unskilled and a lorry-driver as skilled says little more than that the first is generally a woman and the second a man. The common use of one classification scheme, to do with skill, as a surrogate for another, to do with gender, illustrates the complexities of the interdependence of social structures created by the fact that they reciprocally confirm concepts and that these need not be what they claim to be. In other words, the problem of attributing to one structure something which derives from another is exacerbated by the fact that social scientists encounter this same problem within their object of study, in the actions and in the accounts and classifications used by the people they study.

In response to these kinds of problem the best course for social scientists is to pursue our qualitative questions. What is it *about* the structures which might produce the effects at issue?: e.g. is there anything intrinsic to specifically capitalist interests that should make women, rather than some other group, the ones discriminated against? What is it about the job of typing or the sex of a worker which gives rise to the skill classification?

Social structures not only coexist and articulate but endure. The most durable social structures are those which lock their occupants into situations which they cannot unilaterally change and yet in which it is possible to change between existing positions. If a worker gives up his or her job and joins a commune, a replacement is easily found and the structures of capitalism continue to be reproduced. However, the members of the commune will find it extremely difficult not to use and conform with at least some of the commodities and practices of the social structures which they are trying to escape, thereby helping to reproduce them. Incidentally, it should be noted that although structures are invariant under certain transformations and often difficult to displace, this does not mean that they can never be transformed gradually, from within. For example, religious structures, teacher–pupil relations and the marital relation have all changed slowly but significantly, as balances of power and constitutive meanings and practices have shifted.

Structure, agency and reproduction

Now it is common in social science to talk of the '*reproduction*' of social structures, but the concept of reproduction is surrounded by traps for the unwary. Social structures do not endure automatically, they only do so where people reproduce them; but, in turn, people do not reproduce them automatically and rarely intentionally. As Bhaskar puts it: 'People do not marry to reproduce the nuclear family or work to reproduce the capitalist economy. Yet it is nevertheless the unintended consequence (and inexorable result) of, as it is also a necessary condition for, their activity.'[17] Similarly, whether we realize it or not, speech is enabled and constrained by the structure of language, but language can only be reproduced through speech or writing. Hence, while certain actions are only possible within particular social structures, the existence of the latter depends upon the continued (contingent) execution of those actions.

Although social structures are difficult to transform, the execution of the actions necessary for their reproduction must be seen as a skilled accomplishment requiring not only materials but particular kinds of practical knowledge.[18] Actors are not mere 'dupes', 'automata', or 'bearers of roles', unalterably programmed to reproduce. The very fact that social structures are historically specific – that societies have existed and do exist without nuclear families, private property, prisons, etc. – ought to remind us of the contingent status of social structures. (While the elements of structures are necessarily related, it is contingent whether any structure, *as a unit*, exists.) It is therefore not sufficient to explain the *existence* of a structure merely by referring to its constituent internal relations and necessary conditions. It may be correct to say that the rise of the mass-produced motor-car presupposed the provision of cheap fuel but that does not explain its development. In other words, while abstraction by means of structural analysis is useful it does not explain origins. The assumption that such inferences can be drawn purely from this kind of analysis is the prime error of functionalism.[19]

These kinds of qualifications and warnings are necessary on account of the widespread currency of unsatisfactory resolutions of the problem of 'structure and agency'.[20] 'Structuralist' approaches drew much of their strength through countering the individualist and voluntarist view that social processes were reducible to the apparently unconstrained actions of individuals. But in stressing the way in which actions take place within social relations and are rule-governed and constrained by conditions not of the actors' choosing, the activity of the agents and their skills were ignored, so that it appeared that the conditions did the acting. At worst, the 'subjects' were 'written out' altogether, producing a dehumanizing social science.

There is an additional but more general risk in the over-extension of structural analysis and approaches which emphasize the rule-governed character of action; this stems from an unacknowledged effect of the observer's standpoint on what he or she sees: another kind of intellectualist fallacy. From the point of view of the actor or participant, actions are not easily distinguished one from another, their goals are often unclear and their execution is always vulnerable to unexpected diversions. To the spectator, the risk and contingency are less apparent and, when reported, the time dimension tends to be compressed or ignored altogether, with the result that uncertain strategies appear *ex post* as the routine and mechanical execution of well-defined, perhaps reified, 'actions' undertaken according to firm 'rules' and 'roles'. At the same time as this 'hypostatization' takes place, practical knowledge is codified as if it were propositional in form.[21] This can cause considerable misunderstanding and mistrust between intellectuals and 'ordinary people', in that the latter feel that far from illuminating their experience, the intellectuals are denying it in the process of claiming to know it better. Once this happens, it opens the door to the mutually-reinforcing poles of academic-élitism and anti-intellectualism. Like all variants of the intellectualist fallacy, this is more than a frame of mind: it is conditioned or reciprocally confirmed by the practice of intellectual production, with its privileged niche in the social division of labour which distances its occupants from practical knowledge.

'Old hands' at social science often become unaware of the fact that they make this kind of abstraction, but newcomers tend to be very struck by it, especially where they encounter descriptions, usually in the passive voice or third person, of practices which they themselves have experienced 'in the first person', as it were. As Williams notes, if the abstractions of structural analysis are taken as giving a total picture (i.e. as if they were not really abstractions), anything 'moving' or 'live' which does not fit into the 'fixed forms' it identifies tends to be dubiously categorized as 'subjective' or 'personal'.[22] While these are serious occupational hazards in any study of social structure, the proper response is not to abandon structural analysis, for this would give actors' accounts a false privilege and open the doors to 'voluntarism', that is, the view that what happens is purely a function of the unconstrained human will. Rather we should keep in mind not only the power of this mode of abstraction but also its limits. The above errors lie not in using structural analysis as a mode of abstraction but in using it as if it could provide *concrete* descriptions on its own; it provides a possible beginning to research but not an end.

Contentless abstractions

Sometimes the aspect of an object which is abstracted cannot exist in an abstract form but only in particular concrete forms, which this 'contentless abstraction' ignores. For example, all commodities must have 'use-value' if people are to buy them. But they do not have 'use-value in general', only particular kinds such as the quality of being nutritious or providing some kind of entertainment. Such examples seem harmless enough until we come to put some 'explanatory weight' upon them or try to measure what is abstracted. As might be expected, whether some abstractions are contentless or not is sometimes contentious; a particularly controversial case is the concept of intelligence as measurable on a single scale.

There are also cases where abstractions become virtually contentless not because there is nothing they could refer to but because their sense-relations are too weakly articulated to allow unambiguous reference. An abstract concept might be denoted by the symbol p, which in turn might refer to an object P. The danger of taking abstraction to the extreme form of mere notation is that we are easily led to forget P, and what kind of thing it is, so that our manipulations of logical or mathematical formulae 'take on a life of their own' and we lose our grip on our knowledge of those material and causal (as opposed to logical) properties of P which determine what it can and cannot do. There are some who would interpret this loss of contact as an advantage as it suggests the possibility of models or theories as ordering devices which can be applied to a diverse set of objects (e.g. catastrophe theory). This, of course, only begs the question. As Marx said of Hegel, it involves the fallacy of taking 'the things of logic [or mathematics] for the logic of things'.[23] I will return to and develop this point later.

Generalization

The discussion so far has stressed the *qualitative* aspects of objects and their substantial relations, whether necessary (internal) or contingent (external). In fact, it is far more common in contemporary social science to give precedence to the search for formal relations of similarity and dissimilarity, and the study of quantitative dimensions of systems. Although both foci are needed I believe the first to be under-emphasized, partly as a result of the dominance of ordering framework conceptions of theory which tend to encourage the belief that objects are relatively simple and transparent and that the main problems concern their quantitative analysis. However, having counteracted this emphasis, I have no intention of denying the significance of quantity and the methods for studying it. Although structures are constituted by internal relations which must be understood qualitatively, they may in some cases be affected by size or quantities. Physical structures such as bridges have quantifiable limits to their load-bearing capacities and the survival of capitalist

firms is dependent upon changes in quantitative variables such as
rates of profit. Also, we usually need to know how many instances
of a structure there are, together with its dimensions.

A more orthodox approach, which gives greater prominence to
quantitative descriptions and formal, as opposed to substantial,
relations is 'generalization'. A generalization is an approximate
quantitative measure of the numbers of objects belonging to
some class or a statement about certain common properties of
objects: e.g. 'most Third World countries are heavily in debt
to advanced industrialized countries'; '85 per cent of low-paid
workers are women'. Sometimes they incorporate the ambiguous
term 'tends' as in 'offenders tend to be young', which might
suggest a necessary relation, but the most usual interpretation
is one which remains agnostic about the causal status (if any) of
relationships. In the search for generalizations we ask questions
like: 'What do these objects have in common?' 'What are their
distinguishing characteristics?' 'How many of these objects have
these characteristics?' Unlike the questions posed in the development of abstractions and the analysis of structures, these primarily
seek out formal relations, and where they do hit upon substantial
relations, they do not ask whether they are necessary or contingent.
Generalizations may also be either simple descriptive summaries
of a given situation or extrapolations – rough predictions of what
other situations might be like. While the former usage is obviously
informative the latter is problematic. Many social scientists have
believed that with further research generalizations of the second
kind might be 'firmed up' into laws of human behaviour, whether
deterministic or probabilistic, although there is scarcely a scrap
of evidence to suggest they are succeeding. In other words, generalizations are seen by some as an end in themselves, and as
central to a conception of social science as the search for order
and regularity.

Later, I shall argue that this goal is mistaken, but at this point
I want to note several problems and limitations which attend the
search for generalizations. First, generalizations which concern
properties allegedly common to different societies at different
times may mislead by 'dehistoricizing' their objects – that is
by giving a transhistorical, pancultural character to phenomena
which are actually historically specific or culture-bound.[24] As was
noted in Chapter 1, this is not just a problem for history and
anthropology but for all social sciences; even in understanding

our own contemporary society we must be aware of what is or isn't historically specific. Labour is a genuinely transhistorical necessary condition of human existence, but as such it cannot be treated as sufficient to explain concrete work-related practices in particular societies, such as the need to find a job in capitalism. Likewise all societies use tools, but to reduce 'capital' to tools is to empty the category of its historical content and hence to mystify its determinants. The more a social object is internally related to other objects, the less likely is it to be invariant across time and space. Therefore constitutive meanings are particularly variable and unsuitable as objects of generalizations of the second, predictive, kind.[25]

Second, to say that a range of objects has a certain property to some degree (e.g. '90 per cent of tenants are single') says nothing about whether this is a contingent or a necessary fact: which of these is the case would have to be determined by other means than generalization. (Even if 100 per cent of tenants were single, it might still be a contingent fact.)

Third, generalizations are sometimes ambiguous because of the problem of 'distributive unreliability'.[26] Tests might show that in a sample of people 80 per cent do x and the remainder y. This can be interpreted either as an effect of the presence of two types of people, one of which always does x and the other y, or else as a generalization about a homogeneous population in which each member has the same propensity to do x or y. These interpretive problems are common in social research, but there is a tendency to overlook the former possibility.

Fourth, generalizations are indifferent to structures. Even where they refer to like-constituted entities they say nothing about whether each individual is independent of or connected to any other. This is a different point from the previous one which concerned the lack of specification of the status of the relationship between each entity and a given characteristic. Here it is the relationships between the entities which is unspecified; we do not know from the generalization whether they are purely formal relations of similarity or actual connections. Groups whose individual members are not (substantially) connected in any way (e.g. persons aged 65+) are termed 'taxonomic collectives' by Harré.[27] While it is reasonable to say their members have something in common, they might be said only to exist as a group in the mind of the classifier.

Fifth, careful scrutiny of inferences drawn from generalizations is also needed to avoid the 'ecological fallacy', that is, the spurious inference of individual characteristics from group-level characteristics:

as when from the fact that a high proportion of Negroes in a community goes together with high crime rates we conclude that Negroes commit more crimes than whites. This, of course, is invalid because the community-level correlation may also be due to Negroes being more often *victims* of crimes. An even more striking example is the following: from the fact that juvenile delinquency and senile dementia are correlated at the community level, we can hardly conclude that they are often found in the same individuals.[28]

Usually, ecological fallacies are less obvious than this, but their disclosure and avoidance require that generalizations and other statements of formal relations are supplemented by qualitative analysis of the individuals involved and the substantial relations into which they enter.

Sixth, generalizations need involve little abstraction; having discovered a quantifiable aspect of a population in which there is a semblance of pattern, abstraction often tends to stop. Although regularities are often sought at the level of simple events or objects they fail to disclose their concrete character by making it difficult to relate particular, identifiable individuals because of the preoccupation with group-level formal patterns. The five previous problems might all be said to follow from this. Together they cast doubt on the possibility of discovering universally applicable generalizations or 'proto-laws' in social science.

In the 1960s, two Americans, Berelson and Steiner, completed the unusual project of compiling an inventory of scientific findings in the human sciences. They took it to be the job of social science to find 'valid generalizations to explain and predict the actions, thoughts and feelings of human beings'.[29] Their book, which presents most of the findings in terms of generalizations about common properties among apparently externally-related individuals, is a testament to the weakness of this approach. Many of the findings are trivial ('People like to be liked'), or feeble ('An organization is more likely to be strongly centralized during external crises than during normal periods').[30] Others treat conceptually-linked practices as equivalent to mere empirical regularities in intrinsically meaningless behaviour[31] ('Mobile persons identify in norms, standards, values, appearance and behavior with the upper level to which they aspire') Still others produce the impression of regularity not by abstracting from the incidental characteristics but by ignoring variation in the essential features of the phenomena of interest. For example:

The degree of urbanization increases sharply as industrialism increases. It follows that those parts of the world still mainly in the peasant agrarian stage of economic development manifest the least urbanization. . . . As of 1950, the (Pearsonian) correlation between degree of industrialization and degree of urbanization, as measured by our indices, was .86, taking the countries and territories of the world as our units.[32]

The problem with this example is that 'urbanization' and 'industrialism' mean radically different things at different times and places; for example, capitalist and precapitalist cities and industry have only the most superficial (and the most asocial) of similarities.[33] Small wonder that such generalizations rarely prove universal even when their meaninglessness is overlooked.

So the value of generalizations depends upon the qualitative nature of the objects to which they refer. They can only supplement but never replace qualitative methods such as structural analysis. I mention this not to try to ban generalization but to make its use more effective.

Causation and causal analysis

Abstraction and generalization are essentially synchronic, at best allowing only indirect reference to process and change. The explanation of the latter requires causal analysis. Causation has proved a particularly contentious concept in philosophy and several different versions of it form integral parts of competing philosophical positions. As is always the case with metaphysical issues, particular interpretations can only be justified in terms of their compatibility with our most reliable beliefs, and this will be my tactic in defending a realist stance on this issue.

My purpose here, as elsewhere, is to legislate and hence to distinguish better from worse features of lay and scientific thinking. The point of providing a 'second-order' account of causation and causal analysis is not to displace 'first-order', substantive causal accounts but to 'reconstruct' and hence clarify the most reasonable of them. I must therefore warn the reader that although some of the terminology in the following second-order account is unfamiliar, it is intended to clarify something that is thoroughly *ordinary*. This needs saying because the effect of many philosophers' accounts of the subject is to make it appear the special preserve of esoteric, 'scientific' knowledge and hence to derogate or ignore even those lay causal accounts which are quite reasonable. The orthodox literature in the philosophy of science is extraordinarily narrow in its selection of exemplars of scientific practice and cavalier in its assumption that they are applicable to quite different fields. To those who are familiar with this literature the following realist account will seem strange and indeed questionable, though I doubt if it will appear so to newcomers to the subject. In order to avoid a disjointed presentation, I will once again have to postpone replies to some of the probable objections until Chapter 5.

To ask for the cause of something is to ask what 'makes it happen', what 'produces', 'generates', 'creates' or 'determines' it, or, more weakly, what 'enables' or 'leads to' it.[34] As soon as we reflect upon such words, it becomes clear that they are metaphors (and not quite 'dead' ones at that) which allude to or summarize an enormous variety of means by which change can occur. More specific references to causal processes are given, *inter alia*, in the transitive verbs we use in everyday life and in many social scientific accounts: 'they *built* the house', '*restructured* the industry', '*enclosed* the commons', are simple causal descriptions, that is, accounts of what produced change. Like any description they can, of course, be 'unpacked' and replaced by more detailed accounts and these in turn may also use transitive verbs. As explanations, these informal kinds of causal account are characteristically incomplete, but for dealing with more mundane processes they may be quite adequate and one would certainly be hard pushed to say much about society without using them. In order to clarify the nature and limitations of these and other types of causal description and explanation it is now necessary to proceed to a more formal discussion.

On the realist view, causality concerns not a relationship between discrete events ('Cause and Effect'), but the *causal powers* or *liabilities* of objects or relations, or more generally their ways-of-acting or '*mechanisms*'. People have the causal powers of being able to work ('labour power'), speak, reason, walk, reproduce, etc., and a host of causal liabilities, such as susceptibility to group pressure, extremes of temperature, etc. Often the causal powers inhere not simply in single objects or individuals but in the social relations and structures which they form. Thus the powers of a lecturer are not reducible to her characteristics as an individual but derive from her interdependent relations with students, colleagues, administrators, employer, spouse, etc.[35] Powers and liabilities can exist whether or not they are being exercised or suffered; unemployed workers have the power to work even though they are not doing so now and iron is liable to rust even though some pieces never get the chance to. On this view then, a causal claim is not about a regularity between separate things or events but about what an object is like and what it can do and only derivatively what it *will* do in any particular situation.[36] Hence to say that a person who happens to be unemployed nevertheless could work, given the opportunity, is not to indulge in speculation about what might happen in the future but to say something about what that person's mental and physical state and capabilities are like *now*. Causal powers and liabilities may thus be attributed to objects independently of any particular pattern of events; that is, not only when 'C' leads to 'E', but also sometimes when 'C' does not lead to 'E'. As we shall see, this point is extremely important for causal analysis.

The particular ways-of-acting or mechanisms exist necessarily in virtue of their object's nature. The nature or constitution of an object and its causal powers are internally or necessarily related: a plane can fly by virtue of its aerodynamic form, engines, etc.; gunpowder can explode by virtue of its unstable chemical structure; multinational firms can sell their products dear and buy their labour power cheap by virtue of operating in several countries with different levels of development; people can change their behaviour by virtue of their ability to monitor their own monitorings; and so on.[34] If the nature of an object changes then its causal powers will change too; engines lose their power as they wear out, a child's cognitive powers increase as it grows. Therefore in positing the existence of causal powers I am not invoking fixed, eternal essences.

This conception of causality as a *necessary* way of acting of an object does not, as some have supposed, boil down to the virtual tautology that an object can do something because it has the power to do so. Those who make this objection often refer to the case of the 'dormitive virtue' of opium, this characteristic having been advanced tautologically as an explanation of the sleep-inducing effects of opium-taking.[38] Yet scientists often do postulate the existence of such powers but avoid the tautology by establishing empirically what it is *about* the substance which gives it this power, which can be identified independently of the exercise of that power. A well-known example is the explanation of the power of some metals to conduct electricity by the presence of free ions in their structure. Similarly, it is surely not a tautology to explain my ability to walk and my inability to fly by reference to my anatomy, musculature, density and shape. Nor is it tautologous to explain the ability of certain people to live off rent by reference to their ownership of land, buildings or minerals.

In marxist theory it is common to encounter the term 'tendency' as a synonym for 'mechanism', as in the famous or infamous 'tendency of the rate of profit to fall', and its 'counteracting influences'. These kinds of tendency statements have often been interpreted as mere empirical generalizations about allegedly regular sequences of events, that is, about what on average 'tends' to happen. However, it is clear from the supporting arguments that Marx provided that they describe mechanisms which, he thought, existed necessarily by virtue of the nature of capital, but whose effects, like any mechanism, could be mediated by other mechanisms and variations in conditions.[39] Like many others, I do not accept Marx's claims about this tendency, but it is important not to criticize it on the basis of the misunderstanding that it is merely an empirical generalization. Rather it can be refuted by showing that the particular reasoning used to demonstrate that the mechanism exists necessarily by virtue of the nature of capital is faulty.[40] What is in question here is not the validity of the general causal categories – 'tendency' and 'mechanism' – but the particular substantive use of the concept in this instance.

Wherever possible, we try to get beyond the recognition that something produces some change to an understanding of what it is about the object that enables it to do this. In some cases, such as that of gravity or the connection between a person's intentions and actions, we know little about the mechanisms involved. What we would like in these latter cases, and what we already have in cases such as the conductivity of copper or the erosive power of a river, is a knowledge of *how* the process works. Merely knowing that 'C' has generally been followed by 'E' is not enough: we want to understand the continuous process by which 'C' produced 'E', if it did. This mode of inference in which events are explained by postulating (and identifying) mechanisms which are capable of producing them is called *'retroduction'*.[41] In many cases the mechanism so retroduced will already be familiar from other situations and some will actually be observable.[42] In others, hitherto unidentified mechanisms may be hypothesized. In the history of lay and scientific knowledge there are both cases where such hypotheses have later been corroborated (e.g. viruses, capillaries) and where they have been rejected (witchcraft, heat as a substance).[43] The philosophy of science cannot, of course, provide guarantees of success!

Whether a causal power or liability is actually activated or suffered on any occasion depends on conditions whose presence and configuration are contingent. Whether a person actually works might depend on whether there is a job for him/her. Whether gunpowder ever does explode depends on it being in the right conditions – in the presence of a spark, etc. So although causal powers exist necessarily by virtue of the nature of the objects which possess them, it is contingent whether they are ever activated or exercised. (Note that by 'conditions', we simply mean other objects, these having their own causal powers and liabilities – contrary to common assumption, conditions need not be inert.)

When they are exercised, the actual effects of causal mechanisms will again depend upon the conditions in which they work. *The relationship between causal powers or mechanisms and their effects is therefore not fixed, but contingent*; indeed causal powers exist independently of their effects, unless they derive from social structures whose reproduction depends on particular effects resulting.[44] To say that the relationship of a power to its conditions is contingent is not to suppose that the latter are uncaused, only that they are caused by different mechanisms. It is in view of the fact that causal powers are contingently related to their conditions that when we activate a mechanism for our own purposes we take care to ensure that the conditions under which it operates are those which will produce the desired effect. To take a gruesome example, if bombs were exploded anywhere at any time we would find little regularity in the relationship between their detonation and their effects. In order to get the desired results, considerable care is taken to aim them, that is, to locate suitable configurations of conditions. The explosion of a bomb, when it occurs, happens necessarily by virtue of its structure, but it might do so in a variety of conditions. The objects constituting the conditions have their own powers and liabilities, and so whichever conditions hold the results of the explosion will necessarily occur, differing according to whether the objects are cement, water or flesh. As can be seen, the juxtaposition of necessity and contingency is complex, even in the case of simple events such as this: the relationship between objects and causal powers is necessary; the relationship between these and their conditions is contingent, some of these conditions may include objects which activate the mechanisms. For any particular set of conditions, the results occur necessarily by virtue of the nature of the objects involved, but it is contingent which conditions are actually present (see Figure 7). Moreover, it is contingent whether we know either necessity or contingency.

Processes of change usually involve several causal mechanisms which may be only contingently related to one another. Not surprisingly then, depending on conditions, the operation of the same mechanism can produce quite different results and, alternatively, different mechanisms may produce the same empirical result. At one level this seems unexceptional, although it does not rest easily with the orthodox view of causation in terms of regular associations (or 'constant conjunctions') of causes and effects. For example, the effects of the law of value in forcing capitalist firms to reduce the labour time expended in producing each commodity will vary according to such contingent conditions as labour resistance, availability of new technologies, the nature of the product, management characteristics, etc. Firms may respond in a variety of ways, some speeding up work rates, some automating and others closing down. Conversely, a particular effect, such as the loss of jobs, may be caused by the introduction of new technology or failure to introduce new technology (via reduced competitiveness).[45] Where the operation of two or more mechanisms each brings about the same effect simultaneously, the situation is sometimes said to be 'over-determined'. The low social position of an immigrant woman is overdetermined – by class position and racial and gender discrimination.

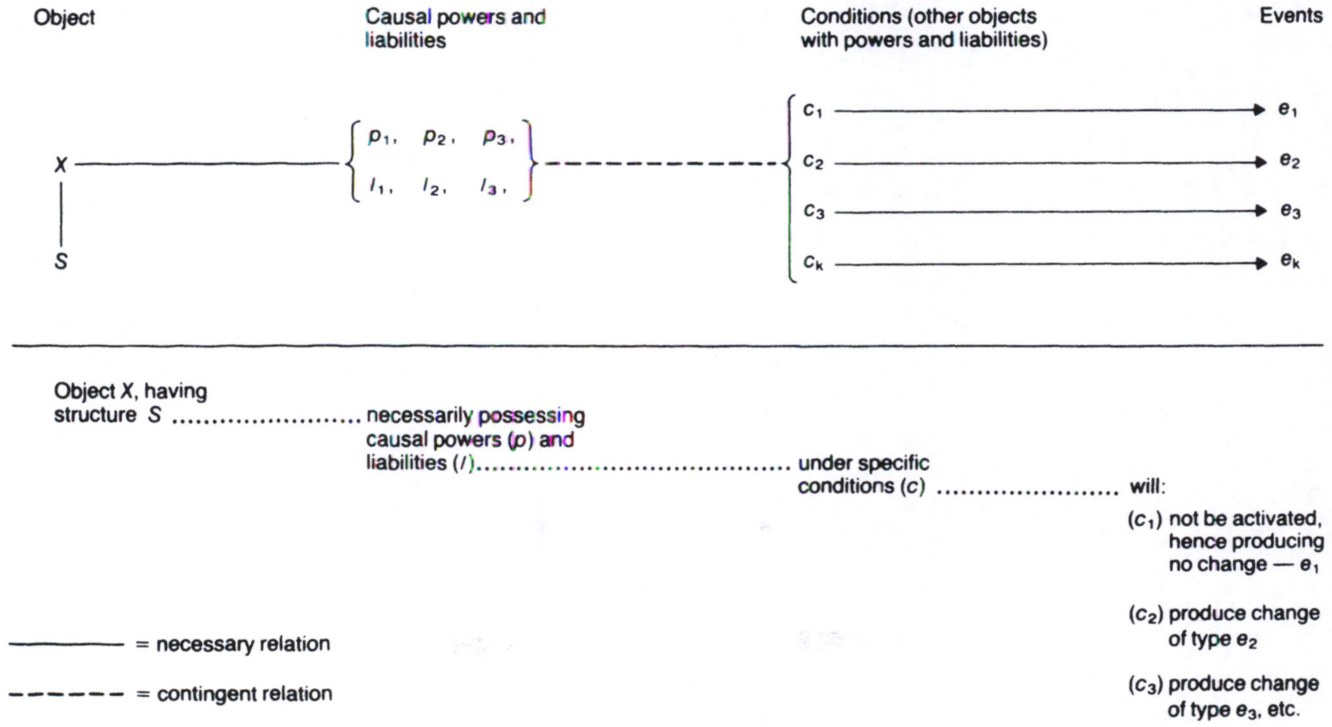

Object	Causal powers and liabilities	Conditions (other objects with powers and liabilities)	Events

$p_1, \ p_2, \ p_3,$
$l_1, \ l_2, \ l_3,$

c_1 → e_1

c_2 → e_2

c_3 → e_3

c_k → e_k

X —— S

Object X, having structure S .... necessarily possessing causal powers (p) and liabilities (l) .... under specific conditions (c) .... will:

(c_1) not be activated, hence producing no change — e_1

(c_2) produce change of type e_2

(c_3) produce change of type e_3, etc.

—————— = necessary relation

-------- = contingent relation

Figure 7 The structures of causal explanation

Inevitably, the exercise of causal mechanisms is often unclear from patterns of empirical events: if I fail to move a heavy weight it does not mean I wasn't pushing; when a plane flies it does not mean the law of gravity is no longer working. Counteracting forces can override and conceal the effects of the operation of a particular mechanism. In the case of pushing the weight it would be easy to establish whether I really was pushing, independently of whether it moved, but other cases may require scientific labour to check. Yet this independence of mechanisms from their effects has crucial implications: but for it we could never intervene in the course of nature, and hence life as we know it, including science, would be impossible.[46] It also means that the discovery of what a given mechanism can and cannot do requires considerable effort and ingenuity and that, as a means to this end, the search for regularities is inadequate.

Note also that contrary to popular myth (derived from the association of causality with regularity), what causes an event has nothing to do with the number of times it has been observed to occur and nothing to do with whether we happen to be able to predict it.[47] Indeed, there are some objects whose causal powers we believe we know, even though they have never been exercised; for example, our causal liabilities with respect to neutron bombs.

Now it might reasonably be objected that many of my examples in this discussion have been of physical causes, with the consequence that the applicability of causal analysis to the study of society might still be in doubt. In particular, one special type of social phenomenon whose causal status is widely doubted is that of ideas, beliefs and reasons. While it might be accepted that people have the causal power to reason and form ideas, the suggestion that reasons can be causes – that is, be the things which produce certain changes – is more difficult to accept. Reasons are very different from the material things in which we more readily recognize causal powers, and their enabling conditions are poorly understood. As was seen in Chapter 1, whereas the natural scientist has only the meanings of scientific concepts to interpret, the student of society has also to understand the intrinsic meanings of social practice. Reasons can also be evaluated as good or bad, false, inconsistent, etc., but it would make no sense to evaluate a physical cause in this way, although we might evaluate its results *for* our own interests.

Yet while reasons are certainly different in these respects from *physical* causes, it doesn't follow from this that they cannot be the causes of certain events.[48] Indeed, why should we want to evaluate reasons if they could not be causes? If repugnant beliefs never did anyone any harm – because they never caused anyone to do anything – there would be little point in wasting our breath criticizing them. And why should anyone bother to argue (reason) that reasons cannot be causes if such arguments could never cause people to change their minds? One may grant that we know little about how beliefs (e.g. my beliefs in realism), intentions (my intention to write about it) and actions (my writing) are connected, but there are few things in life that we do which don't presuppose that reasons can be causes; indeed, in general, communicative interaction presupposes material results.

It was also noted earlier that some social practices are dependent on (among other things) concepts which have been shown to be false or inconsistent. Some possible beliefs are so ridiculous that no material practices could be successfully based on them (e.g. belief in the possibility of walking on water), but others (explanations of our *in*ability to walk on water in terms of witchcraft) may have a limited practical adequacy. In other words, reasons don't have to involve 'true' or coherent beliefs to be causes.

It must also be appreciated that the reasons given by actors for their actions may not always be the real reasons; men who cultivate a macho image may not be aware of it let alone know the reasons for their actions. Indeed, if they were made aware of the real reasons it might (!) prompt them to act differently. Hence the point of critical social science's attempt to reduce illusion in society is to change its effects, not merely to provide an 'academic' critique of an external description of society.

Besides identifying the immediate causes of events, explanations must include references to the necessary conditions for the existence of mechanisms, where we do not already know them. Unless this is done, a voluntaristic account of practice may be produced. Where a process, such as inflation, is co-determined by several distinct mechanisms, it is reasonable to speak of one having more effect than another, but the same does not apply to the existence of necessary conditions (e.g. the existence of exchange) for these are either necessary or they are not. While having a language is not what causes me to write now, it is a necessary condition of my being able to write. Reasons and other causes may be given for actions such as shopping, joining the army, signing a cheque, casting a vote, getting married, granting a loan, imposing tariffs or being polite. But all these actions presuppose conditions such as material resources and social structures, including the conventions, rules and systems of meaning in terms of which reasons are formulated.

Voluntarism is rife in everyday causal accounts. Recently, many managers of firms have found that their workforces have become more compliant. One often sees newspaper reports which attribute this to a new, tougher management 'philosophy', without noting the conditions which enabled this to happen, in particular the threat of the dole queue. And scarcely a moment's thought is given to the kind of social organization of production by virtue of which the distinction between managers and subordinates exists. Although, in everyday life, we can get by without being aware of these necessary, structural conditions and their historically specific and hence transformable character, we can hardly ignore them if we want to penetrate beyond the limited horizons of common sense.

Our level of awareness of the conditions as well as the immediate causes of actions also affects our political prescriptions. 'Managerialist' political interventions are characteristically concerned with mediating the effects of the exercise of mechanisms by manipulating the conditions in which they operate. For example, planning legislation mediates the effects of property development by steering it into particular areas. But radical or revolutionary political changes alter the structures (necessary conditions) by virtue of which the mechanisms exist, in this case by expropriating property capital and nationalizing land.[49] Everyday thinking, being conservative, tends to favour managerialist solutions and one of the reasons for its conservatism is that it ignores the structural conditions of action or treats them as natural and eternal.

Often, an explanation of social practice will involve a (limited, not infinite) regress from actions through reasons to rules and thence to structures. For example, in explaining why building societies grant few mortgages to unskilled workers we might first encounter the reasons given in the actors' accounts (lack of stable income, etc.) together with the actions they inform. These reasons will in turn invoke various rules, whether formal or informal, and in terms of which they make sense (rules governing eligibility for mortgages). Then comes the important stage of asking why these rules exist, that is in virtue of what kinds of structure or object do they exist. The answer might be that as interest-bearing capital building societies have to make a profit (or 'return') on their transactions.[50] As they have to pay interest to their creditors at a rate sufficient to stop them losing assets to competing investment outlets they must therefore minimize any conditions which might reduce their capability of meeting these obligations, such as lending to people who might default on repayments. If we recall our earlier warnings against functionalist explanations, it must be remembered that merely noting these necessary conditions is not sufficient to explain how they are met, if they are. To do this we must refer back to the level of actions. This movement also illustrates the interdependency of structure and agency, once again.

Echoing our earlier point about political prescriptions, note how at each stage in the explanatory movement, different evaluative implications are 'secreted'. At the first level we might judge actors and their reasons as good or bad, at the second the rules particular to the institution, while at the third the wider economic system (together with its constitutive social relations) to which the institution owes its existence might be criticized.[51] Both in terms of explanations and evaluations, competing theories often 'talk past one another' because without realizing it they are preoccupied with different stages in the regress.

One of the attractive features of social theories which try to establish the necessary conditions for the existence of their objects is that they can often be tested quite easily by imagining or actually trying to produce changes in them.[52] For example, one could actually get a job as a building society manager (!) and try allocating mortgages to those who most needed but could least afford them, or alternatively imagine doing this in a 'thought experiment'. If avoiding such allocations is a necessary condition for the existence of the branch then either the branch or the altruistic manager would go. From this it an be argued that policy prescriptions for helping the poor to get mortgages which simply call for more enlightened and kinder building society managers are misjudged.

In everyday discourse and even in some 'scientific' accounts we are often very casual about causality. For instance, a school teacher might say that some children are obedient and hard working because they are middle class. Such statements raise a number of questions: are the children necessarily industrious and obedient by virtue of being middle class or is this a contingent fact about them?; and how is 'middle class' defined here? A more penetrating cross-examination of the teacher's statement might inquire into the nature of the work and the quality of the pupil–teacher interaction in the classroom, for these might affect who works and who doesn't. There might, for example, be other forms of education or schooling to which working-class children respond more fully. All these questions represent a dissatisfaction with an explanation which relies upon a generalization and is therefore ambiguous about the status of the relations to which it refers. Explanations by generalization are only acceptable in the absence of knowledge of causal powers and liabilities, or where the thing to be explained is simply the form of combination and proportions of already-known constitutive processes.[53]

In examining such accounts, it is found that the search for relevant causal powers and liabilities requires a clarification of the kinds of abstractions that are used, in order to improve the qualitative understanding of the processes, so that conditions and mechanisms can be identified. So causal analysis is usually closely tied to abstraction and structural analysis and hence explanation to description. There is also an interdependence between all of these and the interpretation of meaning. Actions are not only meaningful; they have causes and effects. As reasons can be causes and structures can be concept-dependent, causal, structural and interpretive analysis are interdependent.

Can generalization and the search for regularities ever assist causal analysis? Sometimes the discovery of empirical regularities may draw attention to objects whose causal powers might be responsible for the pattern and to conditions which are necessary for their existence and activation. But in order to confirm these, qualitative information is needed on the nature of the objects involved and not merely more quantitative data on empirical associations. So, for example, in epidemiology, ignorance of the causes and conditions of certain diseases may require a resort to mapping and charting quantitative data on a wide range of possible factors. It may seem reasonable to search for a factor which is common to all instances of the disease and hypothesize that this is the cause, or else a factor which is only present where the disease occurs.[54] While they are worth trying, both methods fail to address the problem of finding a *mechanism* which *generates* the disease, as opposed to a factor which merely covaries with it. The weakness of the search for mere associations is illustrated in the well-known story of the drunk who tried to discover the causes of his drunkenness by using such methods: on Monday he had whisky and soda, on Tuesday gin and soda, on Wednesday vodka and soda and on other nights when he stayed sober, nothing; by looking for the common factor in the drinking pattern for the nights when he got drunk, he decides the soda water was the cause. Now the drunk might possibly have chosen alcohol as the common factor and hence as the cause. However, what gives such an inference credibility is not merely the knowledge that alcohol was a common factor but that it has a mechanism capable of inducing drunkenness. The example is certainly not far-fetched, for in many possible applications in social science there is not one but several equivalents of the soda water. Alternatively, instead of looking for similarities between situations in which a common result occurs, we sometimes seek causes by looking for differences between situations in which different results occur. Again this method seems sensible enough but inconclusive. If we have two comparable situations in which different results occur and then discover some other difference between the two situations, it does not follow that it is the one which *makes* the difference to the results. And again, to check whether it is we have to identify mechanisms. Neither common nor distinguishing properties need be causally relevant.

Statistical techniques are often used to identify common and distinguishing properties. Obviously, we don't try to correlate anything with anything, but use available qualitative and causal knowledge to narrow down the list of possible factors to those which might have relevant powers and liabilities. However, all too often the qualitative investigation is abandoned just at the point when it is most needed – for deciding the status and the causal (as opposed to statistical) significance of whatever patterns and associations are found. When this happens research may occlude rather than reveal causality. For example, there have been many studies of housing allocation which start and end by seeking associations among 'factors' and 'variables' – without regard to whether they might be causes or conditions or parts of structures – and which have overlooked obvious mechanisms such as the rule-following actions of housing officials. Through theoretical and methodological inhibitions like these, it is sometimes possible for social scientists to know less about their objects (though more about their models!) than the well-informed lay person.[55]

In the defence of this kind of work, it is often said that progress is inhibited in social science by the lack of theory[56] and the impossibility of experiments. The former judgement is based on the misconception that theories can only exist in the form of ordering structures for data, with the result that other forms of theory are ignored. While experiments are indeed impossible, they are not always necessary for discovering mechanisms, though they are helpful for clarifying their effects since conditions are controlled.

The defence also overlooks the advantage which social scientists have over natural scientists of an internal relation between knowledge of society and its object which gives easier access to mechanisms. There is no need, for example, to conduct experiments on or search for regularities between redundancy notices and redundant workers, in order to understand the mechanism involved. Again, to appreciate this we should remember that many causal mechanisms are ordinary and fairly well understood by actors. A causal mechanism doesn't have to be represented in an esoteric formula to be one.

Conclusions

By way of summary, the relationships between the abstract and the concrete and between structures, mechanisms and effects are represented in Figure 8. The horizontal dimension represents a variety of structures, mechanisms and events present in a complex system. When activated, particular mechanisms produce effects in 'conjunctures', which may be unique. According to conditions, the same mechanism may sometimes produce different events, and conversely the same type of event may have different causes. Abstract theory analyses objects in terms of their constitutive structures, as parts of wider structures and in terms of their causal powers. Concrete research looks at what happens when these combine. In the vertical dimension, some readers may want to add a fourth level above events to cover meanings, experiences, beliefs and so forth, but as these can form structures, function as

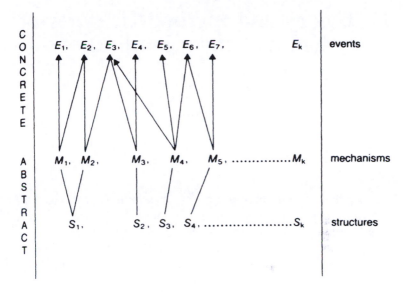

Figure 8   Structures, mechanisms and events

causes, or be considered as events, I would suggest that they be taken as already included.

4 Theory and method II: types of system and their implications

One of the central themes of our argument so far has been that questions of method cannot be answered without careful consideration of the nature of the objects under study. Thus, in the previous chapter, we saw how different forms of analysis and explanation were related to different kinds of object. Having discussed this relationship at a simple level in terms of abstraction, causal analysis and generalization we can now look at some further qualities of objects of study and their implications for method. Of particular importance are 'stratification', 'closed and open systems' and spatial form, which have major implications for explanation and prediction, and which help to explain the manifest differences of method between particular scientific disciplines. As in the previous chapter, the discussion will switch between questions of objects and methods, but by the end it will be possible to develop and synthesize some of the most general principles introduced in Chapter 3, regarding abstract and concrete research, theory and empirical research.

Stratification and emergent powers

It is often assumed that a useful way of understanding a complex object is to break it down into its constituent parts, either by abstraction or literally by taking it to bits. For example, to understand something like employment change, it seems sensible to break down or 'disaggregate' the aggregate statistics in the hope that complexity and irregularity might be reduced to the effects of a combination of simple and regular components. Many researchers have been seduced by the simple idea that if only individuals and their attitudes, etc. were understood, the macro patterns of society would become intelligible. But it is not always so straightforward. We would not try to explain the power of people to think by reference to the cells that constitute them, as if cells possessed this power too.[1] Nor would we explain the power of water to extinguish fire by deriving it from the powers of its constituents, for oxygen and hydrogen are highly inflammable.

In such cases objects are said to have '*emergent powers*', that is, powers or liabilities which cannot be reduced to those of their constituents.[2] This phenomenon suggests that the world is not merely differentiated but *stratified*; the powers of water exist at a different stratum from those of hydrogen or oxygen. Emergence can be explained in terms of the distinction between internal and external relations. Where objects are externally or contingently related they do not affect one another in their essentials and so do not modify their causal powers, although they may interfere with the effects of the exercise of these powers. Mere aggregates, including 'taxonomic collectives' (see above, p. 101) consist of externally-related individuals and hence lack emergent powers. Disaggregation, as a step towards explanation of the whole, therefore presents no problem. In the case of internally-related objects, or structures such as that associated with our landlord–tenant relation, emergent powers are created because this type of combination of individuals modifies their powers in fundamental ways. Even though social structures exist only where people reproduce them, they have powers irreducible to those of individuals (you can't pay rent to yourself). Explanation of the actions of individuals often therefore requires not a micro (reductionist) regress to their inner constitution (though that may be relevant too) but a 'macro regress' to the social structures in which they are located. Likewise deferential individual behaviour needs to be explained in connection with a social structure concerning status. The action of purchasing presupposes the insertion of the buyer in a structure of exchange, the action of the prime minister a political hierarchy, and so on.

It is possible for higher stratum objects such as human beings to react back on lower stratum processes by manipulating them according to their laws or necessary ways-of-acting. By such means as agriculture and contraception we can intervene in biological processes, including those which constitute us.

A fortunate consequence of the stratification of the world is that we don't have to work back through all the successive constitutive strata in order to understand objects in any specific stratum. Although the existence of social phenomena presupposes biological phenomena, the objects of the latter can usually be taken as given. Similarly, biological phenomena have emergent powers and exist at a different stratum (or group of strata) from the chemical phenomena which constitute them, and likewise, the latter, in turn, exist at a different stratum from the objects of physics. *Reductionist* research overlooks stratification and finds itself drawn into such regresses. Disregard of stratification and emergent powers is also evident in research which investigates relationships (usually quantitative) between objects which are treated merely as 'factors' or 'variables' and which may belong to quite different strata. Such indifference to stratification (and structures) invites misidentifications of causality.

The evidence of stratification in the objects of the natural sciences is relatively good, but rather patchy as regards society. It is certainly more difficult to interpret interdisciplinary divisions as reflections of divisions between strata in the social sciences. The difficulty probably derives partly from the highly developed ability of human beings to manipulate systems at different strata and the capacity of individuals to develop conceptions of mechanisms which only social structures can actually possess. In addition, the fact that individuals and institutions operate in many different structures also creates difficulties for deciding by virtue of what structure a particular power exists. Many of the social sciences straddle several strata in their attempt to synthesize whole systems of social practices, including the processes by which high strata react back upon the whole. The study of the interaction between 'individual and society' is a very general example of this concern, although in many cases it has foundered on the assumption that society is just an aggregate of individuals and hence lacking in emergent powers.[3]

Some of the most common and interesting disputes between theories and disciplines are actually about where in a group of strata a particular object belongs: is the subject-matter of psychology socially-determined and hence historically and culturally-specific or is it transhistorical, pancultural and perhaps asocial? If consumer preferences are a determinant of economic behaviour must they be explained by economists or do they constitute a different stratum which is properly the concern of psychology? In large part the answer to such questions requires further empirical research, but philosophical analysis can at least eliminate a few non-starters. Behaviourism, for instance, illegitimately reduces meaningful social action to intrinsically meaningless physical behaviour. Meaningful action is always associated with physical processes (at least neurological ones) but meaning itself is an emergent property which must be understood 'at its own level'. Likewise, the debate over socio-biology can be clarified considerably by using the concepts of stratification and emergence.

This is not to pretend that such problems are easy to resolve. Consider the common-sense belief that people sometimes fight because it is 'human nature' to do so. The usual knee-jerk response from radicals is to insist that human nature is socially determined. Yet the reply is also inadequate for it is patently false to suggest that the physical is an epiphenomenon or ghost of the social. Indeed, human beings must have a particular physical make-up or nature for it to be possible for them to be conditioned by social influences in consistent ways. There are also cases, such as human sexuality, in which the biological may be socially mediated *in every instance and respect*, but this does not mean that what is mediated cannot be biological.[4] Whether people are 'naturally' aggressive, or males, patriarchal or whatever can only be decided by research which pays careful attention to stratification and emergence and is alive to the problems of defining the 'natural' and the 'social'. It should be noted, however, that even if it were found to be true that people are aggressive in virtue of their physical nature rather than social conditioning, it would in no way license an abandonment of attempts to use our social powers to override such tendencies.[5]

Closed and open systems and regularities

Given the independence of mechanisms from their conditions, causation need not imply regularity in patterns and sequences of events. Yet some areas of knowledge abound with impressive examples of precise empirical regularities. It is often assumed that the extent to which such regularities have been found is a measure of the maturity of a science, with the obvious implication that the social sciences are immature. Realism offers a different approach to the phenomenon. Instead of assuming that they exist universally so that they are just waiting to be discovered, with the implication that success or failure reflects only on the competence of the investigator, realist philosophy reflects upon the conditions which must hold if regularities are actually to occur, that is, it asks what a system and its constituent objects must be like for regularities to be produced.

Apart from cases of accidental and usually transitory regularities arising from the chance mutual compensation of changes in a number of processes, the following conditions must hold:[6]

1 There must be no change or qualitative variation (e.g. impurities) in the object possessing the causal powers if mechanisms are to operate consistently. This is termed by Bhaskar the 'intrinsic condition for closure'. Other things being equal, a clockwork mechanism whose spring suffers metal fatigue will not produce regular movement. Similarly, a pressure group undertaking a political campaign will not produce regular effects if the internal organization of the group disintegrates.

2 The relationship between the causal mechanism and those of its external conditions which make some difference to its operation and effects must be constant if the outcome is to be regular (the extrinsic condition for closure). If the political sympathies of the public are changing for reasons independent of the pressure group's campaign, the effect of the latter cannot be expected to be manifested as a regularity.

Both 1 and 2 imply that no new emergent powers are developing in the system.

If *both* the intrinsic and extrinsic conditions are met, a *closed system* exists in which regularities are produced.[7] Most systems we encounter violate these conditions in some way and therefore any regularities they produce are at best approximate and short-lived; these are *open systems*. However, within local regions of open systems, closed or quasi-closed systems may occur, perhaps where one mechanism completely dominates or overrides the effects of others.

In the objects of study of the natural sciences, closed systems may exist naturally (e.g. the solar system) or may be artificially produced in experiments or machines. The whole point of experiments in science is to create (usually simple) closed systems by producing the appropriate intrinsic and extrinsic conditions, so that regular sequences of events result, thereby revealing more clearly the operation of mechanisms.[8] Where anomalous experimental results occur, the usual first response is quite reasonably to check that these conditions have been met.

Now at one level the significance of closed and open systems may seem obvious enough, but few philosophers have recognized either the rarity or the twin conditions of existence of closed systems. Perhaps also, through their disregard of science as an activity or labour process (as opposed to sets of ideas), they have paid little attention to the role of the artificial production of closed systems. The precision and predictive success of some of the natural sciences has not been bought purely by the application of appropriate analytical methods but by the achievement of *physical control* over nature. The latter is not merely a by-product of the former but one of the causes of its success. In taking closed systems, and hence regularities, to be universal, philosophers of science have not surprisingly given enormous prominence to the experience of physics, and to a lesser extent chemistry, as exemplars of 'science', while saying little about other natural sciences such as meteorology in which closed systems are rare. When a warm air mass rides up over a cold one, the effects can be explained and very roughly predicted, partly on the basis of knowledge derived from the 'closed system sciences'. Failure to discover precise, enduring regularities in meteorology reflects not its 'immaturity' but the fact that its system of interest is open. Not surprisingly, sciences and their methods vary according to the nature of their objects.

The social sciences deal with open systems but lack the advantage of their equivalents in natural science of having relevant closed system sciences on which to draw. One of the main reasons for the openness of social systems is the fact that we can interpret the same material conditions and statements in different ways and hence learn new ways of responding, so that effectively we become different kinds of people. Human actions characteristically modify the configuration of systems, thereby violating the extrinsic conditions for closure, while our capacity for learning and self-change violates the intrinsic condition. Paradoxically, it is because most systems are open, and many relations contingent, that we can intervene in the world and create closed (non-human) systems. At the most, social systems can only be quasi-closed, producing regularities that are only approximate and spatially and temporally restricted. A considerable part of human labour and communication is devoted to the creation of closed or quasi-closed systems, with the aim of taking advantage of and controlling mechanisms of value to us, be it photosynthesis in edible plants or the synchronization of labour in a factory. Many forms of social organization tend to produce approximate regularities in patterns of events by enforcing rules or by subordinating workers to machines, which routinize and control the spacing and timing of particular kinds of action. The conditions for closure are therefore of practical as well as academic importance.[9]

However, the 'regularities' which result vary from case to case and do not approach the universality and precision of those available to physicists and astronomers. In any case, patterns of events, be they regular or irregular, are not self-explanatory, but must be explained by reference to what produces them. For example, the (approximately) regular flux of traffic in and out of the city is an effect of the rules governing the working day and the separation of home and workplace.

Within limits, social organizations, and some advanced kinds of machine such as 'autopilots', can ensure the production of regular behaviour even where they encounter variable and indeed unpredictable conditions. Although the patterning and sequencing of inputs and conditions is not predictable, the general nature of each likely input or condition is known so that it can be responded to when met. By such means institutions are able to fashion fairly uniform products out of variable material.

Although the twin conditions for closure are not widely known *formally*, there are some common procedures in social science which take *partial* account of them. For example, it is generally recognized that most social events are the outcome of what Mill called a 'plurality of causes',[10] and it is usually hoped that any irregularities can be shown to be merely the combined effect of separable regular processes. So in analysing any one 'cause' we try to 'control for' the effects of others. However, the controls rarely approach the satisfaction of both conditions for closure.

One other common response to the ubiquity of open systems is simply to *assume* them to be closed. Assumptions of equilibrium in economics and isotropic plains in geography fulfil this function in the development of idealized, hypothetical models. Whether the intrinsic and extrinsic conditions for closure of a *real*, as opposed to hypothetical, system can be satisfied depends on the time period under consideration. Obviously, if a slowly developing system is examined over a very short period of time it will appear to approximate the conditions for closure.[11] This characteristic invites the exploitation of the trivial case in which the illusion of closure is created by treating the dimensions of an open system measured at a single point of time as if they were invariant over time and hence as 'regularities'. In fact some social scientists seem to have acquired the habit of using the word 'regularity' to refer to 'relationships' or formal associations which only hold for a single point in time. However, assuming a system is closed does not make it so, nor is it clear that a hypothetical closed system model 'approximates' a real open one. Novelty, becoming and qualitative change – albeit at widely differing rates – typify human action.

Laws in science: causal and instrumentalist[12]

The above realist concepts of causation and closed and open systems also have major implications for the understanding of scientific *laws*. Conventionally, laws are defined as well cor-roborated or confirmed statements about universal empirical regularities of the type 'If C, then E', and causation is understood as regularity in the sequence of events. On the realist view, causation involves changes *in* C or E and causal knowledge concerns powers or liabilities and only derivatively what they will do or what their effects will be. Accordingly the realist concept of a causal law is different: 'The citation of a law presupposes a claim about the activity of some mechanism but not about the conditions under which the mechanism operates and hence not about the results of its activity, i.e. the actual outcome on any particular occasion.'[13] As already noted, the law of gravity does not cease to exist when the customary regularities of objects falling downwards at certain velocities fail to occur, as in the flight of birds. Rather, its effects are modified by other mechanisms, which might equally be referred to by law-statements. Just as causation concerns necessity and not universality, regularity or generality, so it is with causal laws. They refer to the causal mechanisms which exist necessarily by virtue of the nature of their holders and not to the contingent matter of whether the mechanisms happen to be in conditions in which they can produce regularities.

In social science, particularly history, there has been a long and rather pointless debate about the possibility and legitimacy of 'explanation without laws'.[14] The debate has usually been conducted with all sides accepting the following erroneous assumptions:

1   that causation is indicated by regularity – indeed that the latter is a necessary condition of the former;
2   that laws refer to universal empirical regularities, plus in many cases:
3   that reasons cannot be causes;

and either

4   that hermeneutics can be eliminated so that the methods of social science are identical to those of natural science;

or

5   that the task of social studies such as history is to understand the meaning of their objects and *not* to explain them causally.

It should be clear that, as mirror opposites, 4 and 5 can both appeal to 3 for support. Those who accept 2 rarely realize that the fact that such laws have been discovered in some sciences (e.g. physics) but continue to elude others (e.g. history) reflects the former's access to closed systems and the latter's restriction to open systems. (If you want to annoy advocates of 1, 2, 3 and 4, try insisting that they give a single non-tautological example of a well-corroborated, precise, enduring universal regularity or 'law' governing social phenomena.) Our realist arguments that causation, and hence causal laws, concern necessity and not universality and regularity, and that reasons can be causes, simply *dissolve* the debate about whether we can explain 'without laws', and also the debate between 4 and 5. Included in the former are debates about explanation between traditional ('regional'), 'ideographic' approaches and 'nomothetic' or 'scientific' ('spatial analysis') approaches in geography; between 'classical' and 'behavioural' approaches in the study of international relations; between 'political philosophy' and 'political science'; and between interpretive and positivist approaches in psychology and sociology.

In everyday life, as in history and other social sciences, we frequently explain both by reference to causes which will never be repeated and hence which do not form part of 'regularities'[15] and by reference to reasons; often they may be one and the same thing. Philosophers and historians who have wanted to insist on 1, 2 and perhaps 4 have wasted a great deal of ink and energy in dreaming up ingenious ways of explaining unique events such as the causes of the First World War by citing them as instances of universal regularities.[16] Not surprisingly, such attempts look quaintly absurd. (Some don't even deal with social phenomena.)[17] By contrast, those who are tempted by 5 make it impossible to understand how social change is produced though they may allow that non-social processes can be causally explained.[18]

The belief that laws refer to universal regularities in patterns of events gains support from instances in natural science such as those expressed in the famous equations $E = mc^2$, $PV = RT$, etc. These refer quite unequivocally to regularities among events and not to the causal mechanisms which produce them. I shall call them 'instrumentalist' laws as they provide a way of *calculating* the dimensions of a system.

Instrumentalist laws fulfil a different function from causal laws and are subject to different limitations:

1   Being descriptive of regularities, they are, for the reasons given above, restricted to closed systems in their application.
2   As Harré points out, for such laws to be applied successfully, the properties referred to by the variables which describe the system (e.g. pressure P, volume V and temperature T) must be externally related such that 'they can be varied separately while retaining their identity'.[19] When the values of the variables in the equation change they do not cease to refer to the same objects. Processes in which the elements interact causally but retain their identity are called 'parametric' by Harré. However, because the *qualitative* nature of many social phenomena varies according to context, they cannot be treated as parametric and as possible objects of instrumentalist laws.[20]

Actions cannot be understood independently of the contexts which are constitutive of their meanings: they rarely retain their identity as the context is changed.

3   As instrumentalist laws do not refer to mechanisms and hence do not identify what produces changes, they are not explanatory in a causal sense. Given certain information, they tell us what the value of some unknown variable will be. However, it is possible for references to mechanisms to be made elsewhere in a theory associated with the equations.[21] Without such support instrumentalist laws and theories are merely calculating devices.

4   Where closed systems exist, instrumentalist laws or models can be used successfully for making such calculations *even though they may fail to identify and adequately conceptualize relevant causal mechanisms and conditions.* If outputs are regularly related to inputs then *any* formula which fits the regularities will do. It may help readers to grasp this point if they reflect upon cases where they have been unaware of the existence of certain components of a smoothly-running machine – until, that is, it has broken down. For example, it would be easy to devise a formula for relating the speed at which a record player turntable revolves to the settings of the controls. Such formulae need not include variables which refer to the mechanism underneath the turntable; indeed, this might be completely unknown; and 'theoretical' terms may make no reference to actual objects but merely serve as logical ordering devices. Causal knowledge may seem unimportant as long as the machine is running smoothly (i.e. remains a closed system) and we may take the instrumental attitude that all that matters is that it works and never mind how. (At the risk of committing an offence of heresy against some of the most prestigious sciences one might also suggest that their access to closed systems permits them a similar attitude.)[22] And as long as closed systems are available we need not worry too much about conceptualization as a means of identifying causal mechanisms. In such circumstances, the ordering-framework view of theory is in its element and conceptual problems seem of little practical relevance. Even so, when the machine breaks down and the outputs vary independently of the inputs – i.e. when the system ceases to be closed – we become aware of the presence of intervening mechanisms and try to identify

them by dismantling it. Likewise, in a social crisis, hitherto unrecognized mechanisms become apparent (although few of the constituent processes are likely to be parametric, as they are in a machine). A full *causal* explanation of the motion of the turntable would require reference to such mechanisms, regardless of whether they happened to be producing regular motion, and their identification need not depend on the ability to calculate their effects quantitatively. Likewise, in social systems (which are invariably open), knowledge of, say, the mechanisms by which political consensus is maintained need not depend on an ability to calculate their effects quantitatively.

It can therefore be seen that the effects of having closed systems are double-edged: on the one hand it facilitates analysis, as mechanisms and their effects stand in stable relationships; on the other hand the regularities may conceal certain mechanisms. Yet the problems are more serious where the closed system is a hypothetical one rather than one which is both actual and physically manipulable. In the case of a real closed system such as the record player turntable, certain asymmetries in causal relations may be discovered by examining the effects of manipulating different elements or 'parameters'. We can learn that although the turntable can be made to revolve at 45 r.p.m. by operating the appropriate controls, reversing the procedure and trying to change the control settings by manually rotating the turntable does not work. The closed systems which astronomers study are real but not manipulable and hence causal inferences have to be made more indirectly by observation or reference to other relevant sciences. By contrast, the logical or mathematical manipulation of a hypothetical closed system represented by symbols is a poor guide to causal structure, for the rules governing these kinds of manipulation need not correspond to the laws governing the possible ways-of-acting of real objects; models may be run backwards, effects can be used to calculate ('determine') causes and hence efforts to calculate and 'predict' may rest upon mis-specifications of even the basic asymmetries of causal dependence. Later I shall argue that this problem is endemic in quantitative modelling in social science.

If instrumentalist laws are useful under certain conditions for calculating unknown variables, they are presumably also useful for *prediction* and it is to this subject, and its relation to explanation, that I now turn.

Prediction

Consider the following widely held assumptions about the nature and role of *prediction* in science:

1 Predictive success is the primary goal of any science, natural or social.
2 Prediction and explanation are *symmetric*: explanations can serve as predictions and predictions as explanationns. The only difference besides that of tense is difficulty, it naturally being harder to predict what has not yet happened than to explain what is already known to have occurred.
3 *a* Predictive ability is the most stringent test of theory and a measure of the maturity of the sciences.
   b The 'soft' sciences are weak at prediction not because they deal with intrinsically unpredictable objects but because they have not yet developed theory and scientific methods.

All of these can be shown to be mistaken.

1 is certainly false as regards social science and probably false for many natural sciences. In comparison with the number of explanations produced, predictions are relatively rare, especially accurate ones. Those who accept the scientistic view expressed in 3 and want to claim for their work the honorific label of 'science' are prone to exaggerate their number and significance and to gloss over their relative lack of accuracy and reliability. The pretence of similarity with closed system sciences is often made by stretching the meaning of 'prediction' to cover cases where no claims about future data are made, such as the practice of 'estimating' the characteristics of populations from samples. On the other hand, those critics who accept 2 and 3 but want to deny social studies the status of science tend to highlight rather than conceal the lack of successful social prediction. For example, anti-marxists are particularly fond of giving enormous prominence to the handful of predictions made by Marx and Engels. Yet compared to their commitment to explanation, Marx and Engels took little interest in prediction.

In order to show why prediction is less common than explanation in social 'science' and why 3 is mistaken it is first necessary to examine proposition 2. 'If we can explain how something works we can also predict its behaviour, and vice versa.' Such arguments look plausible until we begin to consider examples of non-explanatory predictions and non-predictive explanations. While instances of the former are quite widely known (e.g. prediction by curve-extrapolation), the latter are less commonly recognized or else regarded simply as *incomplete* explanations. Non-predictive explanations can easily be interpreted in the terms of a realist account of causation. We can explain the ways of acting of objects by reference to their structure and composition and know under what conditions mechanisms are activated without being aware of when or where those conditions and mechanisms exist. It is therefore possible to know what makes an event happen, when it does happen, but future occurrences can only be reliably predicted where the necessary and sufficient conditions are known to exist or to be about to come into existence.

In closed systems, objects and their relations are stable. Abstract explanatory knowledge of mechanisms can more easily be supplemented by information on system states and hence successful explanatory predictions derived (though their predictive success does not depend on the adequacy of the explanation). However, the possibilities for accurate and reliable explanatory predictions for open systems are remote. The prospects of acquiring information on not only the number and nature of the mechanisms but their configuration so that the results of their interaction can be predicted are small. In other words, it is unlikely to be practically possible to discover the extent to which the intrinsic and extrinsic conditions for system closure are *not* satisfied.

Perhaps the most famous example of non-predictive explanation is the theory of evolution. The mechanisms referred to in the theory are not sufficient on their own to predict the course of evolution. But does this mean that non-predictive explanations are just *incomplete* explanations? To answer this we must consider whether it is reasonable to expect to have a knowledge of all the contingent relations which might obtain in the future, e.g. in this case the relations between organisms and their environments.

Let us consider a further example, from another open-system natural science. Geology is only able to provide non-predictive explanations of the occurrence of oil deposits.[23] The necessary conditions for the occurrence of oil are known but these are not, on their own, sufficient to determine its presence. For example, it is known for which rocks and structures the presence of oil is physically impossible (e.g. granite intrusions) or possible (e.g. certain types of sandstone). The mechanisms which actually produce oil are also known, but since the relation between these and the appropriate types of lithology is contingent and the systems in which they occur open, we cannot expect to be able to predict the occurrence of oil with great confidence. We can know where to look from our knowledge of necessary conditions but we still have to drill to see if any exists. The 'incompleteness' of the explanations which prevents geologists from providing accurate and reliable predictions derives not from any lack of abstract knowledge of mechanisms but from a lack of empirical knowledge of contingent relations. It is not the causal explanation which is incomplete but the system description and this is only to be expected, given the changeable form of contingent relations in open systems. Were that description to be completed (e.g. were we to know in which appropriate sites the organisms from which oil is formed actually happen to be present) then there would be little left for us to predict. Because so many philosophers of science have imperialistically prescribed the practices possible in closed system sciences for all types of knowledge, they have tended to underestimate the importance of non-predictive explanations. Yet it is explanatory predictions (or predictive explanations) which ought more reasonably to be regarded as the special case.

Non-explanatory predictions are more widely recognized, but again their conditions of success vary significantly according to whether the systems to which they apply are open or closed. As already noted, given a quantified closed system, it is possible to fit models which predict accurately but do not correctly identify causality. Barometer readings can be used to predict changes in the weather, and vice versa, but in neither case could the prediction serve as an explanation. Non-explanatory predictions are inevitably less reliable for complex open systems. Social scientists wishing to predict often find themselves pulled in two opposing directions. On the one hand it is tempting to improve predictive success by modelling all the main processes thought to be responsible for the events to be predicted. This option runs into the problem of representing unknown and unstable contingent relations. Such models can also be extremely complex, data-hungry and unwieldy and produce considerable error amplification so that the results may not justify the effort. On the other hand, non-explanatory predictive methods such as simple curve-extrapolation are easy to use and despite their opaqueness as regards causality, often produce better results.

It might even be possible to get the best predictive results on the basis of a spurious correlation. As the rate of inflation has correlated more strongly with the incidence of Scottish dysentery than the money supply, the former would have proved a better predictor of inflation than the latter. Economists would not use the spurious correlation, however, not only because of its absurdity, but because it seems unlikely that such accidents could persist in the future.

In practice, then, open system predictive methods are neither completely non-explanatory nor fully explanatory but a compromise usually taking the form of a model in which some of the main processes are summarily represented by 'variables'. These 'empirical models' are fitted to existing data and extrapolated forward. They involve curve fitting[24] but the curves are fitted to relationships which *might* be interpreted as causal: they do not attempt to model actual processes closely. One would not expect to see every economic agent and every causal mechanism and condition responsible for affecting the rate of inflation to be represented in a predictive model. Nor, on the other hand, would an abstract explanation of the relevant mechanisms be expected to tell us when and where appropriate conditions for their existence and activation will exist. Abstract explanations do not concern actual events but what produces them. Concrete explanations require additional empirical knowledge to provide a description of how and in what conditions *these* mechanisms exist and how they interact in *this* particular system. Conversely, predictions concern actual events but need not consider what produces them.

Now social scientists often mix up the goals of explanation and prediction and appeal for justification to the 'symmetry thesis' in which explanations are treated as 'postdictions', i.e. accounts of past processes which would have served to predict the event-to-be-explained even before it occurred. Particularly in research using statistical methods it is common to treat the operation which would have predicted the event as its causal explanation, yet non-explanatory postdictions are no less possible than non-explanatory predictions.

So explanation and prediction differ in more than just tense and difficulty – they are different kinds of operation conducted for different ends. Predictions give us grounds for expecting something to happen (e.g. the first signs of the contraction of a disease),[25] while (causal) explanations tell us what makes things happen. The latter can only serve as grounds for reliable predictions under special conditions not generally found in social science. We must make up our minds which we want – explanation or prediction: dual purpose research is liable to fall between two stools.

So far, for the sake of moving from the simple to the complex, I have once again relied rather heavily on physical examples and have treated social sciences as in the same position as open system natural sciences. But there are some additional and more familiar factors which make prediction even more difficult in social science than in disciplines such as ecology. Popper argued that prediction of anything other than the very short-term development of societies was in principle impossible on the grounds that social change depends on (among other things) the growth of human knowledge and this in turn cannot be predicted without knowing its content now.[26] There is also the widely noted phenomenon of self-fulfilling and self-negating predictions which render the interpretation of predictive success or failure opaque. (Did the predicted outcome occur/not occur only because we made it/prevented it?) Yet this is merely a manifestation of something far more fundamental but often overlooked; namely that what happens *generally* – and not just in response to predictions – depends on what people *do*.[27] Social change does not happen to us, it is *made* by us – although not in the conditions or with the resources of our own choosing. Some of those conditions are natural ones, beyond our control, but others are the (often unintended) consequences of earlier human actions.

There is therefore (to say the least) something strange about the treatment of predictions of social change as equivalent to predictions of natural change. I don't try to predict whether I will write another page by examining my past behaviour – I decide to do it. I don't make the prediction and wait to see if it comes true; I make it come true. Similarly, the announcement of an election is a statement of intention not a prediction. This is not to say that the fact that people make their future renders prediction totally redundant in social science, although it certainly limits its scope. No society exists in which people act together in unison as a single 'subject of history'. What 'we' do, we do against, as well as with, others, though the relative importance of collective and competitive actions varies according to the type of society. The actions of individuals or institutions are not 'pre-reconciled' before they are done, but have to be made on the basis of assumptions – or if you will, 'predictions' – about what others will do.[28] Uncertainty about the future is not like uncertainty about the present: the one depends on what we do, the other concerns what actually exists. And even if a unified collective subject did exist, predictions of a sort would have to be made.

The idea that all predictions – natural or social – are essentially the same is also *dangerous* for its reifies social action, denies our powers as agents or 'historical subjects' and encourages the profoundly defeatist and reactionary belief that what is must be. The danger is especially great in approaches which 1 are preoccupied with the search for order regardless of the qualitative nature of order; 2 misleadingly treat relationships measured at a single point in time as 'regularities'; and 3 extrapolate these into the future as if they were regularity-type or instrumentalist laws of nature. Perhaps the richest source of such naïveties is textbooks on statistical methods which give examples of the search for order in relationships such as that between social class and the degree of racial prejudice, in the hope of predicting them. If we respond by complaining that 'the point (of social science) is to *change* such practices', we are likely to be told that increasing predictive ability will forewarn us so that we can make them self-negating predictions. But approaches which assume an instrumentalist, regularity theory of laws and causation fail to provide information which could be used to change such situations, i.e. concerning *mechanisms*, but merely seek order in patterns of events or 'symptoms'. By contrast realist approaches do not lead directly to prediction but seek out the generative mechanisms and conditions which produce the events we want to change. By providing information on the necessary conditions both for the existence and the activation of the mechanism, and in some cases on the way conditions mediate its effects, we increase the chances of either removing or changing the mechanism, preventing its activation or suppressing the damaging effects of its exercise.

Such knowledge may also provide, as a by-product, explanatory predictions of a very conditional kind: 'if mechanism M is present and so are conditions C_1 and C_2, event E_1 will occur, while if C_3 is present, E_2 will occur'. Often the structures and mechanisms involved will themselves undergo change, or new, unforeseen and causally-influential conditions will arise, so that the prediction turns out to be incorrect. But if it does, the underlying theory is likely to survive this 'falsification', because of the absence of a closed system which could give the 'test' some significance.

In addition a sort of 'prediction' might be made which doesn't involve specifying future events, their dates and magnitudes, but merely asserts that given the presence of certain phenomena, others must be present too, perhaps in a particular configuration: 'if x is internally related to y then x will not be present without y and vice versa'. But then this is not so much a prediction as a claim about necessity in society, about what it is possible or impossible for certain objects or structures to do. For example, a theory of political organization might relate the scope for democratic control to the scale of the institution concerned and the number of matters on which to decide. An economic theory of diminishing returns could be regarded as predictive, but only in the sense that it makes some claims about what is materially possible or impossible for production of a certain kind. They say what their objects are capable of, not what they will do under particular contingent conditions.

In other words, what can be promised in terms of the scope for prediction in social science is much less than the orthodox regularity theories claim, but the miserable failure of the latter to achieve accurate prediction attests to the unfeasibility of their programme. This is because it is based upon an inappropriate model drawn from natural science; few natural scientists study an object which is itself learning to organize nature and society in new ways, creating new possibilities and impossibilities. But in so far as what cannot be predicted can nevertheless often be controlled, its unpredictability need not be seen as a problem.[29] Moreover, and paradoxically, those social processes which have been made most regular and hence are most easily predictable (e.g. regarding the rhythm of the working day) are generally uninteresting objects of prediction. The most important social objects of prediction are generally those actions which produce significant effects (good or bad) but which cannot be socially controlled under the prevailing mode of social organization. (Included among these are, of course, many individual actions which no one would *want* to control.) So what we most want and need to predict is dependent on the kind of society, though equivalent claims might, of course, equally be made about explanation. What is less frequently recognized, however, is that the difficulty and degree of success of prediction depends on the nature of the object.

Let us consider an actual example. In the current context of the world economic recession there has been a resurgence of interest in the idea that capitalist development occurs in 'long waves' of fifty to sixty years in which upturns are marked by the emergence of clusters of growth- and employment-creating new technologies which provide the basis for the ensuing long boom.[30] The system moves towards recession as these technologies cease to add jobs and job-replacing technological change predominates. This is, of course, an extremely crude summary of just a part of the theory, but it is enough to illustrate the problems of prediction. Although not all researchers in this field agree that the long waves have actually occurred in the past, among those that do there is naturally an interest in whether they are necessary features of capitalist development such that the sequence will continue as long as capitalism continues. Inventions play an important role in this theory. As these depend on the growth of future knowledge we cannot expect to predict them: necessity may be the mother of invention but it is not a sufficient condition. Nor do inventions, once made, necessarily become products which can be produced profitably. In models of economic growth, technological change is an *embarrassment*: as it is a 'motor' of growth it can hardly be ignored, although some models do just that, yet it is virtually impossible to model predictively. Moreover, as we have discovered to our cost, it is contingent whether new technologies create more jobs than they displace. Many of the technologies which have formed the crucial clusters have been contingently related to one another and their 'take-off' has depended on many contingent social and political conditions. Consequently, any predictions worth considering are bound to involve a long string of conditions covering not only some of the circumstances in which mechanisms operate but about whether some of the mechanisms will actually be present. Although there may be so many qualifications that it does not seem worthy of the label 'prediction', it may be useful for drawing attention to what we must *make* or prevent if a certain goal is to be achieved.

In response to assumption 3 (p. 130) it can therefore be seen that the uneven success of prediction across the 'sciences' has plenty to do with the nature of their objects and little to do with their 'maturity', as the rhetoric of scientism would have it. If the scientistic view were to be taken seriously it would lead to some surprising judgements; modern geological and geophysical science would appear less mature than ancient astronomy because despite its sophisticated theory and technology it is less successful in predicting the disposition of its objects than the latter (even where it concerns things that already exist!).

These differences also show once again that knowledge can only reasonably be judged in the context of particular subject–object relationships; that is, in terms of what it is about together with its intention. Where it concerns human action, prediction is almost certain to be highly inaccurate, but in so far as it stimulates action this may be better than having no prediction. Indeed, to paraphrase Mill, a great deal of our knowledge that is insufficient for prediction may nevertheless be most valuable for guidance.[31]

Rational abstractions and 'chaotic conceptions'

Abstractions can be made in various ways, but we are now in a position to propose a distinction between 'rational' and bad abstractions or 'chaotic conceptions' as Marx called them.[32] A rational abstraction is one which isolates a significant element of the world which has some unity and autonomous force, such as a structure. A bad abstraction arbitrarily divides the indivisible and/or lumps together the unrelated and the inessential, thereby 'carving up' the object of study with little or no regard for its structure and form. Figure 9 attempts to illustrate the difference.

A fairly uncontroversial example of a bad abstraction or chaotic conception is the concept of 'services', as in 'service employment'; this covers an enormous variety of activities which neither form structures nor interact causally to any significant degree and many which lack anything significant in common. Now it will be recalled that the effect of the inclusion of an inadequate concept in a set of

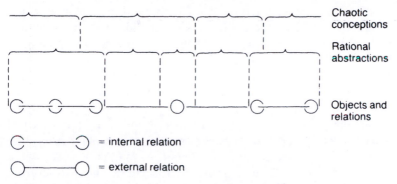

Figure 9 Rational abstractions and chaotic conceptions

beliefs depends upon how much 'explanatory weight' is put on it, or on the extent to which our actions are guided by it. There are therefore many situations both in everyday and scientific practice where such chaotic conceptions can be used unproblematically as simple categories for descriptive purposes. But a concept like 'services' creates problems as soon as anyone attributes unitary causal powers or liabilities to the objects falling in that class, so that, for example, employment in fields as diverse as catering, computer services, local government and plumbing is imagined to behave similarly.

Now I realize that the calls for 'rational abstractions', 'careful conceptualization' and the like might seem too much like trite appeals to virtue which none would refuse, let alone think worth mentioning. Yet you don't have to look far in social science to find substantial bodies of literature based on chaotic conceptions. Particularly common are searches for empirical regularities in quantitative relationships between objects which are internally heterogeneous and hence unlikely to behave consistently; for example, the relationships between 'service employment' and 'levels of economic development'. Much of this kind of work is supported by the erroneous assumption that common properties or, alternatively, distinguishing characteristics of objects will necessarily also be causally-significant properties, and more generally by the assumption that causation has something to do with regularity.[33]

Finally, abstractions, whether good or bad, can form part of the *object* of study in social science and have real effects. For example, the use of money presupposes a 'real abstraction' from the diverse characteristics of concrete types of labour and commodity.[34] Since their effects will depend on their adequacy, we can neither ignore them nor abstain from evaluating them.

From abstract to concrete: the example of marxist research

As an illustration of the way in which theoretical and empirical research are combined in the move from the abstract to the concrete, I have chosen the application of marxist theory, which has the advantage of being unusually formalized in its structuring of the abstract and concrete.[35]

Figure 10 sums up the hierarchy of types of concepts which might lie behind a conceptualization of a concrete event or conjuncture. These range from the most basic principles of historical materialism, some of which refer to transhistorical necessities (e.g. that people must be able to reproduce themselves and hence to find food and shelter as a necessary condition of being able to produce art, science, etc.), through historically specific concepts such as 'feudalism' or 'surplus value', through the 'tendencies' or mechanisms which are possessed by social phenomena (e.g. the tendency for money-capital to flow towards the most profitable types of investment), towards the more 'concrete' level at which these are experienced or 'lived'. At none of these levels – not even the most basic – is the knowledge to be taken as infallible or purely *a priori*.[36]

In moving from abstract concepts of these objects, structures and mechanisms, step by step towards the concrete, 'theoretical' claims (e.g. about the relationship between capital and surplus value) must be combined with empirically discovered knowledge of contingently-related phenomena. Thus, for example, the law of value, which concerns mechanisms which are possessed necessarily by capital by virtue of its structure (as consisting of competing and independently directed capitals, each producing for profit and being reliant on the production of surplus value, etc.), produces effects which are mediated by such things as the particular kinds of technology available, the relative power of capital and labour and state intervention. In other words, the contingently-related conditions are never inert, but are themselves the product of causal processes and have their own causal powers and liabilities. Although the coming together of two or

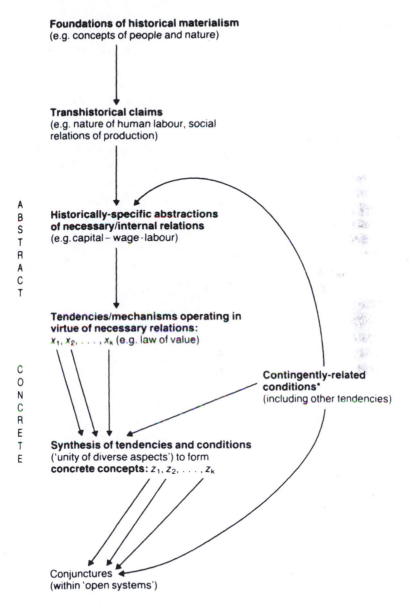

Foundations of historical materialism
(e.g. concepts of people and nature)

Transhistorical claims
(e.g. nature of human labour, social
relations of production)

A
B
S
T
R
A
C
T

**Historically-specific abstractions
of necessary/internal relations**
(e.g. capital – wage - labour)

**Tendencies/mechanisms operating in
virtue of necessary relations:**
$x_1, x_2, \ldots, x_k$ (e.g. law of value)

C
O
N
C
R
E
T
E

**Contingently-related
conditions***
(including other tendencies)

Synthesis of tendencies and conditions
('unity of diverse aspects') to form
concrete concepts: $z_1, z_2, \ldots, z_k$

Conjunctures
(within 'open systems')

* The theorization of these, and their explanation by means of abstraction,
  is often not the sole prerogative of marxism.

Figure 10   The relation of abstract and concrete

more entities may be contingent, what occurs when they are so combined happens necessarily in virtue of their natures.

Now no theory of society could be expected to know the nature and form of these contingent relations in advance, purely on the basis of theoretical claims. The move from abstract to concrete must therefore combine theoretical claims with empirical research aimed at discovering 1 which kinds of objects are present (e.g. is the economy capitalist or what?); 2 what are the contingent forms they take (e.g. is it mining capital, commercial capital, etc.?); and 3 under what conditions do they exist in this instance (e.g. political environment). Because of the need to incorporate empirical knowledge of contingencies at each stage, the move from abstract to concrete cannot be deductive, for the conclusions are not wholly derivable from or 'contained' within the meaning of the premises. For example, in order to move from transhistorical claims (e.g. 'all production is carried out under social relations') to historically specific claims ('capitalist production presupposes a propertyless class of workers'), historical information not implicit in the former has to be added.[37]

Note also that in developing concrete analyses, marxist theory, like any other social theory, has to incorporate knowledge produced outside its own range. For instance, a study of the labour process might have to draw upon knowledge from engineering. Some of these contingently-related phenomena may be theorized satisfactorily outside marxism, some may need re-theorizing, while the theorization of others may show marxist concepts and theoretical claims to be in need of revision themselves. Marxist theory would certainly seem to have a broader scope than other social theories and although there might be possible senses in which it could be said to be 'totalizing', it would be absurd to suppose that it is complete or self-contained such that its application never required it to incorporate knowledge from outside. Marxists are unlikely to challenge the technical knowledge of an engineer, although they might have different interpretations of the social context of technology. Conversely, non-marxists may accept some of the most basic claims of historical materialism or about some limited aspects of more concrete statements, though their 'penumbra of meaning' will vary according to other elements of their discourses.

Finally, it should be noted that this movement from abstract to concrete is less in evidence in the interpretation of meaning.

Although it is common for certain key concepts to be selected out – often with little concern for the violence done by such an abstraction – we do not interpret the meaning of actions or discourse by moving from abstract to concrete in the manner suggested above. Rather our understanding follows hermeneutic circles or spirals, relating parts to wholes, and elements to what precedes them and what is expected to follow them. Nevertheless, to the extent that social relations and practices are concept-dependent – as are all those mentioned in the above example – the movement from abstract to concrete must be combined with interpretive understanding. Awkward though this may sound, to some extent social scientists do it intuitively. As before, the point of the above reconstructions or formalizations is not so much to provide recipes for research as to assist in the process of making these reasoning processes more transparent and self-conscious.

The theoretical and the empirical revisited

Having introduced these realist ideas, it is now possible to make our hitherto very broad view of theory more precise and specify its relation to empirical research. In the sense defended in Chapter 2, theories are examined sets of concepts which are used in making empirical observations and identifying objects no less than in explaining them. Now the identification or definition of an object will usually refer to significant causal powers or liabilities that it possesses (e.g. 'labour-power' itself, 'child-minder', 'invalid'). We can now add that in addition to conceptualizing phenomena, *theories make their strongest claims at the abstract level about necessary or internal relations, and about causal powers, or in other words, about necessity in the world. Where relations between things are contingent, their form must always be an empirical question, that is one which must be answered by observing actual cases.* While theories supply ways of conceptualizing the objects, they are obliged to remain agnostic about relations which are contingent. So, for example, physical theory makes a strong claim about copper's power to conduct electricity, but does not commit itself on whether any particular piece of copper will ever be in a position to do so. And similarly with social theory: given that capital cannot exist as such without wage-labour, theoretical claims may be made about this relation. If General Motors could function in its present form with serf-labour, the theory really would be in trouble, but it quite properly does not commit itself on the contingent matter of whether that labour is American, British or Turkish.

If we made a mistake in an *empirical* claim about a contingent matter, such as the number of workers in General Motors, it would be unlikely to warrant a challenge to basic theory. We quite rationally place considerable weight upon theoretical claims and we are obliged to take their refutation seriously. Conversely, we neither place much confidence in claims about contingent matters nor worry much if they are refuted. As will be shown later, failure to heed this distinction generates unreasonable expectations about the nature and implications of tests in social science.

Note that to say that we cannot reasonably make strong *theoretical claims* about contingent relations, that is about relationships which are neither necessary nor impossible, is not to put the phenomena involved in those relationships beyond the reach of theory.[38] The relation between the offices of insurance companies and public parks in my home town is contingent. No strong theoretical claims could sensibly anticipate their coexistence, for the simple reason that each could well exist without the other. But this does not put insurance companies and parks beyond the scope of separate applications of theory; theories of financial capital or of public goods might well be deployed in their explanation and their description is not theory-neutral. In some cases, the same theory may have some applicability to both of the contingently-related objects, though it still could not be expected to make strong claims about their co-existence. Again we find that there is no justification for a simple opposition or dualism of theory and empirics, for although they have certain contrasting aspects they also presuppose one another.

So far we have stressed one side of this interdependence – the way in which empirical studies are theoretically-informed. But empirical research can also be theoretically-inform*ative*; though guided by existing theory it can yield new theoretical claims and concepts. Thus research on the economies of the Eastern Bloc has enabled the identification of certain necessary properties of complex, comprehensively planned economies which tend to cause poor co-ordination and continual shortages.[39] These were partly anticipated by critics of socialist organization who hypothesized what self-interested economic actors would do in such a context (e.g. in the absence of competition, unemployment, bankruptcy or accountability to customers); some were discovered first by the actors themselves through their own practice, and some were discovered later by academic empirical study. The existence of these different (interacting) routes to the development of new theories is quite typical in social science.

The relationship of theory and empirics is generally closer in social science than in natural science. Where structures are highly context-independent, as they tend to be in natural systems, then once their properties have been understood their theories should not need continual revision, as they are applied to different cases. Where structures are undergoing transformation, at different speeds in different places, as is common in societies, concrete and abstract research need to be in far closer dialogue than is ever necessary in their natural science equivalents of pure and applied research. An engineer isn't likely to find the laws of physics changing in her attempts to apply them and she therefore doesn't need to be a theoretical physicist. But a student of society is quite likely to be faced with change in social structures themselves and is obliged to do some theorizing about their changing nature and powers. Thus the nature and powers of the 'service class' have changed and vary over space, as have those of institutions such as building societies, the welfare state, large companies, youth, and so on. Unlike atoms, such objects have histories and geographies, and these not only provide a setting or back-cloth but can make a difference to the social structures themselves. The results of studies of all but the more durable social structures are therefore likely to be theoretically-informed and informative *narratives* rather than formal analyses of apparently timeless mechanisms. The former may be unpalatable to those wedded to a conception of science derived from closed system natural sciences, but they reflect the fact that social systems are not only open but embody learning processes which produce continual innovation and qualitative change.[40]

As a final point in this 'normative explication' of the terms 'theoretical', 'empirical', 'abstract' and 'concrete', I want to free them from their common association with notions of *familiarity*, in which it is assumed that theoretical matters and abstractions are unfamiliar, abstruse and esoteric while empirical matters are the opposite. In fact, everyday knowledge includes concepts which are abstract in the strict sense and many commonplaces embody what we have defined as theoretical claims (e.g. 'we are all mortal'). Similarly 'concreteness' as I have defined it certainly cannot be exclusively associated with familiar, lay knowledge; if anything the contrary applies because in everyday situations we often only need to understand objects superficially and partially rather than as 'unities of diverse determinations'.

The association of the theoretical with the unfamiliar only serves to obscure more important philosophical distinctions and to exaggerate and mis-specify the differences between lay and scientific knowledge. It should not really seem surprising, but 'familiarity' is not a philosophically significant variable. It also helps to appreciate the possibility of relating theory to empirical research if we suspend this association of theory with the difficult and unfamiliar and if we remember that concepts do not have to be given their technical names to be used. Often those who complain about the integration of theory and empirical research can only recognize theory when it is separated out and the names of its concepts paraded up and down the page.

Spatial form and abstract and concrete research[41]

While it is common to argue that social phenomena are historically-specific and that method should take account of this, little interest has been shown outside geography in their geographically variable character; indeed most social scientists ignore space. Yet space would seem to make a difference to what happens in the world. The spatial relationship between job vacancies and job seekers makes a difference to the operation of the job market; a vacancy is of no use to the unemployed if its location is inaccessible.

Imagine social processes represented as tracing out paths in space–time. What happens to objects, whether people or things, depends on contacts and connections made within space–time; where are we in relation to others? Whom are we likely to come into contact with? What happens depends on the content and form of the social and physical environment constituting space–time. Virtually everything we do in the course of our lives depends on being in the right places at the right times. Normally we abstract objects out from this concrete setting without a second thought and come up with categories of roles, institutions, occupations, etc., which are treated as independent of space and time.[42] First we tear things out of their context, then forget that context and treat the objects as spaceless, timeless data, and then proceed to wonder how we might explain them, which involves trying to reconstruct some kind of appropriate causal context in the absence of information on their spatio-temporal form. Though not entirely unreasonable it is worth reflecting on the extraordinary nature of this way of explaining social life. Are social scientists therefore wrong to ignore space? The answer depends upon whether they are concerned with developing abstract social theory or explanations of particular concrete objects. To demonstrate this I will have to make a brief digression on the nature of space.

Like many metaphysical concepts, 'space' is both mysterious and thoroughly familiar. The common-sense view is that space exists independently of objects and can therefore be empty and that objects are located within it. This involves an absolute concept of space. It is incoherent because 'what is empty is nothing and what is nothing cannot be'.[43] On such a concept, space as nothingness can hardly be said to have an effect, as might be inferred when we speak of the 'friction of distance' or the 'effect of space'. By contrast, on a relative concept of space, space is constituted by matter, by objects having spatial extension. Terms like 'friction of distance' should really be interpreted as a shorthand for frictions between particular substances which constitute space, and, as we know from natural science, the coefficient of friction varies from substance to substance.[44]

However, the important but difficult point about space is that while it is constituted by objects it is not reducible to them. Following Harré,[45] the subtleties of the relative concept of space can be explained by considering the spatial relations between the following sets of letters:

ABC

PQR

The spatial relations of B to A and C, and Q to P and R are exactly equivalent: swapping B with Q would not change this spatial relation of 'between-ness', though depending on what kind of things A, B, C, P, Q and R are, it might activate or de-activate certain causal powers. In other words, although space can only exist in and through objects, it is independent of the particular *types* of object present. What kind of things the letters stand for makes no difference to the spatial relations, though it certainly does to the activation and effects of causal processes. It is this independence of spatial relations from the type of objects composing them that gives the absolute concept of space a certain plausibility. But given that 'space *as such*' is literally a contentless abstraction there can be no 'science of space' as some geographers used to believe. The 'fetishization of space' consists in attributing to 'pure space' what is due to the causal powers of the particular objects constituting it. In reaction to this, some proponents of the relative concept of space have made the converse mistake of supposing that space is wholly reducible to the constituent objects, whereupon it becomes impossible to see how space makes a difference, in any sense.[46] Whether an object's causal mechanisms are activated and with what effect depends on the presence of certain contingently-related conditions; this in turn depends on the spatial form. For example, when we speak of being *surrounded* by things we are talking about a spatial relation, but 'being surrounded by' has no material implications unless the objects concerned are such that their contact will activate causal mechanisms, as would happen if we were surrounded by poisonous gas! While the abstraction of space from substance may seem harmless enough, and indeed is built into the structure of western languages, it is full of traps for the unwary, as the recent history of geography has shown. The most common case arises when theorists who are anxious to correct false impressions produced by aspatial analyses find themselves attributing powers to space itself, in abstraction from the particular objects constituting it. Even those who advocate a relative concept of space in philosophical discussions sometimes fall into this trap in concrete research.[47]

But if we cannot abstract form from content and hope to say anything about the world, can we abstract content from form and hence have an aspatial science? By and large, as Saunders points out, major social theorists such as Durkheim, Marx and Weber abstracted from space.[48] We shall argue that where the development of abstract theory is concerned, this has *some* justification.

Social processes do not take place on the head of a pin. All material social objects necessarily have spatial extension, sometimes a particular spatial configuration of their elements, and particular powers of movement. In so far as these are necessary properties, theory should take account of this or at least avoid negating them for they make a difference to what happens.[49] Moreover, social science deals with systems whose spatial form can be deliberately arranged so as to manipulate and take advantage of the constituent causal mechanisms, be they those of new towns or communication systems. As with any manipulation of nature this involves exploiting contingency so that certain effects are realized. Abstract social science cannot ignore the fact that the possibilities and problems of reproducing social forms depends on the integration of their elements in space–time and several theorists have drawn attention to this in their abstract work.

Thus the operation of property capital necessarily involves access to and monopoly over the use of space, the hyper-mobility of images and of money capital relative to people is an important characteristic of modernity, and so on. Some of these spatial characteristics may be of great social significance, but what we can say about them in advance, at the level of theoretical claims is inevitably vague at best. This is because while no material processes are aspatial, most social processes have a significant degree of 'spatial flexibility' which, within limits, enables the same or very similar social structures to be reproduced in a variety of different configurations. For example, for capital accumulation to occur, capital needs to be accessible to a labour force, and labour markets have spatial constraints created by the time and expense of linking up dispersed workers and jobs. Nevertheless, this doesn't say much about space, nor could it be expected to say much more, for the variety of spatial configurations which meet this constraint is considerable. Which spatial forms do eventuate will depend on a host of contingently-related processes. Similarly, capital's ceaseless pursuit of economies also leads to 'time–space compression', as the costs of overcoming distance are lowered, the division of labour extends and the world 'shrinks'. Again while this is of considerable social importance the claim is necessarily vague because the actual configurations compatible with such a tendency are enormously varied and depend again on contingent relations to other processes and circumstances.[50] So abstract theory ought to have some spatial content, in order to register the necessary spatial properties of social structures. But within limits there is usually a considerable variety of possible forms which they can take and an even greater variety of spatial forms of the contexts in which they can be situated. Given these innumerable contingencies, the spatial content of social theory is inevitably restricted.

Where social theories go beyond the analysis of structures and mechanisms to the postulation of their possible effects (perhaps by assuming a hypothetical closed system), the abstraction from space may produce serious errors. Perhaps the most famous example of the difference that space makes is the case of the (aspatial) perfect competition model which becomes a model of spatial monopolies as soon as the abstraction from space is dropped.[51]

In empirical research on concrete objects and processes, the situation regarding space is different. Since it involves investigating the actual workings and effects of mechanisms in contingent circumstances, then it will generally be necessary to take account of their spatial form since it makes a difference.

In closed system natural science the contingencies of spatial form are either rendered constant or are a matter of indifference where they concern spatial relations between objects which do not causally interact. For example, in an experiment on the mechanics of levers or the periodicity of a pendulum we must take careful note of the spatial extension of the relevant objects, but it makes no difference whether it is conducted in London or Tokyo.[52]

In social systems we have both a greater degree of context-dependence and a continually changing jumble of spatial relations, not all of them involving objects which are causally indifferent to one another. Not surprisingly, regularities are at best transient and spatially limited. *Even though concrete studies may not be interested in spatial form per se, it must be taken into account if the contingencies of the concrete and the differences they make to outcomes are to be understood.* However, given the complexity and openness of social systems, it is seldom practically possible to do more than approach this goal without starting a reductionist regress. For instance, in our labour market example, it would not be feasible to take into account spatial form as it relates to each pair of vacancies and job-seekers, although it would be possible at least to break the national data down into fairly discrete labour market areas. Nevertheless this would still only approximate the effect of the spatial form of the market for it would 'scramble' the concrete form of relations within each area. A considerable amount of social research is weakened by this largely unnoticed scrambling of causal form; at worst the degree of abstraction from the actual forms in which objects relate is such that the process by which mechanisms produce their effects is simply obscured – they become lost in an aggregate, 'de-spatialized, statistical soup'. Hence it is no surprise that in social science the parameters of a model fitted to one set of data rarely apply to another. In some cases, the effects of this scrambling may be mitigated by the spatial flexibility or robustness of many processes which enables them to operate in similar fashions despite differences of context. But the less explanations of actual events take account of the contingencies of spatial form, the less concrete they can claim to be.[53]

Conclusion

In these last two chapters I have deliberately alternated between discussions of the nature of objects of study (types of relations, structures, causal powers, closed and open systems, spatial form, etc.), methods (abstraction, structural analysis, generalization, causal analysis, etc.), objectives (explanation, calculation, prediction, understanding) and types of propositional knowledge (concerning laws, theoretical claims, empirical questions). I hope to have shown that there are interdependencies, in the form of compatibilities and incompatibilities, in the relations between these spheres such that not just any type of knowledge or statement can be successful regardless of context. For example, the possibility and practical adequacy of calculating or predicting the dimensions of a system depend upon whether it is open or closed. In arguing for such forms of interdependence I have also tried to indicate how certain widely circulated conceptions of science which differ from that set out above can draw a degree of credibility and indeed feasibility when applied to restricted objectives and types of object (e.g. prediction and closed systems). Nevertheless, they trade upon implicit assumptions that these restricted conditions are in fact universal. Likewise it is important not only to criticize common-sense conceptions (e.g. of absolute space) but to comprehend them by seeing if there are any aspects of their objects, objectives and methods in which they have some practical adequacy. Examined knowledge, be it 'science' or humanities, is not content with partial practical adequacy, with 'making do', but seeks to maximize its adequacy in all spheres. To achieve this and to understand the differentiated character of the relation between subject and object we must therefore abandon the usual methodologists' quest for the holy grail of a single model for all purposes – which is not, of course, to encourage people to use any old methods for any purpose or to lapse into a permissive eclecticism.

The methods introduced in this chapter have been primarily qualitative. I shall examine quantitative methods more closely in Chapter 6, although those who require further discussion of contentious philosophical issues may want first to consult Chapter 5.

5 Some influential misadventures in the philosophy of science

As I warned at the beginning of Chapter 3, realist interpretations of knowledge and science diverge significantly from orthodox philosophies of science. The latter have had a far-reaching influence upon the practice of social science, and one which in general I believe to have been damaging. It is only for this reason that I now want to pause in the elaboration of a realist approach to social science in order to devote some attention to key elements of the orthodoxies. In so doing I hope to answer some of the probable objections to the foregoing arguments by undermining the philosophical position from which the critics might draw support. This will also help to add substance to the criticisms of the unsatisfactory nature of generalization and of some other approaches and methods to be discussed in subsequent chapters.

As I pointed out in the Introduction, this chapter is primarily intended for those who have already encountered some of the main debates in the philosophy of social science and who therefore might raise such objections. If they so wish, other readers may proceed directly to Chapter 6.

Atomism and the problems of induction and causation

The *problem of induction* is probably the favourite puzzle of philosophers of science. It concerns the fact that we are not logically entitled to assume that because a particular sequence of events has always been observed to occur in the past it will do so in all cases. From our knowledge that the sun has always risen in the morning it does not follow logically that it will continue to do so. Valid inferences about infinite sets of events cannot be made on the basis of finite sets of observed events. This problem has been dubbed 'the scandal of philosophy' because of its seemingly outrageous implications. If true, we lack any firm grounds for trusting past experience in our actions. Mechanisms may cease to exist or operate in the future and there is no necessity about their ways of acting. We can't learn from experience – not even from our mistakes, for what has been mistaken in the past need not be mistaken in the future.[1]

Closely related is the *problem of causation* in which causation is conceptualized as a regular sequence or constant conjunction of events which has been observed to occur. The problem consists in that given such a sequence, in which C is followed by E, we are not justified in saying that C and E are causally connected. All that we can observe and hence all that can be known about the situation is that event E followed event C. Even if it were established that some constant conjunctions were indeed universal, the relation of C and E would still be contingent. On this account any notions of 'cause' or 'forcing' or 'production' are purely 'psychological' in origin. Some versions exclude the concept from science altogether. If true, it implies that there is no real difference between an allegedly causal process (such as the workings of a clock) and an accidental sequence or association, for on this view causation is nothing more than regular succession.

The premises of these problems, especially the latter's description of causation, will appear strange in the light of the expositions of the previous chapter and their conclusions difficult to reconcile with our experience. Yet their logic is impregnable. In response, many are tempted to appeal to the success of induction in science and practical life, yet as philosophers delight in pointing out, such an argument is circular because it tries to justify induction by induction. But there are other responses. I shall attempt to show that although the arguments of the problems of induction and causation are valid, their conclusions need not be accepted, because they follow from unreasonable, indeed absurd, premises. It will also be shown that many discussions of the problem of induction have in fact confused two separate problems, and that in so far as induction is used in science, which isn't much, its description must be modified.

From the way the problem of induction is set up we have a picture of observers trying to make inferences about as yet unobserved events from those that they have observed. There is no mention of the fact that observation is conceptually mediated, that the objects can only be known under a particular description, or of the fallibility of those observations that have already been made.[2] Moreover, the problem as usually defined presupposes the highly implausible doctrine of atomism. Like any metaphysical[3] belief, atomism cannot conclusively be shown to be true or false – only more or less plausible in the light of its compatibility or incompatibility with our most reliable knowledge. Atomism has two branches. The ontological branch – concerning the theory of what exists – holds that the world consists of discrete, distinct atomistic elements existing at discrete, distinct points in time or space. Being atomistic these basic elements have no internal structure or differentiation and no causal powers. The various objects that we know are nothing but different combinations of these atoms. All relations between objects are external and contingent, so that all sequences are accidental. These assumptions are matched by the epistemological branch – concerning the theory of knowledge – which depicts observation as fragmented into simple, unproblematic, indivisible 'readings'. The two branches are mutually reinforcing: if objects or events are 'punctiform' their observation as such is also more plausible, and vice versa.[4]

Now although the concept of theory-neutral observation is hardly ever supported today, the unacknowledged retention of atomism makes it difficult to appreciate fully the sense in which observation is theory-laden. For if objects and events are atomistic rather than complexly differentiated and structured it is not clear why so much intellectual labour needs to be expended in developing concepts or schemata by means of which they can be observed. Attention is instead shifted to the activity of creating ordering frameworks.

Often this reductionist view of observation and its objects is 'secreted' by the fetish for representing ideas by symbols. Once the whole discussion is framed in terms of the status of the knowledge we derive from observations $o_1, o_2, \ldots o_k$ about events $e_1, e_2, \ldots, e_k$ it is easy to forget that much of our work as scientists (or 'intellectuals') is involved in finding concepts which enable us to grasp the often complex and subtle differentiations both between *and within* the changes or objects which we reductively call 'events'. (Philosophers are not immune to the prejudice that replacing an idea of a symbol is enough in itself to increase the rigour of an analysis: 'mental hygiene' has its penalties.)

Not the least absurd aspect of the epistemological branch of atomism and one which has generally not been ditched along with theory-neutrality is the assumption that observation is 'punctiform' rather than continuous.[5] As we shall see shortly, this generates ridiculous implications as regards our perception of change. How philosophers ever came to persuade themselves of such an extraordinary notion is perhaps a little easier to understand in the context of the now largely abandoned quest for an absolute foundation for knowledge. One of the forms this took was an attempt to ground knowledge in certain incorrigible observation statements; the search naturally gravitated towards the simplest, most primitive observations which, it was hoped, would not be contestable. Punctiform observations fitted the bill better than messy, continuously variable ones. Likewise, simple objects of observation appeared to be more suitable 'anchor-points' than internally differentiated, multi-faceted objects. However, this particular quest for certainty seriously backfired in the shape of the problem of induction itself, for the assumption of atomism entailed the assumption that all relations were external and contingent and this in turn meant that there could be no certainty or even confidence about sequences and patterns even if there could be certainty about their constituent atoms.

Atomism generates further problems for understanding change. One of Zeno's famous paradoxes showed that on an atomistic conception of time as consisting of discretely distinct points movement is unintelligible. If an arrow can only be at a single distinct point in space and no other at each discrete point in time, then it cannot move. As Georgescu-Roegen argues: 'That which is in a point cannot be in motion or evolve; what moves and evolves cannot be in any point.'[6] The notion of an 'instant' of time is nonsensical; both motion and rest must occupy time *as duration* to be discernible. So, if we submit to the habit of splitting up the description of, say, the growth of a plant into distinct stages occurring at discretely distinct times we can hardly expect to learn *how* it happens.

If the assumption of non-continuous time is dropped, the remaining assumption of atomistic objects still presents problems for understanding change. The only intelligible types of change are then locomotion and change by replacement, a typical model of change (and hence causation) being that of one billiard ball striking and moving another. This may indeed occur when rigid objects collide, but the possibility of change occurring through qualitative transformations internal to objects is dogmatically excluded since all objects are taken to be reducible to structureless and powerless or causally inert atoms which cannot change.

If the assumptions of atomism are dropped it becomes possible to see that some changes are changes *in* rather than between things, and hence can occur necessarily, by virtue of the nature of those things. Only with an ontology which admits both external and internal relations, internally structured and differentiated objects having causal powers and liabilities is it possible to distinguish between qualitative change and mere successions of events and hence between necessary or causal changes and relationships and accidental ones.[7] The basic flaw of the problem of causation is simple: if we have arbitrarily ruled out, at the start, the possibility of real connections between and within things by assuming atomism, it is no surprise to find that we cannot recover causal connections by an argument starting from those premises. On the realist account, external, contingent relations are admitted but not universalized; there are also internal, necessary relations, such as those between objects and their causal powers.

In order to reply to the problem of induction it is also necessary to eliminate a common confusion that has arisen through the conflation of two separate problems, one ontological, concerning what might exist, the other epistemological, concerning the status of our knowledge. The first, called by Harré and Madden the 'big problem of induction',[8] concerns the idea that it is logically possible that the world itself may change so that past arrangements no longer hold – water is no longer water, earth no longer earth as we know it, etc. Now it is essential to realize that this does not, as many have thought, entail that everything in our present world is only contingently related, including even the relation between objects and their properties. Unless we fall for this common non-sequitur, with its implication that we have no grounds for relying on present knowledge, there is no need to lose sleep over the big problem. Should the terrible day come when the world suddenly changed fundamentally (rather than merely being perceptibly transformed gradually) and should we ever survive it, we would presumably notice it and start to rebuild our knowledge again – crucially by trying to discover new natural necessities. Until that day we have no need to abandon our knowledge of natural necessity in the present world. Making inferences about infinite sets of events on the basis of finite sets of observed events is certainly risky and logically unjustified where the 'events' are, indeed, contingently related, but it is not where they are necessarily related.

On the realist view, nature's uniformity – to which many scientists have appealed – derives not from the 'accidental' regularities of sequences of contingently related things but from the internal relations, structures and ways-of-acting of things themselves.[9] Moreover, it is only on such a view that the concept of 'physical impossibility' is intelligible. In the atomistic framework in which the 'big problem of induction' presents itself at every moment, not just as a threat but as an actuality, there is nothing to stop the proverbial camel passing through the eye of a needle. If objects lack structure and causal powers and liabilities and are always unconnected to one another, then anything can happen and the structure of knowledge is built on sand.

The second or 'little problem of induction'[10] with which this is widely confused is that all our knowledge is, in principle, fallible. As such, it is not really a specific problem of induction at all but a general one, bearing as much upon those observations we have made as upon those we have yet to make. But this possibility of our being mistaken – which stems from the nature of the relationship between our knowledge and the world – does not entail that all relations in the real world itself are external.

Having dealt with the *problems* of induction I now want to discuss briefly the circumstances in which inductive inference is used. Induction is not the only mode of inference and discovering and predicting regular sequences of events is not our only interest. Scientists and laypersons are also and perhaps more often concerned with what kinds of thing exist, what their make-up, powers and liabilities are and hence with explaining what happens rather than predicting what will happen. The postulation of causal powers involves not induction but retroduction. If subsequent investigation of the nature and constitution of objects shows the retroduction to be successful, so that we can claim to know the causes of some process,[11] then we don't need to rely on inducing from past sequences.[12] And as already noted, in the case of spurious relationships, such as the strong correlation between the incidence of Scottish dysentery and the rate of inflation, we would not risk inductively inferring that the association will continue – not because such an inference would fall foul of the *logical* (big) problem of induction but because we feel confident from our knowledge of the objects concerned that they are not causally related.

In other cases where a causal relation is suspected but not confirmed, we may choose to heed inductive inferences if possible outcomes are sufficiently important to us. If people who work with a certain chemical have been found to contract a disease, we will probably make the inductive inference that in future people who work with it may contract it too. Even though we may not yet have successfully retroduced and identified a mechanism which could produce the disease, we may decide that by virtue of the kinds of things chemicals and people are, it is quite likely that the causal mechanism responsible for the disease has something to do with such conditions. Such inferences carry no warrant derived from *logic*: there are no logically valid reasons for refusing to work with the chemical. But then they are not simple inferences that a regularity observed for a finite sequence of instances will be universal. Rather our reasons depend on judgements of possible causal powers and possible consequences of either heeding or ignoring them. In this example, there are four possibilities to evaluate:

1 The chemical is hazardous and we continue use;
2 The chemical is not hazardous and we continue use;
3 The chemical is hazardous and we discontinue use;
4 The chemical is not hazardous and we discontinue use.

To summarize then, where we have good knowledge that events are causally connected, we don't *need* induction; where, on the basis of such knowledge we know that the events in question actually are only contingently related (the Scottish dysentery–inflation case) we don't *use* induction; and where we are uncertain about whether the events are necessarily or contingently related (the work–hazards case) we decide what to assume or do, not by referring to arguments about the logical problem of induction, but by making practical judgements about the possible consequences for action of alternative hypotheses being correct. The conventional account of induction and causation empties our knowledge of all content save that contained in simple punctiform 'observations' of apparently simple and punctiform 'events': the uncertainty about relations *between* objects is the complement of a naïve atomistic conception of our knowledge of objects themselves.

Necessity

These orthodox accounts of induction and causation and their attendant problems either make no reference to necessity in nature or explicitly exclude it. I now want to clear up some common confusions about necessity on which this exclusion is based and also to counter charges that there is something tautological about explanations which refer to necessity.

The main problem is a confusion between logical necessity or possibility, which concern relations between statements, and natural or material necessity or possibility which concern relations between things. Now it was noted earlier that conceptual changes are generally introduced in order to try to improve the practical adequacy of our knowledge, or to improve the ability of our concepts to 'map' the structure of the world.[13] When we feel confident that we have discovered a necessary or internal relation in the world we may sometimes reflect it in our discourse in the form of a 'conceptual necessity', by making the reference to the relation part of the definition of the objects involved. For example, it is true by definition that a father (in the biological sense) is a man who has or has had a child.[14] But this is not *just* a tautology or an arbitrary definition, for the conceptual necessity is used to denote an empirically discovered natural necessity in the relationship between males and procreation. It is not merely due to the quirks of our definitions that a child cannot come into the world without having had a biological father and mother. Apparently, certain aborigine peoples are not aware that the male has any role in procreation and so do not have any equivalent in their language for the word 'father'. Following discoveries of such natural necessity, what were previously understood as contingently related elements are sometimes made part of the definition of objects. Definitions are not just invented arbitrarily: where they are intended to refer to real objects, they can be made to 'map' or 'take up' natural necessities into the language in the form of conceptual necessities.[15]

However, not all necessities that are discovered are 'taken up' into the language in the form of conceptual or logical necessities, for some can be described by contingently related statements.[16] The material relationship between human survival and eating is recognized as necessary but this has not been 'taken up' into the definition of human beings so that it appears as merely a logical truth, true only by definition, probably for the good reason that it would not differentiate us from other animals. So when we encounter statements such as 'a capitalist who ceases to accumulate capital ceases to be one', which appear at first sight to be merely matters of definition, it needs to be asked whether any real object or structure is like such a definition, e.g. could this object retain characteristics a, b and c if d were lost. So long as a, b, c and d can be identified independently (which need not imply that they can exist independently), it is possible to determine whether the claim is true *only* by definition or whether it is 'true' of the real world.

An infinite number of definitions and other logically necessary statements could be dreamed up about the world, most of them absurd, but only a few would successfully identify necessity in the world. I could claim that a capitalist cannot cease to read the *Financial Times* and still remain one, but provided other allegedly necessary characteristics of being a capitalist (e.g. advancing money for the production of goods for sale at a profit) were independently identifiable we could easily check whether the claim was 'true' of the world or practically adequate – that is, whether its logical structure successfully 'mapped' the structure of the real world.

Now many philosophers have attached considerable significance to the distinction between analytic statements, which are true or false by definition, by virtue of the meanings of the words they contain, and synthetic statements which are 'true' or 'false' by virtue of the way the world is (or is believed to be). The previous argument showed that this distinction is unsound because at least some definitions are based on empirical knowledge of the way the world is.[17] Logical necessity and natural or material necessity are distinct and the latter can be represented in our discourse by different logical forms – definitions, conceptually necessary or conceptually contingent statements. We try to find material necessity by seeking out *material* connections which constitute certain properties of the objects so related, not by seeing what statements logically entail what other statements: logical form matters a good deal less than is generally thought in orthodox philosophy of science.[18]

The empirical (*a posteriori*) origin of our claims about necessity in the world can be seen more clearly by considering the process of scientific change. This often follows the realization that relationships formerly believed to be contingent are in fact necessary. For some cases the reverse may occur, usually through the discovery of a formerly hidden 'third variable' which is responsible for the effect which used to be attributed to the first or second variable. Consider again the example of the relation between males and reproduction. Even when discovered as necessary, our knowledge of it is not beyond revision. As soon as it is asked by virtue of what property are males necessary for reproduction, it becomes clear that modifications of the original claim are needed because of the possibility of artificial insemination, though it would seem exaggerated and unreasonable in this case simply to say that the initial claim was utterly false. We can summarize these arguments as follows:

Domain of thought objects	– includes both logical necessity and contingency; statements of *either* form can be used for referring to natural necessity, but always under some particular description (within some conceptual system) which is, in principle, fallible and hence revisable
Domain of real objects	– includes both necessary and external relations, and both causal and accidental relations.

Recalling the common confusion of the two problems of induction, we might also add that the fact that the relationship *between* the domain of thought objects or discourse and the domain of real objects is contingent has got nothing to do with whether relations within the latter are contingent or necessary.

The accusation of 'essentialism'

From the point of view of orthodox philosophy of science (e.g. Popper), realist concepts such as natural necessity, mechanisms, and powers are guilty of (among other things!) 'essentialism'. I shall counter the implied objection by examining and criticizing the doctrines of essentialism and by showing that they are not those of realism. According to Popper, essentialism is:

1   The doctrine that it is the aim of science to discover the true nature or essence of things and to describe them by means of definitions.
2   The belief that knowledge or science starts with observations of individual events and then proceeds by simple inductive enumeration until their universal 'essential' properties are grasped by intuition. These are then made part of the definition of the phenomenon in question.[19]

Other doctrines often described as essentialist are:

3   That the essences so discovered are unchanging.
4   That every object has some ultimate, single essence.
5   That we can attain absolute, incorrigible knowledge of the essence of an object.

The 'sin' of essentialism lies in the arbitrary nature of these doctrines, particularly 3, 4 and 5, in the implication of 2 (and 5) that observation is theory-neutral, but above all, in the dangerously dogmatic character of 5. If this is what essentialism is, it is certainly wrong, but equally certainly it is not what realism is, at least in its modern versions.

Against 1 and 5 we have argued that such simple notions of truth are suspect and that we could never know if we had attained 'absolute' truth. Also against 1, I have just shown that we can express our (fallible) knowledge of necessity in the world in terms of *either* definitions or logically contingent statements and that which we choose is of little importance. 2 has been emphatically rejected in Chapters 2 and 3 and in our discussion of the problem of induction. I have insisted on neither 3 nor 4; there would seem no reason for restricting the properties of objects in this way. Some may indeed be changeable without affecting the others (in which case we may wish to describe them as less essential) but others may be interdependent, so that changing one changes the others and hence (if you like) the 'essential' nature of the object. Even if such properties are finite in number, we have no grounds for assuming that we shall ever know them all, and indeed the history of chemistry, for example, shows that a succession of properties of the elements has been discovered (e.g. colour, weight, melting point, malleability, valency, specific gravity, atomic weight) with little prospect either of any end to the series or of the properties all reducing to a single fundamental 'essence'.

Those who believe realism to be guilty of essentialism might clutch at the remaining straw of the concept of 'natural necessity' as incriminating evidence. Even if they appreciate (as many critics fail to do) that the concept of natural necessity is different from that of logical necessity, and that the contingent status of our knowledge doesn't entail that all events or objects are contingently related, they might still argue that there are no *positive* reasons for believing that some relations are necessary. Stated baldly, in isolation, the assumption of natural necessity seems just that – mere assumption. But so too does the assumption of universal contingency, or atomism. Like any metaphysical belief, as already noted, either assumption can only be evaluated in the light of its compatibility with knowledge which advocates of either position both agree is reliable. Shortly, we will present the strongest defence of natural necessity, by arguing that the case for the prosecution itself presupposes it.

To newcomers to philosophy, I may seem to be attacking rather academic targets, having no obvious practical significance for science or everyday knowledge, but in fact the argument has wider implications in that it serves as a warning against the often misleading structure of discourse.

Where a theory contains many conceptual necessities it can appear to be what Marx called an '*a priori* construction',[20] or set of purely analytic truths. Whether this matters depends on whether the *a priori* elements are grounded in real necessary connections. If what are actually contingently related are made into matters of definition (e.g. the relation between consumer preferences and consumer demand in the concept of revealed preference[21]) then there are grounds for complaint. If, on the other hand, the everyday definitions of two or more objects are independent of one another, it does not always follow that their objects are. Such definitions often refer only to characteristics which can be used for identifying objects as distinct from others and omit those which connect them. 'Production' and 'distribution', as economic categories, are usually defined independently of one another so that logically one does not entail the other by virtue of its meaning. But if we 'unpack' their concepts and examine their objects in their material contexts, it becomes clear that their objects are internally related: for production to take place there must already be a distribution of the means of production,[22] and distribution is materially dependent on the production of things which can be distributed.

The limits of logic

The above arguments could be taken to suggest a more general one concerning the limitations of *logic* in reconstructing and constructing knowledge. Logic concerns the principles of sound reasoning, according to which conclusions follow necessarily from premises.[23] As such, it not surprisingly occupies a special place in most accounts of science. It is important to appreciate that its subject matter is the formal relation between statements or terms in an argument and not the referents of those terms; it does not concern the relation between statements and the real world, or the relations between material objects themselves. Like algebra, logical systems are purely formal, neutral, timeless and contentless; the terms in the logical relations can refer to anything or nothing. A *valid* argument is one for which it is contradictory to accept the premises but reject the conclusion. Whether an argument is valid or not is a separate question from that of its truth or falsity (or practical adequacy) as regards its relation to the real world.

In his interesting book *Logic and Society*, Elster suggests that logical models carry abstraction to its ultimate limit in only recognizing the three degrees – none, some or all, or impossibility, possibility or necessity.[24] They eschew the use of real numbers in quantifying objects and qualitative and spatio-temporal descriptions such as hot, cold, comic, serious, now, here, there, etc. The radical nature of this abstraction can be appreciated by comparing a detailed account of a particular causal process with the usual formal representation 'if C, then E' or 'C $\supset$ E'. In studying the principles of logic we need not worry about this abstraction, but wherever they are applied to arguments about substantive, concrete objects, it is essential to check that what is excluded by the abstraction is not crucial to the problem under discussion. If this is not done we may be misled in our interpretations of the world by the logical structure of discourse. It has already been shown, for example, that from the fact that certain terms may be logically independent, it does not, as is often thought, follow that the objects to which the terms refer are materially independent. Also, in the criticism of atomism, I referred to one of Zeno's paradoxes which showed a clear non-correspondence between atemporal logic and material processes.

Let us then list what the application of logical principles to interpretations of the world abstracts *from*. First, as with any abstraction, certain properties of objects and their contexts are excluded and hence some of the sense-relations constituting their concepts ignored. This process is taken to the extreme where logical models or formalizations of knowledge gained by other means are used. As might be expected, the ultra-abstract nature of logical models of the world makes them a good match for atomistic conceptions of objects and for contentless abstractions of the type described in Chapter 3. Also excluded from consideration are the conceptual problems of *how* we refer to objects – the fact that we can do so only under particular descriptions and within available frames of meaning – and our attitudes as knowing-subjects to propositions.

These last points might also be true of the reconstructions of explanation offered in Chapter 3, although the types of abstraction were a good deal less extreme and restrictive than that of logical models and many 'first order' conceptualizations found in everyday knowledge were endorsed. Neither the use of realist concepts nor logical models *entails* the neglect of the above issues and indeed they may be combined provided their respective limitations are recognized. However, there is always a danger that particular kinds of abstraction may be over-extended so that they displace others which are better suited in certain domains and, in the case of logic, many philosophers and scientists have been seduced by its rigour and certainty into marginalizing other forms and aspects of knowledge.[25]

This tendency, or perhaps it should be called a condition, is endemic in orthodox Anglo-American philosophy of science. Harré terms it 'logicism', defining it as: 'the doctrine that all metascientific concepts such as "cause", "explanation", "confirmation" and so on can be explicated without remainder in terms of concepts drawn from logic',[26] or more generally the view that deductive logic is the only 'vehicle of thought' worthy of consideration.[27] This has disastrous consequences where it informs philosophical reconstructions of science or knowledge in general, but as will be shown in the next chapter something akin to logicism is also present in quantitative approaches to social research.

I have already commented upon the now abandoned assumption that observation could provide a theory-neutral and hence possibly absolute or infallible foundation for knowledge. Although this version of the 'quest for certainty' is no longer current, those who seek a 'logic of science' seek certainty of a different sort in terms of the analytic truths of logic and mathematics. And again, they characteristically confuse questions of what the world is like and what makes things happen with questions regarding the logical relationships between statements.

What marks out science from other kinds of knowledge, on this view, is the logical structure of its arguments and its openness to falsification. Questions of *content* and hence the diverse nature of the objects of knowledge are considered to be more or less irrelevant, contrary to our realist view. And while modern logicists like Popper do not attempt to exclude metaphysical issues, such as conceptions of causality, they see them as very secondary. They also have an extraordinarily dismissive attitude towards the process by which theoretical hypotheses and claims originate. Such matters are considered to involve merely the 'psychology' of science and to be of interest only to the sociology and history of science, both of which are seen as radically distinct from the philosophy of science. Hence, subject–object and subject–subject relations in which science takes place are understood only in terms of a 'psychological' or 'sociological' dimension (Why was a certain scientist the first to think of a particular idea? Who was he/she influenced by?, etc.), and not in terms of their necessary hermeneutic and conceptual conditions. This is clear from the very choice of the term 'psychology' to cover such matters – as if the development of concepts were simply a function of the individual scientist's private psychology rather than a function of the irreducibly social, intersubjective and linguistic nature of conceptual systems. The misidentification is also evident in Popper's glamorization of the source of scientific hypotheses in terms of some inscrutable 'poetic' quality of 'genius'. The result is that problems of conceptualization are ignored[28] (despite Popper's correct insistence that observation is always guided by theory) and the only problems deemed worthy of comment are those of establishing *validity* and truth or falsity of predictions about simple 'events' or 'instances'.

There is also a disregard of forms of reasoning of a non-logical kind. Concepts can be linked by other means than logical relations of entailment, for example by shared reference to a common object or by metaphors, and while such relations are non-logical, they are, of course, not necessarily *il*logical. We are always faced with the problem of *how* to observe and conceptualize the world and that is not answered for us by choosing one particular logical structure rather than another, because logic is contentless.

If the non-logical conceptual content of science is treated merely as a mental prop for poor logical thinkers who need a little imagery to help them swallow their logic, we lose sight of any idea of what science should refer to, why it does not seek necessity or order in just anything, or why scientific labour takes the form it does – abstracting, experimenting, physically intervening in the world – rather than merely randomly collecting data and trying out hypotheses about order in it.

Not surprisingly, given the pedestalling of logic and the lack of interest in conceptual issues, logicist philosophy of science favours the ordering-framework conception of theory. As a result it has little penetration of what most theoretical disputes are about and is unable to say why we don't seek to fit just *any* data into such deductive systems.

What happens in the real world (concept-dependent phenomena apart) is distinct from the logical relations between statements. The same applies to the non-logical forms of reasoning we use, but these are able to conceptualize matters which logic cannot encompass within its austere abstractions. Causal concepts of 'forcing' or 'producing' are lost as soon as 'causal mechanism A produces change B' is reduced to the status of a logical relation of entailment about a mere regularity (universal or not). Without the concepts of natural necessity and mechanisms which are generative of change, causal relationships become indistinguishable from mere (accidental) universal sequences and concepts such as 'physical impossibility' and 'spurious correlation' become unintelligible.[29]

Non-logical theoretical reasoning is needed to grasp the nature of the relevant mechanisms and structures, although it may be found heuristically useful to formalize such knowledge in a deductive logical structure. So, against the logicist prejudice that such non-logical reasoning is pre-scientific and/or merely part of the 'psychology of science', I would argue that it is not causal, picture-carrying and other (non-logical) concepts which are merely a heuristic aid for understanding logical constructions, but rather the reverse.[30]

Popper and deductivism

The most influential logicist philosophy in social science is that of Popper.[31] Most discussions of his work give pride of place to his arguments about the logical structures of scientific inference and falsificationism – the doctrine that science progresses not by verifying hypotheses, which is held to be impossible, but by falsifying them. Less often mentioned – because most discussants accept them – are his treatment of theory, causality and scientific laws as being primarily about empirical regularities, his denial of material or natural necessity and his acceptance of the atomistic presuppositions of standard accounts of induction. Popper acknowledges that observation is theory-laden, but weakens the point by treating theory as a logical ordering framework.[32] As we have seen, problems of abstraction and conceptualization are relegated to the dustbin of the 'psychology of science' or left to the mysteries of 'genius'.

Central to his philosophy is his belief that science is not inductive, but deductive, and he boasts that he has solved the problem of induction. But a denial that induction is used is not a solution to the problem of induction and in fact he uses the standard exposition of the problem as a critical tool to argue for his own position.

Unlike induction, deduction is a valid form of inference: the conclusions of a deductive argument cannot be rejected without contradiction while the premises are accepted. Popper advocated a 'hypothetico-deductive' procedure in which scientists advance bold hypotheses or conjectures from which testable propositions could be deduced. This enables one to take advantage of an important asymmetry: while affirmation of the conclusions of a valid deductive argument (or an inductive inference) does not prove the premises to be correct,[33] denial or falsification of the conclusions necessarily entails that the premises are in some way false too. This property does not exist for inductive arguments. If, on the basis of our observations, we conjecture that not all but most As are Bs and we then find an anomalous instance of an A which is not B, the conjecture is not falsified. Consider the following hypothetical examples which I have adapted from Harré.[34] That they are taken from natural science is not unfair to Popper, for he believes that social and natural science share the same method of explanation.)

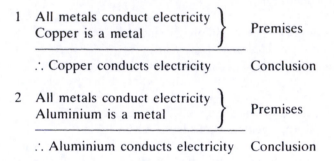

1 All metals conduct electricity   ⎫
   Copper is a metal   ⎬ Premises
                                     ⎭
   ∴ Copper conducts electricity   Conclusion

2 All metals conduct electricity   ⎫
   Aluminium is a metal   ⎬ Premises
                                     ⎭
   ∴ Aluminium conducts electricity   Conclusion

Both 1 and 2 are valid deductive arguments. 2 has been falsified: aluminium does not conduct electricity and so, if it is a metal, the conjectured universal regularity referred to in the statement 'All metals conduct electricity' must be false. The conclusion of 1 does not refute its premises, but neither does it confirm them, for from the fact that one metal conducts it does not follow that all do. Indeed such a conclusion could be deduced from an infinite number of premises, including absurd ones: for example, 'All woods conduct electricity; copper is a wood, therefore copper conducts electricity' is a valid argument. No amount of conforming instances is sufficient to verify the universal claims made in the premises of such arguments, yet only one anomalous instance is needed to falsify them.

This simple strategy, however, fails to circumvent the problem of induction as Popper hoped, for if all sequences of events are contingent and hence vulnerable to the big problem of induction (that the world may suddenly change) at every instant, then (regardless of what mode of inference we choose) what may be falsified today may be corroborated tomorrow. From the fact that we have observed a falsifying instance it does not follow (inductively) that repetition of the test would yield further falsifications. If all events are contingently related, falsifications are of no great significance and conjectures about universal regularities are not bold but foolish. It is only if we presuppose that some relations are necessary that falsifications need be taken as having lasting theoretical significance, so Popper's falsificationism presupposes what he wants to deny.[35] The 'logic of science' cannot evade problems generated at the metaphysical level regarding necessity.

The deductive logical structure that lies at the heart of Popper's conception of science has been widely advocated as an ideal form of explanation, known as the 'deductive–nomological' (D–N) or 'covering-law' model.[36] In this, the event-to-be-explained (or predicted – symmetry of explanation and prediction being assumed) is deduced from a universal (regularity) law and a set of initial conditions. Such an explanatory form could be used to answer the question

Why does copper conduct electricity?

All metals conduct electricity. (Law)
Copper is a metal. (Initial conditions) } Explanans

∴ Copper conducts electricity   Explanandum

(I have again used one of Harré's natural science examples because of the difficulty of finding non-trivial and reasonable universal regularities in social science which could pose as a law of the regularity, instrumentalist type.) But does the 'model' form of explanation really explain? Even if we assumed that the law statement were true, the inquirer would probably already know that all metals conduct electricity and complain that they had not been told why this was the case in the sense of it being explained what *makes* copper and other metals behave in this way. Instead of telling us what *determines* or *produces* the effect the model merely gives us some grounds for having expected the explanandum event to occur,[37] or, to put it another way, it merely provides a way of logically *deriving* the explanandum statement from some other statement. In some cases such grounds for expectations or derivations may be all that is wanted, but it is essential not to confuse this with giving causal explanations, which always involve reference to what generates or produces the event. Moreover, once again, the explanandum event could be deduced from absurd criteria: try replacing the word 'metal' in the example with 'dairy product', 'communist' or whatever you like and the explanation still works in so far as it satisfies the D–N model's purely formal criteria.

Clearly we cannot afford to neglect the question of the *content* of explanations and the need for a *causal* explanation to cite the *mechanism* responsible for the event. On our view, 'copper can conduct electricity because it has free ions in its structure' is an acceptable causal explanation. (We could, of course, ask for the description of the mechanism to be 'unpacked' further, according to our interests.) And whether the event to be explained has only happened once or is an instance of one that has been observed repeatedly in the form of a regularity is a separate matter from that which produces it.

Now it would be possible to fit this kind of explanation into the D–N format, for it doesn't take much ingenuity to dream up a suitable 'covering-law':

e.g.   All metals with free ions conduct electricity
       Copper is a metal with free ions
       _____

       Therefore copper conducts electricity

But the deductive form and the covering law are *redundant* for they add no information about what makes the explanandum event happen. (As Louch notes, attempts to invoke covering laws for social events invariably end up explaining something which is relatively familiar and certain by reference to unfamiliar and dubious claims about alleged regularities.)[38] 'Free ions' attempts to refer to the mechanism. Whether it succeeds in doing so does not depend on whether it is inserted into a deductive argument or not. Accordingly, wherever examples are given of D–N explanations, one should check to see if they owe any plausibility they may have as causal explanations to the unacknowledged inclusion of a reference to a mechanism.

So instead of trying to fit our social scientific explanations into the mould of the D–N model, simple forms can be accepted such as: 'the landed gentry were *taxed* out of existence', or 'the grain exports were authorized *in order to placate the farm lobby*'.[39] If they are to be criticized, it is their *content*, in terms of whether they correctly identify relevant mechanisms, that should be examined. And this in turn requires us to consider something which logicism or 'deductivism' rarely remark upon (despite Popper's insistence that observation is theory-laden) – namely, how we conceptualize the objects referred to in the explanans and explanandum.

In its failure to explain, the deductive–nomological model of 'explanation' bears witness to the poverty of logicism and its confusion of the grounds – particularly pertaining to the logical relations among statements – for expecting things to occur, with the real structures and mechanisms responsible for their occurrence. Yet despite its popularity, particularly as developed by Popper (and Lakatos), it is rarely practised. Many methodologists in social science prescribe its norms to their students but few researchers or students actually use them. The reasons for this are not hard to see once one grasps the significance of the deterministic statements of universal regularities which are supposed to be proposed as covering laws in 'bold conjectures'. If closed systems are unavailable, such hypotheses will be non-starters, even if several protective *ceteris paribus* assumptions are allowed; although to include too many would invite the criticism that the researchers were trying to minimize rather than maximize, as Popper urges, the risks of refutation. In a famous example, the economist R. G. Lipsey wrote a textbook in which it was stated that a hypothetico-deductive approach, permitting falsifications, would be adopted.[40] But it was obvious that if the relationships hypothesized in the book were treated as deterministic universal regularities and assumed to be vulnerable to falsification from any anomalous instance, there would be little theory left. In later editions the author changed the methodological introduction and opted for an approach of which Popper certainly would not approve – proposing probabilistic or statistical laws and 'testing' them to see what measure of inductive support could be found. More recently, following further developments of Popper's ideas by Lakatos, more sophisticated forms of falsification have been sought, although these have perpetuated rather than challenged the regularity (instrumentalist) theory of causation and laws, the doctrines of atomism and logicism and the indifference to the distinction between closed and open systems.[41]

6 Quantitative methods in social science

When you cannot measure it, when you cannot express it in numbers, your knowledge is of a meagre and unsatisfactory kind.
(Lord Kelvin)

When you can measure it, when you can express it in numbers, your knowledge is still of a meagre and unsatisfactory kind.
(Jacob Viner)[1]

The aim of this chapter is to explore some of the problems of the use of quantitative methods in social science. For those who read the preceding chapter, it will also serve to give more substance to what might have seemed – at least to newcomers to the subject – rather academic criticisms. While mathematical approaches are not an integral part of the philosophical and methodological positions I have attacked, the ways in which they are commonly used in social science tend to resonate with those positions.

Advocates of quantitative methods usually appeal to the qualities of mathematics as a precise, unambiguous language which can extend our powers of deductive reasoning far beyond that of purely verbal methods, and, as with logic, the validity of mathematical reasoning is a 'black-and-white' affair, being subject to internal rather than empirical check. This latter characteristic has great appeal for those who are frustrated by the seemingly endlessly contestable character of social science. Yet the recognition of the power and elegance of mathematics should not prevent us inquiring into the limits of its applicability.

Like logic, mathematics is a purely formal language and can be used to refer to anything or nothing. In Chapter 5 it was noted that a valid argument does not have to be 'true' or practically adequate and indeed may be quite nonsensical. So it is with mathematics –

the discovery that a model is free from mathematical errors says nothing about whether it is applicable to the world. The purely formal nature of mathematical reasoning does not relieve us of the need to inquire into its practical adequacy when it is applied: on the contrary, it is precisely because it is neutral that the adequacy of the forms of abstraction used in applying mathematics to the world must be closely scrutinized. As Wittgenstein put it, '(I)n life . . . we use mathematics *only* to infer from propositions which do not belong to mathematics, to others which equally do not belong to mathematics.'[2] Yet one does not have to look far among examples of the use of quantitative methods in social science to see a conspicuous neglect of the problems of using mathematics. Perhaps one reason for this neglect or complacency is the remarkable success of many mathematical representations of the world in the natural sciences, the most famous example probably being Newton's work. As Bernal wrote, 'Newton's contribution was decisive. It lay in finding the mathematical method for converting physical principles into quantitatively calculable results confirmed by observation, and conversely arriving at the physical principles from such observations.'[3]

One can hardly fail to be impressed by such achievements and many social scientists have hoped that the adoption of appropriate methods would enable them to discover their Newton.[4] But if we are to understand why they have been unsuccessful we must ask what real objects and processes must be like for mathematical representations of them to be practically adequate. I shall discuss this question in relation to the two main types of quantitative approach in social science: deterministic modelling and statistical methods. *Whatever the success of my particular answers to this question, I would at the least insist on the importance of the question.*

Quantification

The problem can be posed at its most basic or primitive level in relation to the operation of *quantifying*; namely what must objects be like for it to be possible to quantify them? The answers to this simple question are difficult and complex. In the space available I can only summarize a few points on the subject that have been made by Nicholas Georgescu-Roegen in his remarkable book *The Entropy Law and the Economic Process*.[5]

Practically adequate forms of quantifying using interval scales can only be developed for objects and processes which are qualitatively invariant, at least in their fundamentals. As such, they can be split up and combined without changing their nature. We can measure them at different times or places in different conditions and know that we are not measuring different things. But there are far fewer occasions when we can be confident about this stability in social science than in natural science. Context-dependent actions or properties such as attitudes might therefore be considered unsuitable for quantification. If we do insist on quantifying them we should at least be extremely wary of how the results are interpreted. Only if objects are qualitatively invariant is the order in which we measure or change them irrelevant. The transformation of coal into ashes or the socialization of a child are irreversible processes involving qualitative change and cannot be cardinally measured in any meaningful way. Such objects cannot be modelled as if they were 'parametric';[6] if the objects referred to by the variables of an equation interact in a way which produces qualitative change (e.g. through a learning process), the variables will not be able to make stable reference. Accordingly, assumptions of linearity, additivity and of the possibility of discovering practically adequate instrumentalist laws of proportional variation all depend for their success on a particular material property of the objects to which they refer.[7]

Whether process can be adequately represented mathematically depends on the type of change involved, on whether it is purely quantitative, or reducible to the movement of qualitatively unchanging entities, or irreducibly qualitative. The latter possibility might be divided into cases where individuals still retain their identity (e.g. the process of ageing) and cases where they cease to be identifiable. The first two types of change only affect external relations between objects, and mathematical operations such as addition and subtraction can unproblematically model physical combinations and separations. But in the second kind of qualitative change, emergent powers may arise or be dissolved through such combinations and separations, and hence cardinal measurement will not be practically adequate. One of the least interesting ways of looking at society is by demographic analysis. This conceptualizes individuals as externally related and is therefore 'blind' to social structures and their emergent powers, yet one of the reasons why it is popular is that its mode of abstraction permits quantification. Less 'asocial' approaches are unlikely to find quantification so straightforward, although many researchers nevertheless use it without appreciating the problems. For example, we rarely stop and ponder just how extraordinary it is to treat, say, different kinds of labour as cardinally measurable in units of time or money. As with any kind of abstraction, whether such features cause practical problems depends on the context in which they are used and the 'weight' we put on inferences drawn from them, though it would be foolish to imagine that such measures are always trouble-free. While it is true that many textbooks on applied quantitative methods mention problems of measurement, they rarely prompt much concern because they fail to explore the conceptual and metaphysical problems implicit in their use.

In the case of *social* science there is an additional but rarely discussed complication which derives from the fact that quantification is not just a tool of analysis but part of the object of study. It is hardly surprising that economics is by far the most quantitative of the social sciences given that many of its objects are already quantified, although this simple point is often overlooked by those who prefer to interpret this as evidence of its superiority as a 'science'. But the fact that quantitative data are given *increases*, rather than reduces, the significance of the problems just discussed. The point made in Chapter 1 about the possibility of practices being informed and regulated by false or inconsistent ideas applies not just to the 'soft' qualitative data of sociology and the like but to the 'hard' quantitative data of economics. And despite their pride in their alleged 'value-neutrality', even 'positive' economists sometimes take it upon themselves to criticize modes of quantification or economic calculation (e.g. pricing policies of the public sector) *in* society. These problematic modes are not just limited to non-market transactions but concern all forms of quantification in economies. No economic theory can avoid the issue of what quantitative measures are measures *of*, be it marginal productivity, labour time or whatever.

Mathematics: an acausal language

Having noted these problems, let us now assume that we have adequately quantified our objects of interest and now want to build a mathematical model of the system. At this stage we must be aware of another set of properties and limitations of the use of mathematical approaches.

First, the mathematical operations performed in such a model provide a way of calculating, deducing or deriving certain results from assumptions and data but *not* a way of causally explaining phenomena. Earlier, in the discussion of closed systems (page 117, the example of the record turntable), we saw how the behaviour of such a system might be calculated without any regard for its causal structure. And in Chapter 5, examples of an equivalent non-correspondence between logical (deductive) order and causal order were given. Unfortunately the belief that finding a way of calculating something is necessarily the same as giving a causal explanation of what produced it is endemic in disciplines such as economics which use mathematical modelling widely. Not surprisingly, those who accept this tend to appeal to deductivist philosophers like Popper, who make a principle out of the error.[8]

The use of mathematical models as an aid to causal explanation is inevitably problematic because, as a language, mathematics is acausal and astructural. It lacks the categories of 'producing', 'generating' or 'forcing' which we take to indicate causality. Mathematical functions such as $y = f(x)$ say nothing about what makes y or x, only that quantitative variation in y is formally (not substantially) related in some way to quantitative variation in x. The $=$ sign in an equation does not, of course, mean that the so-called 'independent variable' is the cause of the changes in the 'dependent variable', but merely that the quantities on either side are equal! Any imputations of causality associated with the decision to define one variable as independent and the other as dependent must be based on non-mathematical, causal criteria. (In some cases, however, the grounds for the decision amount to little more than that data are available for some variables, which can therefore be treated as independent, but not for others which must therefore be defined as dependent!) According to the realist theory of causation advanced in Chapter 3, *qualitative* analysis of objects is required to disclose mechanisms. The conventional theory of causation abstracts from such concerns and instead focuses on regular sequences of events. As such, it is more easily associated with mathematical approaches, although clearly this does nothing to remedy its shortcomings, in particular its inability to distinguish causal from accidental relations, as manifested in the problem of spurious correlations.

Similarly, the concept of a 'variable' that is used in quantitative analysis is an *indifferent* one as regards causal explanation: variables can only register (quantifiable) change, not its cause. The vocabulary of mathematics may be useful for recording the effects associated with the exercise of causal powers but other 'languages' are needed to show why objects possess them. Unawareness of this limitation supports the widespread failure in economics to distinguish labour power (or the ability to work) from the exercise of that power – labour. Far from being a minor matter of semantics, this confusion underpins many serious misconceptions about how capitalist economies work, in particular, the belief that wages are a payment for work done. In actual practice, it is impossible to separate work from the results of work; the theorist's abstraction of labour from its effect has no practical equivalent. If workers were to sell their labour, they would also have to sell the fruits of their labour. But unless firms buy in commodities from workers working on their own account, they do not do this. Ford doesn't buy cars from Ford workers; to do so would be to hand over the possibility of making a profit on the cars to the workers! In dealing just with variables and calculations it scarcely seems to matter whether L stands for actual work done or labour power, the capacity to work. But from the point of causal explanation of the origin of profit it is crucial.

Mathematical modellers therefore tend not to be concerned with explaining what it is about social objects which produces certain changes but with representing and calculating the effects of actions. A further reason for this is the inability of mathematics to represent internal relations and hence structures. Moreover, when quantified, relations which are in fact substantial (i.e. involving material connections between objects), internal and/or causal become indistinguishable from purely formal and contingent relations. These limitations help to reinforce the tendency of mathematical modellers in social science to be unaware of the social relations and structures on which the objects represented as 'variables' depend.

Accounting and quasi-causal models

If the language of mathematics is acausal, is there not at least some other sense in which models might be said to 'explain' something about their objects? If by 'explain' we simply mean 'make clear' then, of course, models may explain how component quantities vary. And one of the simplest kinds of model 'explains' change in some aggregate (treated as the dependent variable) by disaggregating it into its components, as one might explain (or calculate) changes in a person's bank balance by reference to the individual withdrawals, receipts and interest payments itemized in the statement of accounts. Indeed, such approaches to modelling are sometimes called 'accounting frameworks'. The model calculates the components of change but does not refer to what causes them to change.

These kinds of quantitative disaggregation often fail to correspond to what might constitute 'causal disaggregation'. For example, in the study of employment change, one obvious method of analysis might involve identifying and quantifying components of change such as plant 'births', 'deaths' and moves, or a sectoral analysis, but the various *causes* of employment change are unlikely to correspond neatly to either disaggregation.[9] Problems also arise where the components are not qualitatively invariant or where they interact causally with one another, or where emergent powers arise or are dissolved through combinations and separations. Attempting to explain the effects of an object which has emergent powers in terms of the relative contribution of its constituents is like attributing a certain percentage of the behaviour of water to hydrogen effects and the rest to oxygen effects![10] Properly applied, the mathematical operations of accounting models should be interpretable in terms of possible material operations or changes. This is not to argue that explanations by calculation are dispensable, for in any *concrete* study it is usually important not only to know what causal mechanisms are present and how they work but also to have a quantitative estimate of their number and their effects (if they are separable).

Besides accounting models there are also models whose independent variables *purport* to be not merely components but causes and conditions of change in the dependent variable. Variation in the latter is not interpretable as the material sum of changes in components but rather reflects how variables which *might* be regarded as causes and conditions *co-vary* with them. (I say 'might' to remind the reader that causal inferences must be made outside mathematics.) Both these '*quasi-causal*' models and accounting models might use an identical equation form – typically $y = f(x_1,$

$x_2, \ldots, x_k$) – but instead of merely noting the evident flexibility of mathematical language we should pay attention to the difference in meaning of the two uses. Particularly in the case of quasi-causal models it is useful to ask in what sense the logical order of the equation can serve to 'represent' the material, causal order of a process like, say, economic growth. Unless an answer is sought to this question, the modeller may lapse into simply 'plugging in' variables into a model so as to cover any phenomenon which might be a 'factor' (another 'indifferent term'), without working out whether they are conditions or mechanisms and if so, of what kind. And possibly, such an agnostic attitude may allow an unexamined combination of accounting and quasi-causal elements in a single equation.

'Theoretical' and 'empirical' models and closed and open systems

As might be expected, whether systems of interest are closed or open also has a strong bearing upon the use of mathematical models. So-called 'theoretical models' invariably posit the existence of a simple, hypothetical closed system, be it a two-sector model of an economy or a Marshallian demand–supply model. As such they can be heuristically useful for clarifying possibilities.[11] So-called 'empirical models' are fitted to actual data, and in social science, whether the researchers know it or not, to open systems. If the mathematical functions are fitted to relationships which are not constant or which do not change in constant ways – i.e. if the system is open – then the model will not have much success at prediction. However, once the components of a system have been quantified, be it closed or open, it is always possible to *fit* a mathematical model to it *ex post*, though only in the former case will it work *ex ante*. Even so, modellers often hope that the system can be decoded in such a way that what appear to be irregular relationships can be shown to be the effect of invariant constituent regularities. Characteristically, the intrinsic condition for closure is ignored even if the extrinsic one is acknowledged and it is assumed that what appear to be open systems are really no more than combinations of closed sub-systems. Nevertheless, the consequences of this misjudgement cannot be escaped if the researcher is trying to model an actual (open) system and indeed certain typical 'symptoms' and responses can be identified.

To illustrate some of these, let us take a very simple example of a mathematical model of population change.[12] Given information on variables such as birth rates per 1000 women in each age group and the number of women by age, we can forecast the number of births in future periods. For the purpose of *ex post* calculations once the model has been fitted, *any* variable can be treated as dependent simply by rearranging the equation – causal order and the order of calculation need not correspond and causes can be calculated from effects if desired. However, when the model is used for prediction and then compared with actual data, the fact that it does not satisfy the conditions for closure will lead to inaccuracies. Even with a fine disaggregation by age, each class is liable to contain different types of individuals with different fertility rates and as proportions of these change and social influences on fertility change, so the age-specific birth rates will vary. One response to this 'symptom' is to disaggregate the model still further in the hope that different groups can be distinguished, thereby reducing qualitative change to purely quantitative change of qualitatively constant groups. Following Bhaskar, this might be called a 'reductionist regress'.[13] Often this reductionist response strategy is in any case counterproductive because it rapidly increases both the complexity of the model, the number of 'unknowns' to be estimated and, with these, the possibilities for error amplification. Moreover, it often loses any degree of regularity which might have been derived from the 'law of large numbers' effect in which variations are averaged out. If the sole purpose of the model is to make simple predictions or calculations rather than explanations it will probably be more practical to choose the level of disaggregation which gives the greatest order or regularity.

Alternatively, or even additionally, a regress in the opposite direction may be tried. In such cases of 'interactionist' regresses,[14] it is recognized that certain parameters are changing, but it is hoped that such variation may be calculated internally within the model. For example, from a study of economic influences upon the birth rate it might be decided to build on an economic sub-system which models this too. Such strategies (sometimes coupled with reductionist regresses!) typified the extravagant monster computer models of the later 1960s and early 1970s, including the MIT world models.[15] They have similar effects on complexity, data needs and error amplification. Ultimately, one is faced with the futility of expecting to be able to model social systems predictively with any accuracy, though as we noted in Chapter 4, we can hardly do without some predictions, even if inaccurate. As with my comments on generalization, I point out these difficulties not to try to ban predictive modelling but to explain the inevitable difficulties and responses.

In modelling hypothetical closed systems, any autonomy of processes from one another and any asymmetry in their inter-dependencies is not apparent – a feature which greatly assists their mathematical representation.[16] In open systems (and closed but manipulable real ones) this autonomy and asymmetry is more apparent (e.g. the partial autonomy of production and supply from consumption and demand), and it is difficult, if not impossible, to model them by means of analytically-soluble equations. Instead, recursive formulations using computer simulation may be required which sacrifice the elegance of analytical models.[17]

Unless a system is particularly well understood, it is rarely possible to specify the values of the parameters of a mathematical model of it *a priori*, and so they have to be 'calibrated'. Usually we have a good idea of the 'sign' of a relationship – whether the variables are directly or inversely related – but are unable to specify the precise form in advance. If the system is closed this need only be carried out once to be sufficient to produce a robust model which predicts successfully. But if the system is open, the model will have to be fitted anew for each and every application, and hence parameters, coefficients and regression lines will vary from case to case.[18] Generalizations, rather than abstractions, are sought, which turn out to be hardly generalizable! Sometimes this kind of exercise is defended as a 'test' of a predictive model, but to fit a model to a set of data is not to predict or test it in any meaningful sense. Even where the 'goodness-of-fit' of certain non-fitted variables is tested, it must be remembered that it is already indirectly optimized through being part of a model which has been fitted.[19]

The presence of uninterpreted constants, parameters or coef-ficients in many models bears witness to the inadequacy of their attempts to produce a correspondence between mathematical and causal order. If they cannot be interpreted as 'standing for' a particular process or characteristic they may more justifiably be described as 'fudge factors' in that their only function is to conceal the inadequacies of the model by providing a means of fitting it to any data set. (With enough parameters *any* model can be fitted to any data.) If, on the other hand, they can be given a coherent substantive interpretation then ideally it should be possible to determine their values *a priori* or within the model rather than leave them to be fitted, although doing so would initiate reductionist and interactionist regresses.[20] Modellers may not be aware of it, but the inclusion of parameters whose values vary from case to case provides a retrospective but uninterpretable way of allowing for the non-satisfaction of the intrinsic and extrinsic conditions for closure and the mis-specification of causal structure.

So the use of 'empirical models' which have to be fitted to each set of data can be seen as an unaware response to the unavailability of enduring regularities which might be made the subject of instrumentalist laws. It also marks an abandonment of deductive logic and with it the belief that science should follow a hypothetico-deductive procedure in which predictions are deduced from hypotheses about empirical regularities and then tested against independent data.[21] Instead of insisting upon successful predictions of this sort, social scientists have been obliged to accept considerably diluted methodological principles. For example, the economist Paul Samuelson has acknowledged that such predictions are infeasible and suggests instead that as a minimal requirement the algebraic sign of the predicted changes in dependent variables must be correct![22] Another economist, Leontief, has noted how, as theorists, economists hypothesize imaginary closed systems in which they can retain the assumptions that scientific 'explanations' or predictions must be deductive in form and concern universal empirical regularities, but they then find that both these tenets must be dropped when the models are 'operationalized' for open systems:

As theorists we construct systems in which prices, outputs, rates of saving and investment, etc., are explained in terms of production functions, consumption functions, and other structural relationships whose parameters are assumed, at least for argument's sake, to be known. As econometricians, engaged in what passes for empirical research, we do not try, however, to ascertain the actual shapes of these functions by turning up new factual information. We make an about face and rely on indirect statistical inference to derive the unknown structural relationships from the observed magnitudes of prices, outputs and other variables that, in our role as theoreticians, we treated as unknowns.[23]

Putting it another way, the 'about face' can be seen as an unaware response to the non-correspondence of causal and logical order. If the system were closed, the implied inversion of causality need not matter for the purpose of prediction, but it certainly makes a nonsense of the theories' explanatory status for open systems. The possibility of getting away with mis-specifications and even inversions of causality in descriptions and predictions of closed systems is manifested in 'identification errors' in which relationships which are determined by, or are the outcome of interactions between, processes are treated as the determinants of those processes. Thus the equilibrium (closed system) assumption in economics allows the treatment of *ex post* demand and supply variables as determinants rather than products of production, distribution and consumption behaviour.[24] Not surprisingly, these inversions cause most disquiet when the 'theoretical models' are put into use.

If modellers abandon deductive form and ignore the alternative of non-predictive causal explanation they are reduced to the 'fitting' of empirical models of 'factors' in the manner described by Blaug:

The journals abound with papers that apply regression analysis to every conceivable problem, but it is no secret that success in such endeavours frequently relies on 'cookbook econometrics': express a hypothesis in terms of an equation, select the best fit, discard the rest, and then adjust the theoretical argument to rationalize the hypothesis that is being tested.[25]

However, while Blaug recognizes and bemoans the symptoms, he fails to comprehend their causes, for he still accepts the twin methodological principles of 'deductivism' and the search for empirical regularities and fails to note the implications of open systems.

The role of assumptions in models

Another way of looking at the relationship between 'theoretical' and 'empirical' or 'operational' models is in terms of the shift from abstract to concrete. Of all the kinds of research, this move is most formalized in work which uses mathematical models to explore the properties of hypothetical systems of successively more complex form, by relaxing assumptions and building on sub-models. Characteristically, however, attempts to carry through the move towards the concrete run into certain problems, particularly regarding the role of assumptions. Now, while assumptions have to be made in any kind of abstract analysis or 'thought experiment', whether qualitative or quantitative, their role is particularly clear in mathematical models and so I will discuss them at this point.

'Theoretical models' are usually based on assumptions which not only simplify the problem at issue but allow it to be treated as a closed system; for example, the assumption of equilibrium in economics and isotropic plains in geography. This is done by abstracting from qualitative variation in their primary variables and by holding other relations which are not of interest constant. These relations may be either necessary or contingent; in the latter case, abstraction can be thought of as a process of 'holding off contingencies'.

These methods may be useful heuristically, but can they help us understand concrete objects, and if so, how? And does it matter if assumptions are 'unrealistic'?[26] The answers depend on the nature of the abstractions, the use to which the model is put and what we mean by 'unrealistic'. If predictions and calculations are needed rather than explanations, assumptions need not be realistic in any sense; all that matters is that the model 'works' in the sense of producing accurate results. If explanation is the primary goal, two possibilities exist:

1   If the model is based on rational abstractions and assumptions merely serve to hold constant certain well-defined necessary relations and to 'hold off' contingent interfering processes, then it may effectively explain (provided it is backed up by qualitative, causal analysis) some of the constitutive processes in concrete open systems. In this case, the assumptions may be 'unrealistic' in the limited sense that they do not hold at the level of actual events. Nevertheless, they do not contradict theoretical claims about necessity in the world, but rather help to expose their objects more clearly.

2   Alternatively, the assumptions may be 'unrealistic' in the more serious sense that they deny what are known to be necessary (and relevant) features of the system of interest; i.e. they postulate as part of their representation of the central processes

of interest a state of affairs which is not merely unlikely or rare but materially impossible.

A well-known example of the second kind of assumption is the representation in economics of market processes as occurring in a timeless world and on the basis of perfect knowledge. Such assumptions may be justifiable for the purpose of calculation or prediction if it can be shown that, in quantitative terms, models based on them approximate results which might otherwise be derived by a complex and cumbersome model using more 'realistic' assumptions.

From the point of view of explanation, the effects of relaxing assumptions of either type are very different: in 1 it leaves the characterization of the basic structures and mechanisms represented in the model intact, though their effects at more concrete levels may be modified; in 2, it can leave it in ruins and hence the 'unrealistic' nature of the assumptions is a serious problem as regards their use for illuminating real objects. It is not just that such models don't happen to match concrete patterns – they don't even grasp the real at an abstract level. (Remember, in our terminology, abstract does not mean 'non-real' but a one-sided aspect of the real.) At best they may be interesting fictions which could never be made true in practice. Unfortunately, they are frequently used in models which are fitted to open systems and treated as explanatorily adequate on the spurious grounds that a fit has been obtained. Therefore, whenever statements such as 'assume we have perfect competition', or the like are encountered, it is essential to establish whether the author is talking about a hypothetical state of affairs which is impossible or a hypothetical state of affairs which is materially possible and an approximation of actual systems: the two options are not the same.[27]

Different criteria regarding the realism of assumptions might seem appropriate for 'praxiological' models, that is, models which are used to work out some *optimum* rather than an actual state of affairs. For example, linear programming models enable us to maximize or minimize some quantity, subject to certain constraints. An economist might use such a model for calculating the maximum output of a set of factories, subject to technical and resource constraints, or the minimum expenditure of time or energy possible for transporting goods to a given number of points. Praxiological models could be said to demonstrate how an idealized rational person would act, not how you and I actually act: so need their assumptions be 'realistic'? To answer this we must examine this type of model more closely. The main concern of such models is 'rationality', but this is a contentless abstraction: even models of rational behaviour must be given some content by assuming that agents have certain powers and liabilities (e.g. perfect or imperfect knowledge) and, implicitly, that they exist within a particular kind of society which makes some actions possible and desirable and others not. Typically, the latter type of assumption is left unexamined and, by default, historically specific contemporary social relations and ideologies (particularly individualism) are treated as universal. In other words, as questions of what is rational behaviour cannot be analysed at the level of contentless abstractions, it is again necessary to decide whether assumptions are unrealistic and whether this makes a significant difference, if we are to judge whether the idealized behaviour is possible in our society.[28]

So the question of the realism of assumptions can only be answered satisfactorily by considering the kind of model in which they are used and the kind of objects to which they are applied, not to mention the meaning of the term 'unrealistic'.

In the process of moving from abstract model towards the concrete, it is often found that many of the contingencies which were 'held off' at a higher level of abstraction are governed by processes which are covered by quite different theories and hence they cannot be modelled without generating an interactionist regress.

Often the shift towards the concrete is simply halted at the first obstacle. The common postponement of the day when the ostensibly 'provisional' assumptions are to be relaxed and the continual experimentation with 'logical puzzles' in preference to analysing real systems in economics and regional science, indicate the dependence of mathematical modelling on closed systems. And the use of 'empirical models' does not normally involve a step-by-step progression towards the concrete by means of 'successive approximations' but rather a leap across the many mediations between the abstract and the concrete, with the result that the representation of the processes actually modelled has to be distorted in order to compensate for the omission of others.

Marx's use of very simple mathematical representations, chiefly in Volume 2 of *Capital*, is interesting in this respect.[29] Before any 'variables' are defined, the concepts of the objects they represent (e.g. value, constant and variable capital) are explored qualitatively with a thoroughness that now seems unusual. The quantitative 'successive approximations' of the 'models' (e.g. from simple to expanded reproduction, from uniform to variable rates of turnover) are preceded by exhaustive qualitative successive approximations. This process is continued until the transformation problem in Volume 3, where Marx is unable to carry the mathematical analysis any further. Those who have solved the problem can only proceed a little further and are still dealing with hypothetical closed systems at a high level of abstraction. The manageability of such equation systems depends on crucial assumptions for retaining system closure – in particular that there is a fixed relation between quantities of use-values and quantities of exchange-values.[30] As Marx realized, such a condition could not possibly be maintained throughout a period of capital accumulation,[31] and since it was the latter that he was trying to explain, the assumption and the mathematical forms of analysis which it allowed had eventually to be dropped in the move towards the concrete. In neoclassical economics, the dominant strategy has been to sacrifice explanatory plausibility in order to retain closed systems and hence calculability. Naturally this is rarely acknowledged, though the point is as good as conceded in the adherence to a predictive criterion and to Friedman's inadequately qualified endorsement of unrealistic assumptions. Marx's strategy was to abandon calculability for the sake of explanation.[32] As was noted in Chapter 4, in neither case can such theories be expected to move far towards the representation of actual concrete cases without conducting empirical research to discover the contingent relations in which the abstracted elements stand, though, of course, the observation will be theory-laden. Often, it will be necessary to shift from analysis by means of formal models to narrative in order to capture the openness, contingency, qualitative change and novelty that characterize social systems.

Statistical methods

There are two main types of statistics: description, for example, measures of dispersion; and inferential, for example, the chi square test. All that needs to be said about the former is that they offer limited forms of description which may usefully supplement qualitative descriptions. However, the more ambitious and demanding project of statistical inference requires further discussion. While many of the limitations of statistical methods are identical to those already examined for 'deterministic' models, their use in the study of open systems for the ostensible purpose of explanation involves some distinctive problems.

Strictly speaking, inferential statistics is a form of inductive inference in which the characteristics of a population are estimated from sample data, though in practice the methods are called upon for the more ambitious purposes of prediction, explanation and hypothesis testing. An obvious reason for adopting such methods is that social processes have an apparently 'statistical' character compared with the more 'deterministic' processes to which natural (closed system) sciences have access.

But before proceeding any further, I must clarify the meaning of 'statistical'. In contrast to 'deterministic' processes, statistical processes, are often said to be 'probabilistic' and involve 'chance' or 'random' elements. This distinction can easily confuse the nature of processes with the nature of our knowledge about them. Most important, there seem to be no grounds in social science for treating 'chance', 'random' or 'statistical' processes as 'uncaused', in contradistinction to deterministic processes.[33] For example, we may prefer to describe the sequence in which the members of a community adopt an innovation as a stochastic process,[34] but this would not mean that we would take the individual adoptions to be uncaused. Sequences or patterns are only random under some particular description; the order of the letters on this page might appear to be random if we abstract from the meaning that strings of them form. So it does not follow from the fact that we can at best only assign a probability for the occurrence of an event that it is not determined.

This argument challenges the common assumption that probability or randomness is an objective property (i.e. a property of objects themselves). The best-known version of the view is the idea that the probability of an event is nothing more than the *relative frequency* of its occurrence, so that, for instance, the probability of a baby being female is simply the relative frequency or proportion of female births. The trouble with this interpretation is that it confuses the meaning of probability with (some of) the *grounds* for assigning probabilities. By contrast, there are also subjective interpretations in which probabilities are measures of our ignorance or confidence. This helps to draw attention to the fact that probability concerns *our expectations* about the occurrence of (future) events, though it says nothing about their causes.[35] Nevertheless, the degree of our (subjective) confidence or ignorance will obviously be affected by the extent of our knowledge of the (objective)[36] causes. If we know nothing about the principles according to which people are selected for jury service then our most reasonable expectation is that everyone has an equal probability of being called. If we then learn the selection rules and obtain information about the number of jurors required and the numbers and characteristics of the population we can redefine the probabilities, assigning zero values to members of excluded groups and adjusting those for people who are eligible.

This suggests that the value of statistics is depreciated as our knowledge of causal mechanisms becomes more complete.[37] However, even where the latter is good, statistical methods may still be used to model the relative quantitative dimensions of a group of processes. In other words, the 'ignorance' which requires us to resort to statistical methods concerns not only causal mechanisms but contingent relations. So even when we know the causes of quasi-random fluctuations in the main processes present it may be preferable to treat them collectively as an undifferentiated random 'noise' for the purposes of modelling them. If the 'disturbances' or fluctuations are non-random and major then they may need to be represented explicitly. Once again we find that, as with other kinds of knowledge, statistics cannot be understood and properly evaluated apart from their practical purpose.

In considering the use of statistical inference in generalization, prediction and explanation, we must note the ambiguities in the meaning of these terms. As we saw earlier, 'generalization' may simply be a description summarizing the characteristics of a population, perhaps on the basis of information in a sample, or else, more ambitiously, an *extrapolation* from the characteristics of a particular sample not only to those of the population from which it was drawn but to other populations at different times and places. Similar uses are common for 'prediction' with the result that modest curve-fitting exercises and estimations of population parameters are often dressed up as bold attempts at 'prediction' in the strong sense.

To a certain extent, the limitations of 'statistical explanations' are well known and teachers of statistical methods usually have their favourite example of a 'spurious correlation' such as that discovered between the birth rate and the number of storks in different regions of Sweden. The problem is usually acknowledged in a token fashion by placing the terms 'statistical explanation' and 'causal' in scare quotes, but the use of statistical analysis is often intended to *suggest* that the quantitative relations so discovered are causal. Regression equations, for example, say nothing in themselves about causal or conditional relations, yet there is a widespread assumption that 'causal analysis' and regression analysis are virtually synonymous; for example, Birnbaum's book entitled *An Introduction to Causal Analysis in Sociology* is largely a discussion of regression and says nothing about what causation is.[38]

The recognition of the possibility of spurious explanation amounts to a realization that regularities are not sufficient conditions for the identification of causes. What is rarely recognized is that they are not necessary conditions either. Because it refuses concepts of natural necessity and causal powers, the orthodox (positivist and Popperian) philosophy of science, to which many advocates of statistical analysis appeal, cannot provide a positive criterion for distinguishing causal from accidental relations. The following view, expressed in 1892 by Karl Pearson, one of the founders of statistical analysis, might now seem extraordinary but at least it indicates one way out of the dilemma. 'Science for the past is a description, for the future a belief; it is not, and has never been, an explanation, if by this word is meant that science shows the *necessity* of any sequence of perceptions.'[39] While I would obviously reject this as a view of 'science', however defined, it strikes me as a reasonable verdict on the role of statistics. More recently, statisticians have tried to make stronger claims for statistics; for example, Blalock has proposed a method of 'causal analysis' based on the comparison of partial correlation coefficients, but this suffers from the same problem and cannot distinguish causes from conditions or accidental formal relations.[40] If such methods are to gain any plausibility they must be supplemented by realist appraisals based on qualitative causal and structural analysis.

In common with many statisticians, Blalock willingly acknowledges that something more than techniques is needed, namely 'theory', although he fails to say what this might involve. However, my impression is that statisticians see theories as ordering-frameworks whose basic building blocks are empirical regularities. The provision of such a theory would only pose anew the problem that regularities are not necessarily causal. Given the disjunction between mechanisms and events, a strong correlation (or some other quantitative association) need not imply causation, nor a weak one absence of a causal or structural relation. If a theory is to help solve this type of problem it must postulate causal mechanisms and not merely specify how total variation in the dependent variable might relate quantitatively to variation in the independent variables.[41]

It has already been shown that a quantitative disaggregation of a system need not correspond to a causal one, and so it is with statistical explanation. For example, a technique such as Analysis of Variance (ANOVA) may be used to attribute a certain amount of total variation in a dependent variable to variation in some other processes. A study of crime rates might break down the data into areal classes, e.g. for inner cities, suburbs and rural areas. If there is a difference between the means for these classes this is termed 'explained variation'. Such exercises can be done quite easily and mechanically, but we must always insist on being told what the results mean in real terms: what does it *mean* to say that a certain proportion of the variation in crime rates is 'explained' by the type of area? or that a certain proportion of intelligence is due to genetic factors? Those whose answer is simply that x per cent of variation is caused by type of area or genetic factors have not thought deeply enough about the question – about the meaning of the terms 'cause' and 'explanation', about what relevant causal powers the objects treated as explanatory might have, and more generally about why quantitative and logical order should correspond to causal order.[42]

If statistical methods are only considered in terms of their mathematical properties or in the 'cookbook' manner, it appears that they can be applied to any subject-matter that can be quantified. Yet their practical adequacy for helping us understand the world depends in part on the type of object to which they are applied. Insufficient attention has been paid to this question in the attempts to transfer statistical methods from natural science to social science. In the search for generality of applications, the particular modes of abstraction which affect the success or failure of statistical analysis in natural science have been overlooked so that *material* restrictions on their use are forgotten, leaving only formal, technical restrictions. Again this comes out in some further ambiguities, this time in the meaning of terms such as 'experiment', 'variable' and 'control'.[43] In natural science an 'experiment' usually involves actual physical control or manipulation of a system of interest, but in social science statisticians often use the term to refer to the control and manipulation of observations of a system which is not itself controlled. Similarly, as Harré and Secord have pointed out, there are two senses of 'variable', one concerning entities which are actually physically manipulated and one referring to a class of entities in which each member has an attribute which is observed to be at a different level, amount or strength. The former is more common in natural science, the latter in social science.[44] In the case of 'control' we can distinguish 1 experimental controls – physically holding something constant which might otherwise vary (e.g. controlling temperature); 2 observational controls – restricting observation to cases where a certain variable or factor happens to be constant, e.g. choosing an ethnically-homogeneous population to study; and 3 mathematical controls – mathematically manipulating some data in order to 'control for' the effects of a variable which has not been controlled or constant in practice.

In terms of deciding whether the controlled variable actually makes some difference, 1 gives us the most direct evidence or 'epistemic access', and 3 the least direct. As I mentioned in Chapter 4, researchers who study objects which can be manipulated have a considerable advantage over those whose objects can only be observed. Although social objects themselves can be manipulated (and not merely the data we have about them), individuals are rarely comparable because of their differing interpretations and pre-understandings of the manipulations, and they certainly can't be treated as somehow 'controlled' in a uniform manner. Compare the following two cases. In the first, a natural scientist chooses a sample of plants with a view to testing their susceptibility to the application of fertilizer. Although the sample is random it might be stratified or limited to a single type of plant in order to avoid the problem of distributive unreliability. The sample is then split in two, one part being used as a 'control group', while a treatment of fertilizer is applied to the other 'experimental group'. Results are recorded and a statistical test run in order to check whether the difference between the two groups might be due to sampling biases. If the null hypothesis is rejected (i.e. the hypothesis that there is no difference between the (sub)sample means) then since only one treatment was applied in otherwise controlled conditions the researcher may feel confident that it was the fertilizer which made the difference.

In the second case a researcher studying differences in approaches to industrial relations of immigrants and indigenous workers takes a sample of each and then runs a test to see if the differences recorded between the two groups on some variable might have occurred by chance through sampling bias.

There is a world of difference between these two cases. In the second we know very well that individuals have *not* been randomly assigned to either group, and the nature of the 'controls' used in the two cases is also vastly different. Because of the uncontrolled (and arguably uncontrollable) nature of the social science 'samples', plus the 'context-dependence' of human action, the differences attributed to the variable ('immigrant/indigenous' are liable to be affected by a range of other characteristics or 'correlated biases'). Distinctions such as immigrant/indigenous blindly subsume a wide range of characteristics (e.g. class and income). Moreover, actual interaction and internal relations (e.g. of status) between the two groups may be overlooked. As the Willers argue, it is therefore pointless to test for statistically significant differences between the groups.[45] In natural science, context-dependence in the behaviour of objects is more limited and stable because they do not actively interpret and learn about their surroundings, or engage in meaningful action. Not surprisingly, the allocation of individuals to control and experimental groups and the avoidance of distributive unreliability are much less problematic, with the result that statistical analyses are less ambiguous. All this is not to say that 'controls' in social research designs are not sensible, only that they can't be expected to do the same job as in truly experimental science.

I would therefore argue that the usefulness of statistical methods depends crucially upon the type of objects to which they are applied and the type of research design in which they are deployed.[46] Evaluation of the possibilities for statistical analysis thus requires a non-statistical examination of the objects of interest. Because there need not be a correspondence between mathematical and causal order statistical techniques themselves cannot be relied upon to evaluate the possibilities. For example, in deciding whether a sample is distributively reliable, we cannot expect to find an answer merely by looking for irregularities or inflexions in curves drawn on graphs, for distributive unreliability may not produce these. Rather qualitative analysis and conceptual preparation are needed.

In principle, it would seem possible to precede statistical analysis by such preparations but in practice the technical requirements of the techniques often inhibit them. Qualitative analysis is liable to encourage the proliferation of variables, and the identification of interdependence, emergence and distributive unreliability, thereby making the techniques more difficult to apply.[47] Those who set great store by the use of statistics may be tempted to ignore such information – sometimes on the dubious grounds that the lack of quantification is indicative of theoretical immaturity. For example, distributive unreliability is often overlooked for the sake of getting the 'advantages' of big samples. This in turn may make the possibility of finding causal explanations more remote by dispensing with descriptions of the causal powers and compositions of objects and by increasing the number of different objects or events to be explained simultaneously.

The weakness of statistics for causal explanation is also evident in the way in which the presence of causal connections and internal relations can be an *embarrassment* in so far as these prove a nuisance from the point of view of meeting the technical requirements of many of the methods.[48] Observations are supposed to be independent of one another so that one does not end up seeking statistical associations among observations of the same individual or connected individuals. The independent variables used to 'explain' variation in the dependent variable of a multiple regression equation are supposed to be independent of one another and their combined effects purely additive. While there are techniques for dealing with failure to meet these requirements, it is striking that the very things we are interested in from an explanatory point of view – interdependence, connection and emergence – should have to be treated as nuisances for many techniques. For example, there are techniques for dealing with the 'problem' of interaction among independent variables in regression but while these offer a way of calculating interaction they do not explain it. So, for instance, in a study of teaching in schools we might find an interaction between teaching method and social class background of pupils which affects performance. Surmounting the technical problem of interaction among the independent variables still leaves the phenomenon to be explained.

One of the most common criticisms of statistical analyses of relationships among variables is that they tend to abstract from qualitative change in their key objects and from changes in context; often the two are linked and internally related. For example, students of industrial change have for many years conducted such analyses, abstracting from the continually changing interdependence between the qualitative nature of particular industries and the competitive environment in which they operate, as if the 'variables' were only externally related and as if the economic environment were just a passive backcloth to the action. What needed to be theorized and measured were not just 'variables' such as investment and employment but the internal relations between the qualitative nature of firms and the economic environment. Given the rapidity of historical change, the results of analyses needed to be regarded as specific to particular conjunctures rather than as revelative of some timeless, context-independent regularities. Similar problems are common in sociology and psychology; the nature of individuals – whether people or institutions – and their social environments are rarely simply externally related and susceptible to treatment simply as variables.[49] This is unlikely to be acceptable to those who suppose that statistical analyses are the only acceptable kind of method, precisely because it is difficult to cope with these aspects using such methods.

The main verdict on statistical methods must therefore be that despite their logical rigour they are primitive tools as far as explanation is concerned. In one sense, the theory of statistics is strikingly attentive to the problem of defining conditions under which each technique can legitimately be used (e.g. what kind of scaling, whether appropriate for non-normal distributions, etc.). These restrictions can be interpreted as ways of preventing inconsistent uses of the acausal language of mathematics in the representation of causal order. Indeed, the choice of statistical in preference to deterministic methods itself represents a response to a property of certain systems of interest. Now, statisticians often rightly stress the importance of understanding the concepts behind techniques and hence avoiding a 'cookbook' approach. But if the assumptions on which the techniques rest are to be shown to be rational and appropriate to actual objects of study, our conceptions of 'causal order', social theory, the nature of explanation and more generally of our object of study must be examined rather than taken for granted. And in this sense, on these questions, the practice of statistical analysis in social science is seriously deficient.

In most cases of which I am aware, the *implicit* conception tends to assume the universality of closed systems, a regularity theory of causation, an atomistic ontology (theory of what exists) and an equivalence of explanation and prediction. Without an explicit consideration of these issues, one tends to be conscious of the problems of these implicit assumptions only at the level of their effects in terms of 'technical' difficulties such as non-linearity and autocorrelation. And if one is unaware of the limitations of statistics one tends to force modes of abstraction and explanation into the moulds provided by the techniques rather than dispassionately assess whether they are appropriate for their objects.

Conclusions

I now want to conclude this chapter by discussing at a more general level the problems associated with quantitative approaches to social science. It is important to understand the nature of the types of criticism involved. I have been concerned with the *limits* to the use of such approaches and some of the assumptions and practices which *commonly accompany* their use. Now the reader may have noticed earlier how structural analysis tends to 'resonate' with marxist (and possibly some other) conceptions of society, but not with individualistic theories which portray society as a structureless aggregate of externally related individuals and causal 'factors'. This latter view resonates more easily with the use of quantitative methods. In noting this, I am not suggesting that structural analysis *entails* marxism or that individualistic theories entail or are entailed by quantitative approaches, but merely that there are 'resonances' which encourage the clustering of certain philosophical positions, social theories and techniques.[50] Any adequate critique of social science must go beyond piecemeal criticisms to the understanding of these resonances. So, for example, it is worth trying to appreciate how the technical requirement of adequate sample size, the assumption of universal regularities, the underestimation of distributive unreliability and of the context-dependent nature of human action resonate and reinforce one another. The blindness of mathematics to internal relations and emergence encourages (*though does not entail*) the belief that complex actions can be treated as reducible to some simple combination of simple behaviours which in turn are regular responses to set stimuli, as if each stimulus and action had the same meaning regardless of context.[51] A further example of this kind of resonance is evident in the tendency of users of mathematical models of social phenomena to reify human practice by interpreting it as mechanical and regular rather than always contingent and liable to transformation.

The views on quantitative methods advanced here are clearly at odds with the beliefs of many social scientists, who would probably regard approaches which do *not* use them as primitive. The fact that many 'methods' courses in social science teaching are limited to little else but statistical methods bears witness to the influence of this orthodoxy. Scientistic prejudices are rife here. Knowledge derived by other means is often patronizingly described as 'merely intuitive', or – curiously– as *a priori*, as if the only kind of observation and hence empirical technique were measurement, which can only be ratified if made repeatedly,[52] and as if a relationship is somehow 'less real' if it has not been observed in a sample of requisite size.

Exaggeration of the power of quantitative methods is often associated with the methodological tendency, noted in Chapter 5, of 'deductivism', which subordinates non-logical forms of reasoning, such as those involved in developing concepts, to deductive logic and which interprets theories as devices for ordering regularities. In deductivism, description and conceptual preparation are seen as unimportant preliminaries to the 'real' business of science – the construction of testable ordering structures or models. There is therefore a clear distinction between description and explanation, and in this respect deductivism echoes the now defunct distinction between theory-neutral observation and 'theoretical terms' which do not refer but merely order data. Consequently, the careful description and conceptualization necessary for the discovery of mechanisms and structures is overlooked.

This is not to say that qualitative and quantitative forms of analysis cannot be combined, only that this is rare – for the reasons given above. Often qualitative, and hence possibly causal, knowledge is actually *discarded*, and not merely temporarily abstracted from, in order to restrict the description of objects to the dimensions which can be quantified. At the extreme, initial conceptualization is reduced to a matter of defining mathematical notation ('K is capital and capital is K and let's get on with the model!').[53] In fact it is not unusual to find that students who are learning how to use quantitative methods and models and who question their descriptive meaning (i.e. inquire into the relationship between mathematical and causal order) are discouraged by their teachers as if such inquiries indicated an inability to understand the methods![54] Often the price of achieving mathematical order and rigour is conceptual sloppiness produced by disregard of the nature of the object being modelled.[55] If modelling is not accompanied by qualitative analysis, complex but nevertheless comprehensible social forms may be reduced to the status of logical categories or 'contentless abstractions' which are easy to manipulate but difficult to interpret. If researchers discard knowledge in this way and start to think simply in terms of 'variables' and their quantitative relationships it is easy to get the impression that there isn't much 'theory' around. Thus it is not uncommon to find users of statistical analysis beginning by ignoring available theory only to complain at the conclusion of their work of a lack of theory! Admittedly, statisticians often remind researchers of the importance of having a theory of the system under study, in order to avoid GIGO ('Garbage In – Garbage Out') applications, but this sound advice is often not followed because the nature of the 'theory' is misunderstood.

Contrasting with the prestigious view of the modeller as the guardian of 'science' is the image of mediocrity increasingly associated with the research project which uses the 'regression bash' as a substitute for thinking. This mediocrity derives partly from the limited scope of the techniques and partly from the way they are frequently used. Reflect, for example, on the primitive nature of the practice of building research designs around the rejection or acceptance of the null hypothesis that two sample means do not differ significantly (not forgetting the possibility that causality need not be reflected in quantitative order)! The preoccupation with statistical significance, sample sizes and response rates stands in bizarre contrast to the lack of concern with the adequacy of the frequently 'chaotic' conceptions whose interrelationships, or rather 'correlations', the statistical analyses are supposed to uncover. We typically find a meticulous statistical analysis of the way in which one set of 'chaotic conceptions', e.g. a sample of firms involved in diverse types of production, competitive situations and financial health, is related to another, e.g. particular geographical areas covered by different planning and economic policies. Apparently, making the basic categories less 'chaotic' would be unacceptable since it would make the sample less 'representative'! Increasing the size of the sample, or indeed, the range of the population may produce some regularity through the effect of the 'law of large numbers', but it does not make a 'chaotic conception' any less chaotic or, to put it another way, reduce distributive-unreliability. 'In Bloggs's study, the value for relationship A was x, in Smith's study y, but then again Jones found a value of z for a slightly similar relationship B.' The conclusions are invariably inconclusive: the studies were done on different populations at different times and places and hence their comparability is uncertain, there is a lack of theory and since no clear pattern emerges, more research – presumably of the same kind – is needed. If we only keep trying, our universal generalizations will turn up one day. Even if this goal is dropped and the results are accepted as spatially and temporally specific the methods are inadequate on their own for explanation and may indeed be dispensable.

Finally, these resonances of quantitative methods can weaken the initial hypothesis on which research is based. Consider a subject like educational performance and social background. One may be tempted to interpret the subject from the start as involving questions about possible generalizations and quantifiable, formal relations: 'How does educational performance *vary with* social background?' As soon as the question is posed in this way we tend to opt without further ado for a quantitative analysis. From then, the next major decision involves choosing 'variables', 'factors' or 'indicators' for which there are data and the result is some (probably non-generalizable) statements about how these co-vary. But it is also possible, though more difficult, to think of such issues causally, in terms of the processes and mediations by which membership of a particular social class, a particular type of educational institution and particular economic circumstances affects attitudes to education, etc. This could be incorporated with empirical study of *concrete* instances of the relationship.[56] This is not simply a more complex version of 'variable analysis', for it involves considerable conceptual and empirical work to distinguish and relate the categories, structures and strata of elements present; how the 'cultural' is related to the 'economic', how responses are mediated by interpretations, how interpretations and individual opinions are related to 'intersubjective meanings' and so on. Nothing is gained by remaining agnostic about such matters or by treating them indifferently as possible 'variables' or 'factors' in the hope that something might come out in the way of explanation in the statistical wash. The distinction between to 'vary with' and to 'causally determine', or that between formal and substantial relations, is by no means as fine or as academic as might at first appear. It marks a divide between radically different kinds of research with very different chances of providing illuminating answers.[57]

7 Verification and falsification

How do we decide whether to accept or reject particular ideas or theories about society? There are some simple and well-known answers to this question which are based on what is assumed to be the best practice of natural science. I will discuss the most popular of these, Popper's 'falsificationism', in the next chapter. Although such accounts tend to encourage optimism about the possibility of clear, decisive tests, it is difficult to think of any examples of them in social science. Indeed, there are many social scientists who are deeply pessimistic about the possibility of arriving at any consensus on the adequacy of social theories; theoretical disputes are seen as endless and progress as rare or uncertain. I shall argue that the orthodox views on verification and falsification are misconceived and particularly inappropriate for social science. As a result the two poles of unfounded optimism and exaggerated pessimism are mutually reinforcing. For the more social scientists orient their work to the prescribed modes of verification or falsification, the more remote the possibility of progress based on adequate assessment of theory: but then the less progress in testing is evident, the more strongly the inappropriate standards are advocated.

Our thinking on this subject is often influenced by 'pop' images of natural science in which theories are first developed, like the prototype of an aeroplane, and then later tried out in a decisive 'crucial test' by comparing predictions with rock-like observed facts.[1] But if this is an inadequate picture of testing/in natural science, it is all the more inappropriate for social science where hypothesis formation and testing are scarcely discernible from one another and the word 'evaluation' seems more suitable than 'test'. I shall argue that these differences are reasonable responses to the differences in their objects.

We must also ask what we want social theory to be adequate *for*: prediction?; practice?; causal explanation?; interpretive understanding?; social self-knowledge?; emancipation? Too few commentators on this subject even bother to ask what is reasonable to expect of knowledge of society and of thinking, self-interpreting beings. The usual procedure is to follow the scientistic prejudice of asserting that natural science offers exemplars of 'high standards' which are universally applicable and towards which social science should strive. If enough people fall for this, anyone who demurs can be attacked for lowering standards.

Any discussion of verification and falsification also presupposes a particular stance on the questions of epistemology and objectivity discussed in Chapter 2. Confusion on the latter questions sows confusion in the former. It might therefore be useful to recall the following points:

1   The distinction between the realm of ideas and the realm of real, material objects. Practice is an active relation between the two, though thought is trapped within the former.
2   Radical scepticism, or universal doubt, has nothing to contribute to the present discussion since testing or evaluation depend on provisional acceptance of certain ideas, e.g. B, in the argument 'not A, because B'. Ideas are assessed and disputes resolved by finding out which of the contested ideas is compatible with (or better, presupposed by) those agreed by all contending parties to be our most reliable and coherent ideas and practices.
3   The concept of absolute truth is incoherent. All knowledge is fallible, though not equally so. The problem is to assess its (relative) practical adequacy, including its intelligibility. Verifications and falsifications are also in principle revisable.[2]
4   Observation is theory-laden but not necessarily theory-determined. Theories are not monolithic and discrete but overlapping and internally differentiated. Their internal structure usually has a substantial degree of redundancy; refutation of at least some of their elements will often not bring the whole structure tumbling down but may merely require minor adjustments of a limited number of concepts. Within theories and sometimes between them it is usually possible to find commensurable (i.e. mutually intelligible) and non-contradictory

sets of concepts which are also sufficiently independent to allow non-tautological cross-checking.

5   Since sense and reference are interdependent a test does not involve merely a comparison between isolated bits of knowledge with individual fragments of reality. The statements under test are confronted not with unmediated facts but other statements about facts. And as any one term's reference to the world depends on its sense-relations with other terms, several concepts are implicated in any test, no matter how specific. Moreover, 'internal' questions concerning the coherence of a theory are not independent of 'empirical' questions concerning the adequacy of its 'external' reference to the world, although some errors in the latter, such as quantitative mistakes, may not prompt any conceptual revisions.

6   In social science it is not possible to conduct experiments in order to isolate structures. This makes evaluation difficult because, as we saw in Chapter 3, different social structures are invariably articulated together and are often implicated in one another's reproduction.

Above all, it must be remembered that in view of these points it is quite unreasonable to expect verifications and falsifications to be absolutely certain and conclusive (unless they concern logical or mathematical truths or errors). They might more accurately be said to involve judgements of superiority and inferiority.

Philosophical criticism

Philosophical criticism itself can play a role in assessing social theory by providing a 'coarse sieve' which can filter out certain misconceptions. For some this will seem like a move from the frying pan into the fire, for if any knowledge is endlessly contested, philosophy is, its questions have a distinctively eternal character. But there are at least some malpractices (such as behaviourism's denial of the meaningful and concept-dependent character of social phenomena), whose persistence, I feel, derives not from the provision of a successful defence but from an ignorance of the arguments against it. This ignorance is partly a function of some prominent features of the sociology of knowledge in philosophy and social science; notably the dogmatic refusal of many Anglo-American philosophers even to acquaint themselves with the Continental traditions of philosophy in which hermeneutics and related schools have developed, and the similar predominance of scientism among social scientists, particularly those who have recently transferred from natural science. Many inter-theory disputes in social science boil down to questions of philosophy and methodology, and while many of these are still highly contested, there are also others where the elements of a consensus have emerged, e.g. the recognition of the theory-laden character of observation. (Remember that given point 2, all that we can expect is that there should be some relatively enduring though not eternal areas of consensus which can provide provisional anchor points for criticism in other areas.)

Existential hypotheses

Moving beyond this philosophical level of criticism, how we assess knowledge-claims depends on their type. One of the most important is 'existential hypotheses' such as 'there is an inter-national division of labour', 'there are class societies', or 'there are particular codes of acceptable behaviour in the company of superiors'. Although many accounts of science ignore such statements, they are an important component of theories, whether formal or informal. Their verification, in some conceptual system,[3] requires the prior establishment of acceptable criteria for recog-nizing the objects in question. It only needs a single instance of the observation of an object of the specified kind to confirm such hypotheses.[4] (Note they do not involve claims about the number of such objects and are not generalizations about regularities in the sense defined in Chapter 3.)[5]

But what about existential hypotheses concerning unobservable objects such as gravitational fields or modes of production? Often, as in the second example, it is not certain that they are unobservable; 'observability' may sometimes be more accurately interpreted as 'familiarity' and initially unobserved objects sometimes come to be observed later. At any rate such claims are not made in isolation, arbitrarily; they are retroduced from our knowledge of more observable or familiar events and objects. For example: 'for it to be possible for profit, rent and interest to exist (all observable) there must be "surplus value"' (unobservable); or 'for it to be possible for children to speak grammatical sentences which they have never heard before they must already possess structures which generate speech'. Obviously the vaguer the definition of the hypothesized entity the less the possibility of either verifying or doubting it. At a minimal level, a certain amount of support may be established on metaphysical grounds. For example, on the basis of the metaphysical assumption that every event has a cause we might accept that an observed change having no observable cause must have an unobservable one. If we went no further than this, we could justifiably be accused of simply invoking convenient hypothetical objects to explain away awkward observations. But existential claims are more specific than this and can draw upon other forms of support. Where existential claims are made about powers and liabilities (e.g. the power to speak), we expect them to be 'grounded', that is, we expect to be told what kind of object could possess such powers and liabilities. The kind of entity involved may be specified by reference to cases or events whose causes and conditions are better known and which are held to be of the same type.[6] Arguments are usually provided to the effect that for the observed effects to be possible, an entity of a particular kind must exist. If other, independent events also point to the existence of the same entity our confidence will be raised. Moreover, once such claims are specified more fully, their objects often become observable.

Not just any kind of entity may be invoked; it must be one whose properties are plausible in the light of our existing knowledge of the world; it must be an object whose existence and characteristics are materially possible, as far as we know. While we can't exclude the possibility that there are entities and mechanisms which are not only unobservable but not remotely like anything we presently know or could conceive of, they cannot be justifiably invoked in explanations. A line has to be drawn somewhere or a 'conservative principle' established, to distinguish the plausible from the idly speculative.[7] If we grant credibility to the latter simply because it hasn't been falsified we run the risk of contradicting and hence prematurely abandoning reliable knowledge; e.g. preferring spiritual healing to modern medical treatment (which is not to suggest that the latter is infallible). To draw the line higher and extend the conservative principle so that all talk of unobservables is banned is also irrational, generating the dogmas that observable events can have only causes which are observable and that the world just happens to be co-extensive with our sensory powers.

Existential claims about observables can be falsified if the space–time location of the entities is specified but found to be occupied by some other object.[8] Where the hypotheses concern unobservables they may be challenged by retroducing more plausible entities capable of producing the observed events, or by showing that the latter can in fact be causally explained by, and not merely derived or deduced from, other observable objects. Whether observable or not, we might also challenge the conceptualization of the hypothesized object (e.g. the debates about the nature of (or the conceptualization of) the state and about modes of production or mental illness).

The assessment of theoretical claims about internal or necessary relations and conditions is more straightforward, provided due care is given to defining exactly which aspects of the objects concerned are necessarily related.[9] That X necessarily presupposes Y can be clearly falsified if X is found or can be produced without Y (and vice versa if the relation is symmetrical). Although verification is less decisive, support for such claims rests upon arguments about the nature or properties of the objects by virtue of which they are believed to be necessarily related. They can be tested in closed or open systems, either by observation or by trying to refute them through practice – by attempting to carry out actions which are hypothesized to be impossible inside or outside the relation in question. Falsifications of this kind are not of purely negative value because they simultaneously turn up new information on the practical possibilities of social action.[10] Precise definition is particularly important where concept-dependent internal relations are concerned, like the marital relation. These may be said to be dependent for their existence on rules, but the definitions and hence the precise forms of the internal relations may change. Assessments of claims about them must therefore take into account their historical specificity if they are to be applicable.

As regards empirical claims about the behaviour or configuration of contingently related phenomena (e.g. certain geographical patterns), it is only worth making strong predictions and taking their falsification seriously if one is dealing with closed systems. If we are confident that the system is closed (having checked the two conditions for closure) and our predictions fail, then this must be taken as a falsification of the instrumentalist laws used to make the predictions or as an indication of an error in the data. Falsifications of predictions of contingencies in open systems whose initial state is incompletely known need not be treated as theoretically significant.

Nevertheless, description and predictions of the state of social systems, including many of their contingencies, are of considerable practical importance to us. The success or failure of our actions depends not only on how well we understand natural and social mechanisms, but on how accurate are our descriptions and predictions of the contexts in which we try to activate these mechanisms to achieve our ends. But while an error concerning contingencies may have serious practical consequences it need not threaten our theoretical claims. For example, an economic policy may fail not because its assumptions (theoretical claims) about the structures and mechanisms of the economy are wrongly specified, but because information about contingent facts such as specific quantities of commodities already in circulation is defective. Likewise failure to realize or predict that the petrol tank is empty has no significance as regards our theoretical understanding of how cars work (provided we know it *ought* not to be empty), though, of course, in practical terms it may be a minor disaster. Since a great deal of social research is concerned not with innovations in abstract theory about necessity in the world but with using existing theory to understand concrete conjunctures of social systems, with all their many contingent relations, it is not surprising that empirical falsifications or critiques of such accounts often have few theoretical consequences. For example, while a critique of an account of a particular episode in history might attack its conceptualization of social structures and mechanisms, there might alternatively be little more to criticize than its judgements about contingent facts. Those who make unfavourable comparisons between the allegedly inconclusive character of the latter critiques in social science and the allegedly decisive character of tests and criticism in natural science often fail to realize that they are quite different kinds of study; social research of this type is concerned primarily with *concrete* accounts of open systems, and ('pure') natural science with abstract claims, usually in closed systems.

Predictive tests

In principle, *predictive tests* seem an attractive proposition because they disallow the luxury of *ex post* rationalization, which may often creep unnoticed into explanations.

Yet attempts to confirm hypotheses by testing predictions derived from them are rare in social science: most predictions that are made of future social events are forgotten. In the few cases where attempts are made to test social theories by reference to predictions, several major problems arise. One is the possibility of self-fulfilling or negating prophecies. Another is known as 'the fallacy of affirming the consequent'. Given a hypothesis of the form 'A, because B', the discovery of instances of A (affirming the consequent) does not in itself prove B was the cause rather than some other, C. The fallacy is common in everyday arguments; for example, it has often been claimed recently that the absence of nuclear war constitutes a 'proof' of the claim that nuclear weapons are a deterrent and have 'kept the peace', but such an argument does not prove the point for other conditions might equally or more plausibly be responsible for the peace.

In social science the situation is often worse because the hypothesis is taken to be confirmed not by the success of its predictions but by the fact that an empirical model embodying the hypothesis has been 'fitted' to the data. As already noted, fitting a model is quite a different matter from testing it, and with enough parameters to be estimated any model can be fitted to a set of data. A successful fit does not necessarily demonstrate a successful causal explanation but rather the contrival of a calculating device, albeit one which will not predict the future development of open systems successfully.

Turning to the use of generalizations and probabilistic hypotheses in predictions, it is well known that these cannot be conclusively verified or falsified by reference to conformable or anomalous instances. Statements of the kind '80 per cent of X's are Y's' or 'the probability of an X being Y is 0.8' can only be verified or falsified in a finite population by exhaustively checking every individual and in an infinite population not at all. Failures of probabilistic predictions based on sample data can always be attributed to the sample. However, even though it is logically permissible to use such a defence it would be considered unreasonable if there were repeated failures.

A popular type of statistical testing takes the form of trying to reject the null hypothesis that there is no significant difference between two sample means. In most applications, the researcher gives a preferred hypothesis for explaining the alleged difference between the sample means. It is hypothesized 1 that there is a significant difference Y and 2 that it is caused by X. But as many statistical methods textbooks rightly point out, rejecting the null hypothesis and hence confirming 1 in no way confirms 2. The belief that it does is another instance of the fallacy of affirming the consequent. To confirm 2 we would have to carry out separate explanatory tests on X, which could show that X, and no other possible known mechanisms, was responsible for Y. So the weakness of this statistical test derives not simply from the fact that it does not prove beyond doubt whether differences in sample means were due to sampling errors, but from the fact that it does not directly test causal hypotheses.

Finally, and contrary to the impression given in much of the orthodox literature, such tests cannot be reduced to the verification or falsification of predictions whose conceptualization is unproblematic. Regardless of whether quantitative errors are found (and in an open system their significance is ambiguous), the concepts implicit in the statistics or model also need to be evaluated.

Causal explanations and explanatory tests

The problems of evaluating causal explanations are not widely understood, partly because of the prevalence of simplistic, regularity theories of causation. As Figure 11 attempts to show, a causal explanation implicitly or explicitly includes several components; it does not merely cite two events, one as cause and the other as effect. We usually have some understanding of the nature of the objects involved (their structure, composition, properties) and can often observe the operation of the mechanism. Claims about powers, liabilities or, more generally, mechanisms possessed by the object X can be checked by our observing, under suitable conditions, how they work and by examining X's structure in order to discover by virtue of what properties these powers exist. For example, we can examine a political structure by virtue of which an occupant of one of its 'niches' can bring about specific

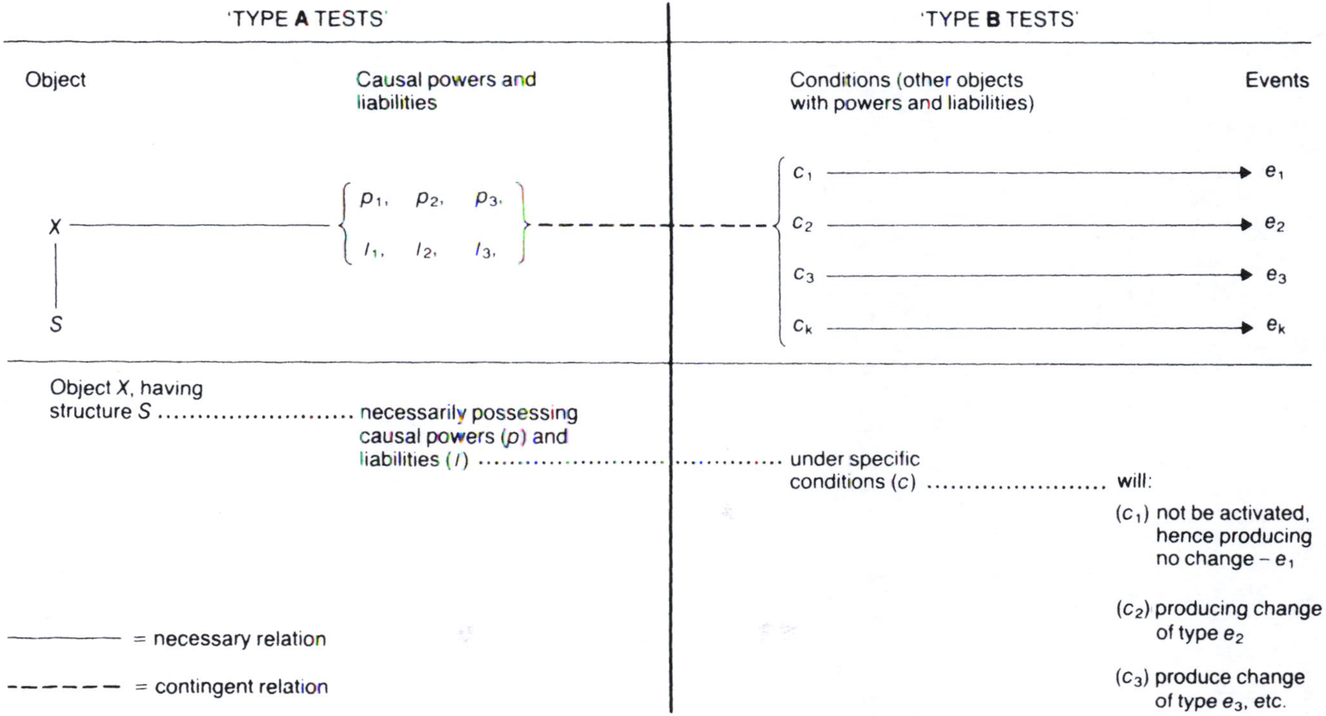

'TYPE A TESTS'   'TYPE B TESTS'

Object	Causal powers and liabilities	Conditions (other objects with powers and liabilities)	Events

$p_1, \quad p_2, \quad p_3,$
$l_1, \quad l_2, \quad l_3.$

$c_1 \longrightarrow e_1$
$c_2 \longrightarrow e_2$
$c_3 \longrightarrow e_3$
$c_k \longrightarrow e_k$

X ——— S

Object X, having
structure S .... necessarily possessing
causal powers (p) and
liabilities (l) .... under specific
conditions (c) .... will:

(c_1) not be activated,
hence producing
no change – e_1

(c_2) producing change
of type e_2

(c_3) produce change
of type e_3, etc.

——————— = necessary relation

– – – – – – = contingent relation

Figure 11 Evaluation or testing of causal hypotheses

changes. Causal explanations may therefore be evaluated in zone A of the diagram. The objects and properties under this heading are not always unobservable or otherwise inaccessible and their identification may be no more problematic than that of events in zone B; indeed, events are often more complex and concrete and may need to be analysed by abstraction before they can even be adequately described. Moreover, explanatory evaluation is often easier in social than natural science because we have 'internal access' through practice to many of the structures and mechanisms, and reasons and beliefs similar to our own may function as causes. Transitive verb causal explanations (see Chapter 3) are particularly open to check. Much more difficult are causal explanations in which it is claimed that reasons function as causes, for sometimes, particularly in historical studies, we lack even the suspect evidence of actors' accounts.

Now the range of conditions c in which X is located may be enormous, but given information on their location and nature, we may be able to predict what kind of events e will be produced. But particularly in the case of complex, open social systems we know little in advance about such conditions and so are unable to make a firm prediction. If they are made, success or failure does not count seriously either in favour or against the causal hypothesis precisely because c are not known. Those who try to use purely predictive tests of causal hypotheses in open systems (relying solely on the occurrence or non-occurrence of events in zone B) are liable to be guilty of 'naïve falsification', in which an anomaly due to interference from some other mechanisms is treated as a falsification of the causal claim in question, e.g. 'aeroplanes are heavier than air but can fly, therefore the law of gravity is refuted'. Alternatively, as we have seen, if a verification is claimed purely on the basis of predictive success in zone B, i.e. 'the predicted event occurred, therefore our hypothesis about its cause, X, must be true', they fall foul of the fallacy of affirming the consequent once again, for it has not been shown that X, rather than any other mechanism, was the cause. In any case, strictly speaking, predictive success in the evaluation of causal hypothesis does not test the claim about the nature of the mechanism or powers and liabilities but rather a hypothesis about some of their effects.

I want to argue that causal claims can be subject to type A evaluation of their *explanatory* rather than predictive adequacy and without any fallacy of affirming the consequent. Although we often cannot predict when an event will happen, e.g. when the fish will be hooked, or when the value of the £ will rise, we can explain how it happens when it does, by closely examining the nature of the objects possessing the relevant powers and liabilities and the mechanisms by which they work, when they work. In the case of the value of the £, we could find out the reasons why currency speculators and others bought sterling. Some of the reasons they give may be based on faulty judgements, but they may still be causes even if false. We would also have to examine the social, institutional and ideological structure and contexts by virtue of which such reasons and powers are held. In other words, the verification of an explanation does not rest simply on the occurrence of certain events in zone B (the consequent), indeed under some conditions X may even fail to produce such events. Rather, the verification rests upon the identification and 'unpacking' of X (the antecedent) and its mechanism(s), that is, on evidence at least partly independent of the occurrence of past events.

The possibility of type A descriptive and explanatory evaluation is underestimated in philosophies of science which subscribe to the view that explanations must be deductive and/or that theories need only be calculating or predictive devices, for it then appears that theories only make statements about the world in their outputs – their predictions, while the rest of their content merely serves as a means to this end and not as something to be tested in its own right.[11] This view is common in the way mathematical models are used in social science, although it need not necessarily be so. The idea that evaluation of zone A might not easily be separated from the formation of its explanatory and descriptive content need not be interpreted as a problem. Evaluation doesn't have to be postponed until we feel ready to make predictive claims regarding zone B on the basis of a provisional acceptance of the content of zone A. Even the process of observation and initial conceptualization might reasonably be said to involve an inbuilt (though, of course, fallible) evaluation procedure, if it is understood on the twenty questions model put forward in Chapter 2. Many would dismiss such tests as feeble in comparison with the allegedly strong tests of predictive performance. However, we have already shown that confidence in the latter is inappropriate, particularly in social science, and it therefore seems unwise to dismiss other options.

In practice many social scientists treat causal hypotheses as claims about regularities among contingently related events. When confronted with open systems but lacking an understanding of their consequences, they then have to qualify the causal claim with numerous *ceteris paribus* ('other things being equal') assumptions. But causal claims are not about regularities but about the production, and prevention, of change. When I push the door but fail to open it, it doesn't mean that I wasn't pushing. No *ceteris paribus* qualifications are needed – if I'm pushing the door, I am doing so *regardless* of whether it is locked, unlocked, barricaded or really a sliding door. While it might make it easier to detect whether I was pushing if the door is unlocked, there are other means of checking. *Ceteris paribus* assumptions are only needed for making predictions of what effect the activation of some mechanism might have; they are not needed for explaining what has already happened or what kinds of mechanism exist.[12]

If we try to evaluate theories by testing their predictions in open systems it is always unclear whether anomalous events indicate non-realization of *ceteris paribus* assumptions or falsifications. This invites the dubious but not uncommon strategy of appealing to the former possibility to protect one's favoured theory from falsification while criticizing the use of the same strategy by opponents as an evasion of falsification. If we rely purely on predictive tests then the problem of avoiding naïve falsification without rendering falsification impossible is a serious one, but there are other ways of assessing theories.

Consider the case of Christaller, an economist who in 1933 proposed an elegant theory explaining and predicting the size, distribution and spacing of settlements.[13] The location of places at which goods are sold was hypothesized to be governed by the sellers' attempts to maximize sales, assuming that buyers minimize the distance travelled to shop. Assuming a fairly evenly distributed population, Christaller derived a general competitive equilibrium solution in which sellers of similar goods were spaced at regular intervals on a triangular grid. By taking into account the different sizes of catchment areas for the sale of different goods he also derived and located a hierarchy of settlements of different sizes. He then tried to apply the model to southern Germany, and as might be expected found many differences between observed and predicted locations. But he warned his readers that such anomalies did not constitute a falsification of his theory, merely an indication of the extent to which *ceteris* were not *paribus*.[14] Now while this might be true (towns can hardly be located on mountain tops or where other extraneous factors override economic forces), such an argument could clearly provide a spurious protective belt for any theory, no matter how outrageous. Despite this possibility and the poor predictive performance of 'improved versions' of the model in other applications, it is still widely accepted as a partial *explanation* in terms of its plausibility as an account of how competitive pressures in space influence location decisions. In evaluating this 'plausibility', researchers had the advantage – not available to natural scientists – of 'internal access' to mechanisms of market behaviour. In so doing they were not affirming the consequent but examining independent evidence for the explanatory hypotheses. Others interpreted the model in a 'praxiological' way as a representation of what a *rational* settlement pattern would look like under certain behavioural and contextual assumptions, and on these grounds found it substantially reasonable. In so far as some aspects of the theory have been criticized and perhaps falsified, it is again in terms of its *explanatory* adequacy (e.g. its failure to specify the kind of socio-economic structure which could give rise to such market behaviour). *Superficially*, when compared with the simple models of verification or falsification popularized by some philosophers of science, the situation might seem to typify social science's alleged immaturity in failing to produce testable theory or to accept the results of tests when they are carried out, with the consequence that no clear progress is made. But rational assessments were made in the best way possible given the non-availability of real closed systems, and progress was achieved in the understanding of mechanisms if not in the prediction of their actual spatial effects.

When considered in the abstract rather than in terms of actual examples, the discussion so far may disturb some readers who may smell a rat in the shape of possible tautologous arguments and spurious, unfalsifiable hypotheses. Can we really justifiably claim that the use of existential hypotheses about unobservables is any better or more testable than claims about occult forces? Can claims about mechanisms ever be tested properly if failure of the expected effects can be explained by appealing to countervailing forces? Consider the following expression of these doubts by Saunders,

Such reasoning produces no more than self-confirming tautologies (e.g. if profit rates are falling, this is due to the inherent tendency for the rate of profit to fall, and if they are not, this is due to the effect of counteracting tendencies). One is reminded of the story of the man on a train journey through the Home Counties who scattered mustard seed from the window in order to keep the elephants away. When told there were no wild elephants in Surrey he replied that this only served to demonstrate the efficacy of mustard seed as an elephant deterrent.[15]

The argument is superficially appealing, but on closer inspection turns out to rest on several errors. The first is the assertion that appealing to countervailing forces necessarily produces 'self-confirming tautologies' and spurious justifications. Consider again our mundane example of this structure of explanation: 'I would have managed to push the door open had it not been locked.' Of course, it's possible that I could use such arguments spuriously (intentionally or innocently); I might just pretend or delude myself that I am pushing the door and try to evade the falsification of the causal claim by appealing to countervailing forces. But the possibility of a foolish use of a concept doesn't disqualify its responsible use and it is not difficult to think of *independent* ways of checking the operation of both the postulated force (pushing the door) and the postulated countervailing force (the engagement of the lock). So such explanations need not reduce to 'self-confirming tautologies'.

But what about social science examples? Consider the following statements, all of which concern a tendency (B) which is overridden by a countervailing tendency (A).

1 (A) 'Had the women not been socialized into a passive role (B) they would not have accepted such boring work.'
2 (B) 'Wages would have fallen (A) had it not been for the defensive power of the unions.'
3 (B) 'The agrarian reform would have been completed (A) but for the military coup.'

How would we test or evaluate such claims? If we took the outcome as proof of the operation of the countervailing force then the justification would certainly become tautological and involve 'affirming the consequent': e.g. 'that the women accepted boring work "proves" that they have been socialized into a passive role'. But there is another strategy, and that is to seek *independent* evidence which 'grounds' the alleged countervailing force, e.g. evidence of the nature of women's socialization; in other words such claims should be evaluated in zone A rather than zone B. While this is often difficult it is rarely impossible. One reason for the difficulty is the possibility of the presence of other, unrecognized causes of the change. All we can reasonably ask is that the possible alternative causes are checked and eliminated, again by looking at the evidence in zone A. (We can hardly expect unknown causes to be assessed!) For example, in the case of 1, managers often argue that women are *naturally* better able than men to put up with boring work and try to justify their belief by saying that the fact that women do boring work proves the point. This, of course, will not do, for it involves a tautology and affirms the consequent. But the claim could be evaluated (and eliminated!) in a non-tautological fashion by asking in virtue of what physical attributes women might have an aptitude for boring work.

What about the specific examples of spurious explanation and testing cited by Saunders? The first is the marxist theory of the tendency of the rate of profit to fall (readers who are not familiar with this may want to skip this paragraph). In fact Saunders offers a caricature of the theory and misrepresents its explanatory structure. Actually, claims for the existence of both the tendency and the countervailing forces are grounded in changes which might be identified independently of the movements of the rate of profit that they are supposed to explain, i.e. without affirming the consequent or constructing a tautology. For example, one of the countervailing forces tending to raise the rate of profit is the possibility of an expansion of the supply of labour which drives down wages and hence lowers costs. Again this explanation can be evaluated non-tautologically. The claim that there is also a different tendency pulling the rate of profit down is more difficult to assess in practice because it is based on an argument about movements of a ratio ('the organic composition of capital') which is virtually impossible to measure. More generally there are major problems in assessing the relative 'weight' of the various tendencies and countertendencies in a specific conjuncture, even if one accepts the possibility of each one. However, these difficulties are not ones of 'self-confirming tautologies'. (Actually I think the theory has other failings, but they are not those suggested by Saunders, nor do they bear upon the topic of verification.)

The second example of the mustard seed spreader serves to suggest that appeals to tendencies or countertendencies are no better than the invocation of purely fanciful and unverifiable forces. But look again at examples 1 to 3: there is nothing fanciful or occult about the causes they invoke. All of them are typical of explanations in social science; indeed it would be difficult to imagine any social research or theoretical disputes in social science which did *not* involve the assumption that some forces may be modified, overridden or blocked by others or which did not assume the existence of unobservables. Provided we remember the possibility of zone A evaluations, it is not difficult to distinguish between serious and fanciful explanations. On the criterion that I have proposed we would have no difficulty in falsifying the claims of the mustard seed spreader, e.g. demanding proof that elephants have not always been absent; if it were proved that they were once present, we would try to eliminate other possible causes of their departure by conducting an experiment on actual elephants. If in turn this proved successful, we would still demand an account of the mechanism and additional evidence of its powers. (The bizarre nature of this response reflects the triviality of the example!) It is precisely those philosophies which 1 make light of existential hypotheses, 2 reduce the role of theory to a heuristic device for deriving statements about observables and 3 suppose that the only things that can be tested at all are predictions about observable events, which offer least resistance to crank explanations that pay no regard to (existing knowledge of) material possibilities.[16]

Interpretations – beyond evaluation?

The greatest degree of pessimism about the possibility of evaluating competing accounts in social science concerns interpretive understanding. How can we decide whether a conservative historian's interpretation of, say, a political movement is better or worse than a socialist historian's? How can we decide what is the real meaning of an ideology? Often such decisions are described as 'subjective', in contrast with the 'objective' decisions allegedly possible in natural science; we either accept the interpretations or we don't. But as was shown earlier, the dualism of subjective and objective is itself highly suspect. We have already seen that the conclusiveness of tests in natural science is frequently exaggerated.

I shall now argue that while there are good reasons why interpretive understanding should be especially contestable, the 'softness' and inconclusiveness of its evaluation can also be exaggerated.

To the extent that conceptual and concept-dependent objects of the social sciences differ from those of natural science we shouldn't be surprised that their cognitive possibilities differ. We can understand and 'use' meanings but we can't pick them up, prod them or measure them.[17] Deciding how to interpret, say, 'patriotism', is simply not like measuring the boiling point of water. We evaluate interpretive understanding not by first setting up hypotheses or predictions and then testing them. Rather the process of interpretation itself embodies a continual monitoring and revision as we read one part of the 'text' in relation to others. Whereas natural scientists operate within a single hermeneutic circle in which the only meanings they have to interpret are those of their own scientific community, social scientists have to mediate between their own frame of meaning and those of actors. This can pose major problems of translation and judgement, especially in history and anthropology where the frames of meaning are likely to be far apart and possibly associated with different concepts of rationality. Nevertheless it must be remembered that hermeneutic problems are not insuperable but rather something we cope with continually in everyday life.[18]

Let us take the relativist reaction to the apparent indeterminacy of interpretation first: all interpretations are interesting and equally valid so we should let a hundred flowers bloom. A more sophisticated variant argues that conceptual objects like texts or ideologies just *are* ambiguous and we should welcome rather than resist this quality.

Who could be against letting flowers bloom? Answer: those who know better than to be cowed by a picturesque but tendentious analogy. Let us be clear what it implies: that the novice's interpretation is just as good as the scholar's; that a racist interpretation of *apartheid* is just as good as a liberal one. On several counts the position is dubious. First it tends to be disingenuous, for its proclaimed liberalism serves to protect the status quo from criticism. Secondly it fails to make sense of the fact that we are rarely indifferent to interpretations and argue a great deal about them. The contestation of meaning in everyday life that we commented on in Chapters 1 and 2 points not only to the fact that it *is* contestable but to the fact that it matters that not

just any interpretation is acceptable. Dissensus over interpretations signifies not that we are indifferent to them but that they
matter.

The exaggerated view of the undecidability of interpretation
stems from an unaware abstraction of meanings from their practical
context, from their referents and users. The meanings that actors
use and understand are embedded in practices and social relations.
They can establish descriptions and evaluations of people and their
circumstances, they can influence our identities and what we can
do in society. And of course they can conceal or misrepresent
too. For these reasons I am not indifferent to being described,
say, as 'a burden on the tax-payer'. Not just any interpretation is
acceptable. Only if such an interpretation influenced no one and
made no difference to their behaviour toward me might I feel
indifferent about it. And it is partly in relation to such descriptions
and practical implications that we evaluate interpretations.

This is not to argue that our interpretations of meaning and society should suppress ambiguity and multiple meanings. If concepts
and situations in society are ambiguous and contestable for us as
researchers, they are likely to be so for actors too. The meaning
of an army parade on Remembrance Day is a deeply ambiguous
event, combining both a recognition of the horrors of war ('Never
again. . .') and a celebration and glorification of the army and perhaps war itself. But to interpret an event as ambiguous or as having
multiple meanings is not to admit just any interpretation for not all
interpretations would recognize the ambiguity. Ironically, if we are
to do justice to ambiguity we cannot interpret it in just any way.

A more convincing angle on the multiplicity of interpretations
has been put forward by Clifford Geertz, who argues that in his
discipline of interpretive anthropology, 'progress is marked less
by a perfection of consensus than by a refinement of debate.
What gets better is the precision with which we vex each other.'[19]
This seems an eloquent and reassuring defence against the familiar
criticisms of the social sciences' 'interminable debates' so often
voiced by those who suppose that they should be more like the
natural sciences. And Geertz's defence has the virtue of resisting
the inference that dissensus implies absence of progress. But I
think we can get a little further still beyond the relativism of the
hundred flowers.

The objects of our interpretations – motives, beliefs, actors'
accounts, constitutive meanings and the like – have a double

determination, not only from their holders' objective material situations but from the conceptual tools available to them in their culture which provide them with ways of interpreting their situations. The student of society must try to comprehend both aspects, often using conceptual tools which are more examined and have developed in very different contexts. In so far as meanings vary across space and time we cannot simply check our interpretations by replicating investigations, as we might an experiment in natural science.

The evaluation of interpretations involves the cross-checking of one concept's sense and reference by another's, in a kind of 'triangulation' process in search of inconsistencies, mis-specifications and omissions.[20] The meaning of each part is continually re-examined in relation to the meaning of the whole and vice versa. Decisions about interpretations are made in the light of knowledge of the material circumstances, social relations, identities and beliefs and feelings to which the contested ideas relate. In so far as reasons and beliefs can be causes of social events, the evaluation of interpretive understanding is not so different from that of causal explanations as is often supposed.

Another strategy, advocated by some anthropolgists, is for researchers to make available to their readers as much of the primary material as possible (transcripts of conversations, interviews, etc.) so that readers do not have to rely wholly on the researchers' glosses and can judge for themselves.[21] This has the virtue of placing some limits – only some – on the usual tendency of researchers to select, filter and mould their primary material and makes their interpretations easier to evaluate. Neither the actors, nor the researchers, nor the readers have any ultimate authority in interpretation; any one of them may be mistaken. The mode of presentation of primary material is not itself neutral and is liable to conceal certain nuances. The researcher may still have the relative – not absolute – advantage of having 'been there' and the reader still needs to consider the researcher's interpretations, but the strategy opens up the conversation a little and makes the researcher's inferences a little more transparent.

A more direct way of assessing researchers' interpretations is of course to ask the actors themselves what they think of them. This need not mean that the actors' views are given any ultimate authority. Academic accounts can refer to unacknowledged conditions and consequences, they must necessarily re-present practical consciousness in the form of a discourse about it, and they can even refer to subliminal meanings. For these reasons an academic account can differ from an actor's account. Sometimes they can contradict one another too. This is an inevitable consequence of the fact that actors' understandings face academic understandings both as object and rival. As we cannot avoid evaluating such accounts (this being necessary for finding the best explanation) we often become embroiled in arguments about rationality and values. And as we saw in Chapter 1 it becomes possible to say without absurdity that it is society, in particular its actors' understanding and practices, that is wrong, not our accounts of them. Natural science's objects do not have any such qualities to evaluate and it is only the observer's knowledge that has to be evaluated, not the object itself. In social science, both the observer's knowledge and the observed's knowledge are under scrutiny. In such circumstances there are no *a priori* grounds according to which we can grant authority to the actor *or* the academic.

To acknowledge this critical relationship between interpretations is not to give a licence to academics to ignore actors' own accounts, or to treat the above reasons for differences between the two accounts as justifications for such a strategy. Interpretations of the significance of 1968 are a good example of academics confusing their own reflection with their object of interpretation. Possibly the significance of the personal experience of academics and people of similar social positions (e.g. media personnel) is greater than their tiny numbers indicate, but so often their accounts fail to note that for most people it was a rather ordinary year in which the celebrated events (celebrated by whom?) were only distinctly and dimly perceived.

Academics therefore need to decide whom the interpretations they provide are of and for. If they are meant to be interpretations of actors' own understandings then that has different implications from developing interpretations purely for the edification of academics themselves, where the resulting accounts are often more a function of the academics' own social position and of academic competition than of their ostensible objects. Of course lay understandings have to be interpreted via the researcher's frame of meaning, but we can recognize that there is an interaction here without supposing that the former can be collapsed into the latter so that the lay criticism of academic accounts can always be dismissed. This is not to say that researchers should never develop their interpretations for their own edification, provided they don't try to pass this off as the same as attempting to represent what things meant to actors. Realism can accept the sense in which interpretive understanding can be very personal, but it does warn of the need to specify the co-ordinates of the author's personal position: if we are to assess interpretations we need to know by whom, for whom and of whom they are made.

Conclusions

To conclude: once again I must stress that the above prescriptions are *formalizations* and *reconstructions* of what I believe to be legitimate methods of evaluation. I think many social scientists already use them extensively, but unfortunately many have been influenced by restrictive accounts of evaluation which suggest that instead they should put greater faith in tests of predictions. If the result were merely that researchers denied in their methodological pronouncements what they practised in their substantive research little harm would be done, but regrettably some of them have taken the advice seriously. By comparison with the situation in natural science, the implications of the character of the relationship between subject and object in social science may induce gloom and despondency in some about the possibility of making conclusive evaluations. Conversely, nothing is to be gained by pretending the interaction does not exist and proceeding as if research were no different from that in natural science, indeed such a strategy is only likely to make things worse. However, in the latter part of Chapter 9 I shall try to show that if we re-examine the *aims* of social science, some of the problems can be turned into solutions.

8   Popper's 'falsificationism'

The best-known ideas on testing in social science derive from the work of Popper on 'falsificationism'. His theory is attractively simple but paradoxical and comes in strong and dilute versions which allow a variety of interpretations.[1] It also glamourizes science by replacing the dull image of scientific progress as a steady accretion of knowledge by means of induction with a portrayal of science as a daring process of setting up and trying to falsify bold conjectures. These characteristics have made it popular despite the fact that it is virtually impossible to put into practice. Like Chapter 5, where some of Popper's ideas were introduced, the following discussion is intended for readers already familiar with some of the debates in the philosophy of science; other readers may wish to proceed directly to Chapter 9.[2]

At the root of Popper's falsificationism is his denial of natural necessity. All relations between things or events are contingent and consequently the big problem of induction (that the world may change) arises at every instant. This is repeatedly conflated with the little problem of induction. Induction is rightly ruled out as a rational mode of inference, but in its place Popper puts not retroduction, which presupposes natural necessity, but deduction. Theories should have a deductive form and produce testable predictions. Deductive theories cannot be said to be confirmed by successful predictions because, as was seen in Chapter 5, any number of hypotheses could be used in the premises of a valid deductive argument and generate successful predictions. There is no equivalent to type A tests because, in ignoring the content of theories at the expense of their logical form, Popper overlooks the ways in which theories relate to their objects other than via predictions of events, such as through existential hypotheses.

Now the most distinctive part of Popper's argument is the claim that while (deductive) theories cannot be confirmed, they can nevertheless be clearly falsified by predictive failure; if the predictions follow validly from the premises and yet are falsified, then there *must* be an error in the premises.[3] Hence the asymmetry noted in Chapter 5 between confirmation or corroboration and falsification. Paradoxically we can apparently only be certain about a theory when it is shown to be wrong.[4]

In order to conform to this deductive structure and thereby expose theories to the risk of falsification, scientists are urged to make bold conjectures about universal regularities; e.g. not 'most X are Y', but 'all X are Y'. Although the latter statement could be described as universal and deterministic, it is, according to Popper, nevertheless about contingently related phenomena. This metaphysical assumption generates vicious paradoxes for Popper. Why should anyone *want* to make a universal deterministic claim about contingencies? If there is no necessity in the world, why should the falsification of a universal statement about events (which as Popper advises should forbid as many outcomes as possible)[5] be of any interest?

Now at least because of the little problem of induction (that all our knowledge is in principle fallible), no successful theory could be proved correct beyond revision, but then neither could any falsifying statements, and effectively Popper acknowledges this. But if, in addition to this, decisive confirmation cannot also be achieved because of the big problem of induction, then as we saw in Chapter 5 neither can falsification. If there is no necessity in the world then what is falsified today could be verified tomorrow and vice versa. It is only if we can justifiably make claims about necessity in the world that falsification can be decisive, although they will still be subject to the little problem of induction, like any other knowledge of the world. Moreover, it is only if there is any necessity in the world that it is worth making bold conjectures about relations.

If there are, as I have suggested, both necessary and contingent relations in the world then the necessary ways of acting of objects will only give rise to regularities in patterns of events if there is a closed system. The existence of a manipulable real closed system is therefore extremely helpful for minimizing interpretive disputes over alleged falsifications of claims about these ways of acting.

According to Popper, even our most successful theories cannot be said to be confirmed or verified, only corroborated or as yet unfalsified. In pure inductive inference, each successful prediction of an event fails to strengthen our theory because there are no logical grounds for inferring that success will continue. This is correct except that as we have seen we are unlikely to rely on pure induction, i.e. on the inference that simply because a particular sequence of events has always been known to occur it will continue to do so. If, however, we take into account existential claims and type A tests then while these are, like any other statements, vulnerable to the little problem of induction, it is absurd to say that an existential hypothesis which has proved successful on one or more occasion is no better than one which has never proved successful. Our intuitive idea that there can be degrees of confirmation or corroboration is therefore quite reasonable. It is only if we have to rely on pure induction from observation of events or on deduction from non-causal premises (because we lack knowledge of the natures and causal powers of objects) that success can be said *not* to warrant increased confidence in our theories.

Popper offers a heroic picture of progress in science in which bold theories are conjectured – the more vulnerable to possible falsification the better – and then attempts are made to prove them false. When this happens, the originators of the theory should not respond by trying to protect their theory by making *ad hoc* adjustments but should welcome it as evidence of progress. Although Popper moderated and qualified this argument by allowing that at least some adjustments might legitimately be made and accepting that it is irrational to abandon even a falsified theory until a better one has been found,[6] it is for several reasons still unsatisfactory.

First, theories are often (quite reasonably) not deductive in structure and falsification of at least some of their claims need not lead to the overthrow of the entire theory. And it seems bizarre to assume that adjustments in response to falsifications must necessarily 'weaken' theories. Adjustments of this sort are most likely to have an *ad hoc* character if the theory is weakly developed in zone A (i.e. if it tends towards an instrumentalist theory). If this is the case, the theorist will lack conceptual constraints on what changes can be made. Instead of restricting changes to those which are intelligible in terms of existing (unfalsified) knowledge of the nature of the objects concerned, he or she will be tempted to change anything provided it removes the anomaly – which is precisely the practice which characterizes instrumentalist social science, particularly mathematical modelling. In other words, *Popper's view of theory and science encourages the very danger he warns us against.*

Second, Popper's lack of consideration of the conceptual content of theories and of meaning change also narrows his perception of the process by which theories are evaluated. Conceptual modifications can be made with or without prompting from empirical falsifications of predictions. (They may be prompted by arguments to the effect that the right answers have been produced for the wrong reasons.) Such modifications do not arise merely from rearranging the logical relations between statements whose meaning is fixed but from changes in the conceptual and pictorial content of the theory and this content must itself be evaluated. In Chapter 5, examples of valid but absurd deductive arguments were given. It is not logical changes which eliminate such absurdities, and falsifications of predictions do not directly expose them. Rather, once again, it is precisely the 'pre-test' conceptual scrutiny that Popper dismisses as outside the 'logic of science' which most directly produces progress on this front.

Third, adjustments to theories in response to falsifications need not necessarily be interpreted uncharitably as evasions but are often *acknowledgements* of refutations. Consider the famous example of Marx's 'immiseration thesis'. This has been interpreted in several ways and it is not clear which of these Marx intended. But that is not important. What does matter is the adequacy of the various interpretations, regardless of their pedigree. If the simple interpretation (namely that the working class is progressively impoverished as capitalism develops) is recognized as false, as it surely must be, and then another interpretation of this thesis is proposed in its place, this should not be taken as an evasion of the first version's falsification but as its acceptance. The second version must then be considered in its own right.

Sometimes, of course, as we have seen, a claim about a process is defended against alleged falsifying instances by appealing to countervailing forces or conditions. In this case, it has often been argued that large sections of the working class of the developed countries would have been 'immiserated' were it not for the immiseration produced by imperialism in the Third World which enabled a rise in real incomes in the former countries as they substituted imports from cheap-labour countries for expensive domestically produced goods. Purely on the basis of philosophical arguments this structure of explanation cannot be ruled out as unfalsifiable and hence illegitimate. Whether it is depends on the kind of *explanatory* evidence available for both the immiseration mechanism and the countervailing forces.[7] Much would depend on whether the immiseration thesis purported to refer to something inherent in the nature of capitalism regardless of its articulations with pre-capitalist modes of production or whether it was a prediction of a state of affairs which was held to be determined by a contingent factor. This is not to underestimate the difficulty of ever deciding what would have happened in history if such-and-such had been different, but non-realists frequently overestimate it by ignoring our knowledge of necessity in the world. That X would have happened need not simply be an inductive inference from cases where it has recurred, it may be knowable (fallibly, as always) from a theory of the nature of some mechanism.

Fourth, Popper's argument in favour of theories which 'stick their necks out' also needs qualification. ('Every good scientific theory is a prohibition: it forbids certain things to happen. The more a theory forbids the better it is.')[8] Now it should be no surprise that theories about open systems forbid less than those concerning systems which are closed or can be closed, and likewise statements about contingencies quite reasonably forbid less than ones about necessity. According to Popper, theories which say 'either X or Y can happen' rather than 'X but not Y will happen' are uninformative. But consider the claim that 'investment either increases or decreases employment'. If this is correct and we formerly imagined that it could only raise employment then it certainly would be useful. But, of course, it would be even more informative if it specified under what conditions either result would occur. The general point to be made here is that methodological prescriptions should not ignore ontology. What theories should prohibit depends on the structure of the world.

Finally, let us consider the prominence given to falsification in Popper's account of scientific change. In its dilute version, it is the simple idea that 'we can learn from our mistakes'.[9] As we have seen the assessment of theory is largely restricted to tests of predicted events, or type B tests in our terminology. If this is so, *what* do we learn when a deductive theory is legitimately falsified (i.e. not naïvely falsified in the sense defined earlier)? Only that we must try a different deductive theory. As deductivism ignores the content of theory and hence cannot distinguish causal explanation from instrumentalist 'derivation', then by default, the content of zone A can only be evaluated indirectly through tests in zone B – and then only when a falsifying instance is discovered! Only then, apparently, do we know something is wrong, but *only* that *something* is wrong and not *what* is wrong. This *constraint* upon learning from experience is all the more serious where, as in social science, type B predictive tests are rarely possible anyway.

This last point implies that far from encouraging social scientists to expose their theories to criticism, falsificationism supplies them with an ideology that this is what they are doing while in fact they are doing the opposite. Type A criticism can be refused on the grounds that it concerns the 'psychology' and not the logic of science, that only type B falsifications of predictions can conclusively settle matters and that assumptions don't have to be realistic. But since it is extremely difficult to produce unambiguous falsifications for predictions about social systems, the claim that they have a superior method of evaluating theory is empty and serves to protect their theories from tests. For example, Blaug[10] and Giedymin dismiss criticisms of the abstractions and explanations of neoclassical economics made on type A grounds, in this way (also by appealing to the argument that assumptions need not be realistic).[11] Blaug's adoption of this tactic is all the more strange as he endorses many of the criticisms that have been made of the unfalsifiability of certain economic theories. Others who have taken this more seriously but who have lacked any alternative to Popperian criteria have not surprisingly lost faith in the possibility of solving theoretical conflicts and despairingly conclude 'it all depends on your theory/paradigm'. Bhaskar's comment on this post-Popperian situation is apt:

the very absence of decisive test situations, coupled with continuing formal allegiance to a *predictive* criterion, serves at once to mystify methodology, protect entrenched (or otherwise privileged) theory, stunt alternatives and/or encourage (a belief in) the unresolvability of theoretical conflicts which, in practice, of course means their resolution in favour of the status quo.[12]

9 Problems of explanation and the aims of social science

'What is a good explanation?' is one of the most common questions that social scientists ask methodologists. It is also one of the most exasperating because little can be said in reply without knowing what kind of object the questioner has in mind and what he or she wants to explain about it. However, some philosophers have tried to give a general answer by arguing that the diversity of types of explanation is only apparent and can be reduced to one or two basic logical forms, such as the 'deductive–nomological model' discussed in Chapter 5. They have also provided as exemplars explanations of simple events: 'why the column of mercury rose'; 'why the radiator exploded', and so on. As I argued in Chapter 5, these models are seriously deficient, even as reconstructions of explanations of simple events. Not surprisingly, the exemplars have not been found very useful by social scientists interested in explaining phenomena as complex as the causes of the First World War, women's subordination or language acquisition in young children.

In this chapter I shall examine some of the problems of 'explanation' in social science in a way which attempts to do justice to the specific nature and complexity of its objects of study. In particular, I shall try to show why characteristically explanations are relatively incomplete, approximate and contestable. I take the difficulties to arise from an interplay between the nature of the object of study, on the one hand, and our aims, expectations and methods on the other. While some of the problems might be said to be self-imposed through the use of inappropriate methods, what is or isn't appropriate can only be decided by reference to judgements about the nature of the thing to be explained. In part, the issue can be clarified by reference to our earlier distinctions between abstract and concrete analysis and generalization, but it also helps to look at the problem in terms of alternative research designs.

Now, in most discussions of method, the basic aims of social science are taken for granted as the development of a 'scientific' objective, propositional knowledge which provides a coherent description and explanation of the way the social world is. I shall call this the *orthodox conception of the aims of science*. But if we pursue the question of difficulty far enough, there comes a point where we have to reassess these aims and ask whether they generate unreasonable or contradictory expectations. I shall call the alternative the *critical theory conception*. When we throw open the whole question of what social science and related kinds of knowledge are *for*, the difficulties become more comprehensible. What is more, some of our judgements about what are problems and what are solutions have to be reversed.

Before beginning, a few words are needed on the question of difficulty, because there is a widespread reluctance among philosophers to accept this as a legitimate concern. It is often dismissed by saying that all science is difficult and that it is characterized by its method and not its object. But if the lack of 'success' in social compared with natural science has nothing to do with its object then one has to resort to blaming it on the incompetence of social scientists and their failure to use proper scientific methods, or on its allegedly shorter history. None of these possibilities can be given much credence. While differences in 'success' may be partly due to uneven use of appropriate methods it is simply dogmatic to refuse even to consider the quite reasonable possibility that the differences in the object of study might have something to do with it. And if my arguments so far have been fair, it is unreasonable to suppose that a single criterion of 'success' can be applied to every type of study; indeed it may be as absurd as trying to evaluate football by the rules of cricket. Certainly any kind of research faces difficulties, but I want to consider some of those specific to social science. And given the importance it attaches to the question of what exists, and the cognitive possibilities of objects, realism is particularly well equipped for this task.

Explanation and the question of difficulty: I orthodox conception

Following Putnam we can distinguish between open system studies like meteorology whose objects are a 'mess' in that they lack structure and those, like the social sciences, whose objects are a 'structured mess'.[1] The former are inherently simpler and in the case of meteorology their understanding can be assisted by relevant knowledge produced by other natural sciences which have access to closed systems. Better-known sources of difficulty are the unavailability of experimental methods and the internality of social science to its object which makes the latter susceptible to change by the former. Some natural scientists have argued that the same difficulty exists in quantum mechanics where the investigation has an unavoidable effect upon the object of study, but since the interaction is not a meaningful one the comparison hardly stands.

This latter difficulty in turn derives from the fact that people are self-interpreting beings who can learn from and change their interpretations so that they can act and respond in novel ways, thereby producing novel stimuli for subsequent actions. In other words, their causal powers and liabilities are considerably more diverse and changeable (even volatile) than those of non-human objects. While they are influenced by material circumstances, their actions do not stand in fixed relations to them, precisely because they are mediated by the ways of seeing available to them, and these can vary enormously. The development of knowledge itself can therefore change its own object in social science. On the other hand, being the subject as well as the object of this problematic relationship, we do at least have the advantage of an internal access to it, albeit a fallible one, of course. In addition, our nature as self-interpreting beings also makes human action particularly context-dependent or 'polyvalent' though not in fixed ways and ensures that complex social behaviour is rarely reducible to a combination of simple behaviours which are invariant across contexts. *Any* explanation, be it of natural or social phenomena, is incomplete for the epistemological reason that all knowledge is revisable, but explanations of social phenomena are also incomplete for the ontological reasons given above that the objects of study are undergoing continuous historical, and not merely evolutionary, change.

'Explanation' is an elastic term covering a wide variety of cases and we must try to come to terms with the range.[2] The danger of producing very formalized and restrictive reconstructions of explanation is that it allows us to overlook the simple point that in our attempts to explain we draw upon everything we know. At the other extreme, it is pointless merely to list everything that passes as an explanation in everyday life without critical comment, for in that case methodology is redundant. Furthermore, although it is easily forgotten in philosophical discussions, requests for explanations and their answers never exist in a vacuum; they are demanded by people with particular levels of pre-understanding and interests. Answers to my requests for explanations of why the bus was late and of the causes of the Iranian revolution will differ in complexity, not just because the latter event is more complex but because my pre-understanding of the former is greater. Therefore, where explanations are discussed in the abstract, readers must imagine a plausible social context in which they might have been proposed. When explanations are abstracted, they always seem incomplete (be they about natural or social objects) not only because of our ignorance, but because of our existing knowledge which makes completeness unnecessary. However, there are other more serious kinds of incompleteness specific to social science, as will be shown shortly. Successful explanation also presupposes that the conceptual frameworks used by the inquirer and respondent are mutually intelligible. This may seem rather obvious, but all too often philosophers' reconstructions of explanations ignore what is often their most problematic feature – the meaning of the terms they use.

In earlier chapters I discussed several types of explanation of relatively simple events and objects. I shall now briefly repeat these before passing on to more complex objects. Events are causally explained by retroducing and confirming the existence of mechanisms, and in turn the existence of mechanisms is explained by reference to the structure and constitution of the objects which possess them. Where the same events are co-determined by several distinct causes, they may also be explained by calculating the relative contributions of each mechanism. However, we must always be alert to the possibility of the event being a result of emergent powers arising from the combination of other objects but irreducible to their respective powers; in such cases, the method of causal disaggregation will not work. Often the problem of explanation lies in the description of the event to be explained, in which case a redescription will suffice as an explanation: 'it was a religious meeting, not a political rally'. Concepts in society must be explained at their 'own level' or, as some would prefer to say, their meaning must be *understood*. While they may be associated with observable physical behaviour (which may itself need explanation), they are not to be reduced to an epiphenomenon or external description of action. At the same time it may be necessary to explain what produces actions by reference to their causes and enabling conditions, which might include other actions, reasons and beliefs; understanding the meaning of an action is rarely sufficient to explain why, how and when and where it is done. More generally, social science is often concerned with explaining actions which in themselves may be relatively well understood in everyday discourse but whose conditions of possibility are largely unacknowledged; in particular, social structures. In some cases, the thing-to-be-explained may be sufficiently specific as to allow explanation purely by reference to abstract theory; for example, the question 'Why do tenants have to pay rent?' However, we frequently seek explanations of things as complex as concrete instances of wars and ideologies and economic development; major research programmes may be needed to provide answers. To do justice to such situations we must return to the relationships between theoretical and empirical research and the abstract and the concrete.

Figure 12, which is based on Figure 8, is intended to clarify the relationships between different kinds of research. In practice, however, a particular project might combine several types. Abstract theoretical research deals with the constitution and possible ways of acting of social objects, and actual events are only dealt with as possible outcomes. Examples include theories of value in economics and those theories of social class which define class in terms of internal relations. Concrete research studies actual events and objects as 'unities of diverse determinations', each of which has been isolated and examined through abstract research. By contrast, the method of generalization tends not to involve abstraction, at least not self-consciously, and treats events and objects as simple rather than concrete. Its main purpose is to seek regularities and common properties at this level. We might also add a fourth type, 'synthesis'; that is, research which attempts to explain major parts of whole systems by combining abstract and concrete research findings with generalizations covering a wide range of constitutive structures, mechanisms and events. Research of this kind is especially common in history and geography, although it would perhaps be fairer to say that ideally it should be interdisciplinary. *Interpretive understanding* is

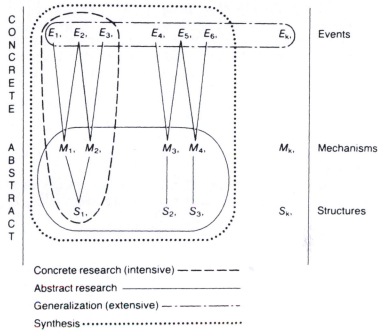

Concrete research (intensive) — — — — —
Abstract research ————————
Generalization (extensive) — - —— - .—— - -
Synthesis •

Figure 12 Types of research

presupposed in all these types of research, though the extent to which it is problematized will depend on the topic; e.g. cultural studies as compared to economics.

Another approach to concrete research but one which cannot easily be represented in our diagram is the method of 'ideal types'. Given the complexity of the world, it is argued that any research must be selective and that consequently researchers specify objects in terms of ideal types which isolate phenomena according to their interests and values. For example, a student of the early industrial city might take a particular example, such as Manchester, or set up a hypothetical 'Coketown' as the ideal type of this phenomenon. The realist objection to this is not directed against the fact of selectivity and the influence of values, for these are unavoidable; rather the problem is that the methodology pays no attention to the structure of the world and hence is unable to recognize that some selections are better than others according to their relationship to this structure.[3] It is because of this arbitrary attitude to ontology that ideal types cannot be represented on our diagram. When ideal types are defined independently of such matters, it is unlikely that much can be learned from comparing them with actual cases, except, of course, that there will be differences. But then the arbitrary freezing of contingent patterns, regardless of the structures that produce them, inevitably obscures whatever significance the differences may have, i.e. whether they are unimportant differences in contingent relations or mis-specifications of structural differences. Not surprisingly, the refusal to grant such differences any significance has invited the criticism that ideal type methodology gives users a built-in protection from refutation.[4]

Now the functions of these different types of research are often misunderstood both by users and critics. In particular, researchers often *over-extend* them by expecting one type to do the job of the others (looking at this from the opposite direction it can alternatively be seen as a form of reductionism).

In the case of abstract research this over-extension might be termed 'pseudo-concrete research' for it makes the mistake of expecting abstract theory to explain events directly, without any need for empirical research into the contingent forms of combinations of abstract elements which comprise the concrete. It reduces the concrete to the abstract. This is a common fault in marxism and sociology. An early opponent of this tendency was Sartre:

Valéry is a petit bourgeois intellectual, no doubt about it. But not every petit bourgeois intellectual is Valéry. The heuristic inadequacy of contemporary Marxism is contained in these two sentences. Characterising Valéry as a petit bourgeois and his work as idealist, the Marxist will find in both only what he has put there.[5]

Similarly, Raymond Williams attacks the tendency in sociology to use 'indifferent' terms such as 'socialization', defined as 'learning the ways and becoming a functioning member of society', which obviously takes place in all societies, as a *substitute* for concrete terms describing the widely differing '"ways" and "functioning"' and the highly differential character of being a '"member" of the society . . .'.[6] The tendency has been particularly evident in recent work on the capitalist state. Many researchers seem to have imagined that the nature of the state, in its concrete forms, could be 'derived' purely from a reworking of the most basic categories of marxist theories, as if the move from abstract to concrete were irreversible and deductive. For several years, 'the debate on the state' consisted largely of arguments between rival pseudo-concrete positions. Even where this research is explicitly abstract it tends to be assumed that the only available source of abstractions is existing (marxist) theory and that one cannot develop new abstractions by starting from concrete objects and different theories.[7] Abstractions are indispensable for providing some of the means by which we study the concrete, but they owe their origins to a *process* of abstraction which takes concrete objects as its starting point and raw material. Abstract research cannot displace concrete research and its dependence on empirical investigation.

However, although there are dangers in trying to extend purely abstract research upwards in Figure 12, it may be possible to extend it horizontally, in so far as the necessary relations discovered exist elsewhere. Because they concern necessity, they are likely to discover relations and properties which are 'general' or widely distributed, although exactly how widely is only determinable through empirical study. Note that the sense of this 'generality' is quite different from that implicit in the concept of generalization. The latter is primarily concerned with discovering similarities and regularities among the features of concrete objects and events but has difficulty finding enduring ones in open systems. Abstraction seeks necessary relations, conditions and properties and does not expect to find successful generalizations at the concrete level; but in abstracting *from* the particular contingencies that co-determine particular concrete objects, they are likely to produce a conception characterized by generality.[8] The landlord–tenant relation is a good example. Not surprisingly, most instances of generality that do exist in open systems derive from necessity rather than from contingent consequences and patterns of events.

The function of abstract research is also frequently misconstrued in empiricist and everyday understanding in that abstract (i.e. one-sided) concepts are wrongly expected to pre-empt the specificities of the concrete. When it is inevitably discovered that they do not they are abandoned through 'naïve falsification'. Perhaps the best-known instance of this mistake is the expectation that marxist concepts of class should enable one to partition the population into classes according to shared attributes at the concrete level, so that income, education and attitudes, etc., polarize neatly round the labour–capital divide. When it is found that this doesn't happen, the abstraction is thrown out on the spurious conclusion that class has been shown not to exist. By such simple misconceptions, numerous social scientists have disavailed themselves of some of their most powerful concepts.

The over-extension commonly associated with concrete research consists in the illegitimate extrapolation (or generalization) of specific findings about a particular (contingent) conjuncture of a system to the rest of the system, when in fact it may be unrepresentative. This involves an extension in the horizontal dimension of Figure 12. Obviously, the more heterogeneous the system, the more hazardous the extension. Although it seems a simple enough error to avoid, the impracticality of doing concrete research on every part of a system of interest makes it a strong temptation. For example, in historical accounts of the industrial revolution, one can easily get the impression that the very particular conditions present in the Lancashire cotton industry were 'representative' of the period; they certainly weren't, though it might be argued that they 'represented' (in a different sense) the shape of things to come.

Similarly with generalization. The patterns it discovers in particular open systems cannot be expected to apply to others with any accuracy, although we may be tempted to try. And for different reasons its role cannot be extended beyond description to (causal) explanation.

A further possible case of over-extension or reductionism is also detectable in interpretive analysis. We have already noted the absurdly imperialist tendency of some interpretivists to ignore or dismiss social science's interest in material processes in society. But even as regards the understanding of concepts in society itself, it often seems to be assumed that *all* that needs to be understood about concepts in society is what they mean, as if the question of how widely they are held and used were of no importance. This syndrome is especially common in cultural and political analysis where researchers generalize from tiny samples with astonishing disregard for the question of their representativeness.[9] Given that consciousness is so context-dependent, it is doubtful whether accurate general statements about things like working-class culture can be derived from limited personal experience or individual case studies. One may grant that the essentially shared, intersubjective nature of language and culture and the pervasiveness of modern communication systems give the consciousness of particular groups common strands, but there then arises the problem of how this insight is to be reconciled with the particularity of the concrete contexts in which people's consciousness is shaped. Although the problem is well known in cultural studies, the awareness is, as far as I can see, insufficiently acknowledged in its methodology, particularly as the range of social groups studied has tended to be rather restricted, at least until recently.

Research design: intensive and extensive

The problems of conducting theoretically informed concrete research can be illuminated further by considering alternative *research designs*. Unfortunately this topic is rarely discussed in a philosophically informed way and is frequently treated as synonymous with the design of research of a very specialized kind – statistical analysis.[10] In designing concrete research we have to keep in mind the nature of our objects of interest. Heterogeneity, complexity and qualitative change and 'polyvalency' are such that few concrete individuals are identical in every respect of interest. (*Note* – I do not want to restrict the meaning of 'individuals' to persons.)

These features affect the ways in which objects can be defined in social science. Now the more properties are used in the definition of an individual, the fewer the individuals who have all those properties;[11] for example, there are fewer members of the class 'self-employed males over forty who vote Conservative' than the class 'persons over forty'. If we want to examine a large number of individuals and make comparisons and generalizations it is necessary to restrict the number of properties used to define them. But because of their heterogeneity and polyvalency, such studies frequently exclude not just inessential aspects but properties which make important differences to the behaviour of individuals. In other words, their samples tend to be distributively unreliable, even when stratified. Indeed, in categorizing a range of diverse individuals by reference even to a fairly large number of character-istics, it is often not clear to what extent each attribute is causally significant to each individual. The alternative is to examine a large number of properties of a small number of individuals, in which case many individuals or other parts of the system are simply ignored.

Consider the following pair of possible research projects on poverty. In one project, a large survey is conducted on a representative sample of low-income households. Data are gathered on variables such as type of employment, if any, income, number of dependants and household structure, type of housing tenure, persons per room, ethnic origin, educational and skill qualifications and so on. The primary and secondary data are exhaustively analysed in order to identify common associations, sub-groups, etc. An enormous amount of descriptive results is produced but explanations are uncertain because of the problem of the ecological fallacy (see above, page 102), the loss of information in aggregation, etc. Another project takes a very small number of households – perhaps fewer than ten – and examines each one exhaustively in terms of its history and its context, i.e. its specific experience regarding housing, employment, education, the welfare state, transport and so on.[12] Much of the information is qualitative and concerns processes, activities, relations and episodes of events rather than statistics on particular characteristics. By looking at the actual relations entered into by identifiable agents, the interdependencies between activities and between characteristics can be revealed; for example, how waged work and domestic work commitments are integrated in time and space. The results are more vivid because they describe individuals and their activities concretely rather than in the bloodless categories of statistical indicators such as 'socio-economic group'. However, there is, of course, no guarantee that the results are representative even if they seem to provide satisfactory explanations.

This dilemma involves a choice between what Harré terms '*extensive*' and '*intensive*' research designs.[13] Superficially, this distinction seems nothing more than a question of scale or 'depth versus breadth'. But the two types of design ask different sorts of question, use different techniques and methods and define their objects and boundaries differently (see Figure 13). In intensive research the primary questions concern how some causal process works out in a particular case or limited number of cases. Extensive research, which is more common, is concerned with discovering some of the common properties and general patterns of a population as a whole. These two types of question are widely conflated and confused, particularly where researchers pose

	INTENSIVE	EXTENSIVE
Research question	How does a process work in a particular case or small number of cases? What produces a certain change? What did the agents actually do?	What are the regularities common patterns, distinguishing features of a population? How widely are certain characteristics or processes distributed or represented?
Relations	Substantial relations of connection	Formal relations of similarity
Type of groups studied	Causal groups	Taxonomic groups
Type of account produced	Causal explanation of the production of certain objects or events, though not necessarily representative ones	Descriptive 'representative' generalizations, lacking in explanatory penetration
Typical methods	Study of individual agents in their causal contexts, interactive interviews, ethnography. Qualitative analysis	Large-scale survey of population or representative sample, formal questionnaires, standardized interviews. Statistical analysis
Limitations	Actual concrete patterns and contingent relations are unlikely to be 'representative', 'average' or generalizable. Necessary relations discovered will exist wherever their relata are present, e.g. causal powers of objects are generalizable to other contexts as they are necessary features of these objects	Although representative of a whole population, they are unlikely to be generalizable to other populations at different times and places. Problem of ecological fallacy in making inferences about individuals. Limited explanatory power
Appropriate tests	Corroboration	Replication

Figure 13 Intensive and extensive research: a summary

ambiguous questions such as 'how much of the variation of y can be explained by x?' and rely on patterns and regularities in events as guides to causality. Typical methods of extensive research are descriptive and inferential statistics and numerical analysis (e.g. cross-tabulations) and the large-scale formal questionnaire of a population or 'representative sample' thereof. Intensive research uses mainly qualitative methods such as structural and causal analysis, participant observation and/or informal and interactive interviews.

The two types of research design also work with different conceptions of groups. Extensive research focuses on *taxonomic* groups, that is groups whose members share similar (formal) attributes but which need not actually connect or interact with one another.[14] Individual members are only of interest in so far as they represent the population as a whole. Intensive research focuses mainly (though not exclusively) on groups whose members may be either similar or different but which actually relate to each other structurally or causally. Specific, identifiable individuals are of interest in terms of their properties and their mode of connection to others. Instead of relying upon the ambiguous evidence of aggregate formal relations among taxonomic classes, causality is analysed by examining actual connections.

Note that the extensive/intensive distinction is not identical to the more familiar distinction between survey analysis and ethnography. Intensive research need not always use ethnographic methods to establish the nature of causal groups and surveys need not be devoid of attempts to understand the social construction of meaning.

In extensive studies, the criteria by which samples are drawn have to be decided in advance and adhered to consistently in order to ensure representativeness. In intensive studies the individuals need not be typical and they may be selected one by one as the research proceeds and as an understanding of the membership of a *causal* group is built up. In other words, it is possible – though not mandatory! – for intensive research to be exploratory in a strong sense. Instead of specifying the entire research design and who and what we are going to study in advance we can, to a certain extent, establish this as we go along, as learning about one object or from one contact leads to others with whom they are linked, so that we build up a picture of the structures and causal groups of which they are a part. This is not intended as a justification for empty-headed 'fishing expeditions'. It is just a counter to the rather peculiar idea that researchers should specify what they are going to find out about before they begin and an acknowledgement of the need to develop research procedures which do not inhibit learning-by-doing.

The rationale behind the use of large-scale, formal standardized questionnaire and interview surveys in extensive research is that by asking each respondent the same questions under controlled (quasi-experimental) conditions, comparisons are possible and 'observer-induced bias' is minimized. Again, like the statistical methods usually used with them, when applied to the highly heterogeneous samples that characterize social science (even when highly stratified), these techniques sacrifice explanatory penetration in the name of 'representativeness' and 'getting a large enough sample'. Extreme standardization which disregards the differences in types of respondents and in the contexts which are causally relevant to them can in fact make comparisons meaningless, because the research fails to register the fact that the same questions can have a vastly different *significance* for different respondents. Even if questions are included which aim to assess this (causal, not statistical) level of significance, the rigidity of the method makes it difficult for the researcher to respond to and follow up such variations. In other words, the technique allows individuals to be compared taxonomically but is weak for researching causality.

By contrast, with a less formal, less standardized and more interactive kind of interview, the researcher has a much better chance of learning from the respondents what the different significances of circumstances are for them. The respondents are not forced into an artificial one-way mode of communication in which they can only answer in terms of the conceptual grid given to them by the researcher. This also enables the researcher to refer to and build upon knowledge gained beforehand about the specific characteristics of the respondent, instead of having to affect ignorance (*tabula rasa*) in order to ensure uniformity or 'controlled conditions' and avoid what might be taken as 'observer-induced bias'. In fact, the belief that traditional, highly-formalized interviews or questionnaires minimize observer-induced bias could not be more misjudged. The rejection of such methods is not a licence for researchers to try to influence their subjects but a precondition of a meaningful type of communication which maximizes the information flow by making use of communicative and social skills, by being willing to adapt preconceived questions and ideas in the course of the interview according to what is relevant to the respondent and by being prepared to discuss, as well as to 'elicit', answers.[15] Where the researcher's questions and emphases are disputed by the subject, this is not something to be repressed by insisting on strict adherence to the questionnaire at all costs. Rather, we should try to learn from such situations: what do they tell us about the interviewee and about our own preconceptions?[16] Such heretical methods are also more interesting and less alienating for both parties, not to mention more likely to produce a high response rate.

Different types of test are also appropriate for intensive and extensive research. As regards the former, we must distinguish between testing to see how general the particular findings are in the wider population (replication) and testing to see that the results really do apply to those individuals actually studied (corroboration). For example, if an intensive study of an institution were based on interviews we might want to check with others in the same institution to corroborate information about common practices. A switch to an extensive study would be needed to test for replication in other institutions.

In evaluating the merits and problems of intensive and extensive research designs we must keep in mind their different roles, which may be complementary rather than competing. Extensive studies are weaker for the purpose of explanation not so much because they are a 'broad-brush' method lacking in sensitivity to detail (they may in fact be used on small groups if their parts are analysed taxonomically), but because the relations they discover are formal, concerning similarity, dissimilarity, correlation and the like, rather than causal, structural and substantial, i.e. relations of connection. They are only likely to produce explanations where they demonstrate that a certain aggregate pattern can be attributed to the effects of separable components, in the manner of the accounting approaches mentioned in Chapter 6, although they do not clearly identify the causal mechanism involved in those components. In seeking universal categories for understanding heterogeneous concrete individuals, and in preferring generalization to abstraction and causal analysis, they are susceptible to the twin problems of 'chaotic conceptions' and distributive unreliability. Causality is difficult to determine because actual connections and interactions between objects are often recorded in aggregates in which the specific individuals entering into the relations cannot be identified.

Also, extensive methods abstract from the actual *forms* in which individuals or processes interact and combine, even though these forms make a difference to outcomes. Therefore explanations of concrete phenomena which abstract from form (including spatial form considered in terms of relative space) must be regarded as being significantly incomplete. Yet few social scientists even recognize the problem, and this despite the fact that variations in form are a major factor in the failure of causal mechanisms to produce empirical regularities.

Certainly, practical difficulties often prevent us from taking form into account; in fact, it would take an extremely selective intensive research design to look so concretely at the production of events and conjunctures. Sometimes it is possible at least to reduce the problem by spatially disaggregating the information; for example, as we saw in Chapter 4, in the case of a study of the job market, it helps to disaggregate into distinct labour markets in which vacancies can reasonably be regarded as within the reach of job-seekers, but even then the representation of the spatial form relevant to the components of the system of interest is only approximated, as regards both those supply–demand relationships which are not contained within the areas defined and the spatial form of relations within each area.[17] If we want to be able to calculate and predict results at the level of events accurately we may be tempted into a reductionist regress by making the spatial units smaller in order to take account of these additional effects of form.

However, for the purpose of explaining events non-predictively we may be happy to make do with such an approximation. Certainly if all that is wanted is an abstract explanation (e.g. of the structures and mechanisms of the job market), it is often possible to abstract from form. *What is important is that the problem of form is at least recognized so that we do not generate unreasonable expectations of concrete explanations in social science based upon inappropriate analogies with closed system natural science in which the difference that form makes is controlled or controllable.* And if we do require very concrete explanations of events, the necessity of using intensive research designs must also be appreciated.

The greater level of detail in intensive studies need not be overwhelming because individuals who do not interact with the group of interest can be excluded even where, on taxonomic criteria, they would have to be included. Precisely because causal groups are selected, the 'logic of the situation' is often relatively easy to discover. For example, in a study of employment change in an industrial sector which I undertook with a colleague, we began to build up background descriptive information by using an extensive method chiefly involving the scrutiny of available statistical information on the industry. While some patterns were discernible at this level, their explanation was largely a mystery. As soon as we changed to an intensive method in which identifiable firms were looked at in their respective competitive contexts, simple explanations of the data quickly became apparent in terms of innovations in product and process technology, achievement of economies of scale, and so on. It was like 'switching the light on'.[18]

However, causal groups are not always small and easily demarcated and often they change radically during the period of study; indeed this may be the principal point of interest. In a related study of the development of the computer industry it was found that despite its internal diversity, the interdependencies between mainframes, micros and software, etc. were such that the whole industry warranted treatment as a single, rapidly changing causal group, for it provided a common environment or context which was causally-relevant to all its parts.[19]

That we should study things in context may seem so commonsensical as to be unworthy of mention, and too vague an injunction to impress those who like their methodological prescriptions to sound more technical. Such a dismissive attitude frequently belies an assumption that contexts (i.e. causal groups) are merely something that one refers to in general terms as part of the 'background' to the research, perhaps in the introductory part of the report, and then proceeds to keep firmly in the background during the actual research. This practice, coupled with the tradition of variable analysis of taxonomic groups, encourages a blindness to or 'scrambling' of structures, causal groups and contexts, rendering society as atomistic, unstructured and unhistorical. Contexts or causal groups are rarely just background; exploration of how the context is structured and how the key agents under study fit into it – interact with it and constitute it – is vital for explanation.

But what of the disadvantages of intensive studies? In order to avoid the converse of the ecological fallacy, it must be acknowledged that the results are not 'representative' of the whole population; indeed, given the nature of social phenomena it would be surprising if many concrete individuals could be said to be 'representative'.

While there is certainly often a problem of 'representativeness' arising from the over-extension of concrete (intensive) studies, we must avoid the absurd dogma that no study of individuals, in the broad sense, is of interest except as a representative of some larger entity. Proponents of extensive methods sometimes argue that intensive research fails to produce 'objective' results because its results are not representative (i.e. not replicated elsewhere). But providing there is no pretence that the whole population is 'represented', there is no reason why an intensive study should be less 'objective' (i.e. uncorroborated) about its particular subject matter than an extensive study. And although at the level of concrete events the results may be unique, in so far as intensive methods identify structures into which individuals are locked and their mechanisms, the abstract knowledge of these may be more generally applicable, although it will take further research to establish just how general they are. In some cases the unusual, unrepresentative conjuncture may reveal more about general processes and structures than the normal one. Rare conjunctures such as experimental communities, social or institutional crises, psychological abnormalities, identical twins reared apart, etc., may lay bare structures and mechanisms which are normally hidden. In other words, precisely because of the contingent nature of concrete conjunctures it is sometimes possible to find situations where certain contingencies are actually 'held off' spontaneously. This allows us to make comparisons with abstract theoretical accounts in which the contingencies are only 'held off' in thought experiments.

Since social structures exist on a variety of scales, from the interpersonal to the international, intensive studies of their reproduction, transformation and effects need not be merely local in their interest. Conversely, extensive methods can be used on small as well as large scales. As they are oriented towards providing descriptive generalizations, it is often said that extensive methods produce results that are 'representative'. But representative of what? As descriptions of a particular open system they are unlikely to represent other systems. Even in the case of the more modest claim that the generalizations are representative of a unique system, it is still not always clear of what they are representative. The most obvious example of this is where a statistical average is found to which no real individuals correspond. This difficulty arises from the reliance on taxonomic rather than causal classification and the usual focus on events rather than structures and mechanisms.[20] However, if the population is not too diverse, it may be possible to define taxonomic classes in which individuals share similar causal powers and liabilities, hence enabling extensive and intensive research designs to become more complementary.[21] Both methods are needed in concrete research although the latter tend to be undervalued; some researchers are perhaps loath to admit that they get more out of intensive studies in terms of explanation for fear of appearing 'unscientific', but I hope to have shown that the fear is unwarranted.

Part of the difficulty of understanding objects as complex as historical movements or the development of a region arises from the fact that they do not constitute clear causal groups; rather, they cut across many structures and causal groups in a 'chaotic' fashion. It is not always possible or desirable to reduce the object so that it is less chaotic, because it may nevertheless be of interest as a whole, perhaps because, chaotic or not, it is to such objects that people respond. For example, governments respond to 'regional development' even though regions are 'chaotic' groups.

It is still, of course, necessary to use rational abstractions in order to understand such objects, although doing so will require reference to things lying beyond the boundaries of the object as originally defined and hence an expansion of an already complex field of study. So, for example, we may find that a subject like the condition of the poor in the East End of London in the nineteenth century will require repeated references to phenomena which lay outside this area and yet were causally connected to it, such as British imperialism.[22] In such wide-ranging studies the temptation to over-extend inferences drawn from case studies is strong[23] and inevitably the best that can be produced is a narrative supported by some results of extensive surveys (or fragments thereof), a few intensive 'case studies' and a host of statements about relatively simple constituent elements or events, all informed by abstract theoretical knowledge.

We can easily criticize such work for its incompleteness and apparently informal character, without thinking what else we could reasonably expect of research on this kind of subject. For example, Blaug derides this approach as 'storytelling', by which he means

the method of what historians call *colligation*, the binding together of facts, low-level generalizations, high-level theories, and value-judgements in a coherent narrative, held together by a glue of an implicit set of beliefs and attitudes that the author shares with all his readers. In able hands it can be extremely persuasive, and yet it is never easy to explain afterwards why it has persuaded . . . because storytelling lacks rigour, lacks a definite logical structure, it is all too easy to verify and virtually impossible to falsify.[24]

Several phrases in this passage suggest a comprehensive mis-understanding of the relationship between theory and empirical research. Given the nature of an open system event or transforma-tion, such as a war, one wonders what a rigorous, 'logical' deduc-tive explanation would look like! Is Blaug suggesting that users of other approaches – deductive or whatever – do not also make value judgements or rely upon the 'glue of an implicit set of [shared] beliefs and attitudes'?; or does he suppose that explanation can take place without a hermeneutic circle or context? If one is unaware of the existence of qualitative methods such as structural analysis and the 'cross-gridding' or 'triangulation' of interpretive analysis, and if one imagines that events can only be explained by deducing them from statements about universal regularities, then the nuances of 'storytelling' will indeed seem baffling. And if one is unaware of the relationship between abstract and concrete, it will always seem vulnerable to naïve falsification. Certainly evaluation of this kind of concrete study is not straightforward, but then there is a huge difference between this and testing a theoretical claim about a particular phenomenon under controlled experimental conditions. To arrive at reasonable expectations of social research we must take account of the kinds of things it has to explain.

Explanation and the question of difficulty: II critical theory conception

So far in this discussion it has been implicit that the aims of social science are to construct a coherent description and explanation of the world and hence to represent and perhaps 'mirror' an object external to itself. As we have just seen, there is plenty of room within this view for disagreements on how such aims might best be realized and whether the supposed practices of the natural sciences should be treated as 'high standards' to which we should aspire, or as inappropriate. However, recalling the arguments of Chapter 1 about the context of social scientific knowledge, I now want to suggest that these aims are overly restrictive and at the limit contradictory. To do this it is necessary to broaden the discussion to embrace the simple but fundamental question: what do we want social science *for*?

First consider the paradox that the very things which make knowledge possible – our ability to monitor our own monitorings, to learn and hence to change our interpretations, actions and responses – are also things which make social science *difficult*, assuming that its aims are understood in the traditional way. Then consider a concrete instance of the difficulty; the problem that in the course of an interview aimed at eliciting an objective account of people's views or experiences they are inadvertently led to revise them as a result of having to reflect upon them, thereby 'distorting' our results. Now the point of all science, indeed all learning and reflection, is to change and develop our understandings and reduce illusion. This is not just an external and contingent sociological condition of learning but its constitutive force, which not only drives it but shapes its form. Without this universal necessary condition, none of the particular methodological and ethical norms of science and learning in general has any point. Learning, as the reduction of illusion and ignorance, can help to free us from domination by hitherto unacknowledged constraints, dogmas and falsehoods. All this may seem very obvious at one level, although it can easily be forgotten as one is socialized into the ways of thinking associated with the conventional view of knowledge as a mirror or external representation of the world. The radical implication of this can be revealed most provocatively by asking what is wrong if researchers stimulate this potentially emancipatory change in others in the process of trying to achieve it for themselves? Then consider a further deliberately loaded question: should the aims of the social sciences be to provide greater knowledge of society as an object or to assist in our emancipation? This ought to strike the reader as strange – surely the answer should be both? But how far is this answer actually presupposed in scientific practice? In natural science there does not appear to be any contradiction in the two

aims since the knowledge which it produces is really external to
its object. But in social science, where the reduction of illusion can
cross the boundary between subject and object, the emancipatory
goal may pose a threat to the goal of objectivity. Again, what
is learning for, if not to change people's understanding of their
world and themselves? Or is it only for the edification of the
scientific élite? Should we first do research on people as objects
and then, when completed, perhaps report it to them so that they
might respond as subjects? The usual answer to the last question
would appear to be yes, although often only a restricted group of
people called policy-makers or decision-makers are granted the
status of subjects.

My point at this stage in posing these apparently rhetorical
questions is not to evade the effort of giving argued answers
but merely to force a deeper appreciation of the significance of
the question of the aims of social science. As we shall see, the
answers are not as straightforward and one-sided as might at first
appear.

The strangeness of social science which resists its immanent
emancipatory role is perhaps clearest in studies which exhaustively
search for enduring regularities in aspects of human behaviour
which are manifestly susceptible to change, such as attitudes
towards other races. It may indeed be useful to find out, at a
given time, the nature and extent of such attitudes, but often
their descriptions appear to be treated as preliminary versions of
law-like statements about eternal regularities. The justification of
the accumulation of this 'external' knowledge of society is then
usually that it can provide policy-makers with information so that
they can change the situation, although sometimes they accede
to calls for 'further research' in order to procrastinate. 'Social
engineering' is an apt term for this kind of intervention because
it suggests that the agent's relationship to the behaviour is, as in
engineering, an external and instrumental one; the object can be
manipulated externally in accordance with its (eternal) laws.

In response to this kind of endless fact-gathering about behaviour, radicals often echo Marx by protesting that 'the point is
to change it'. But they do not mean the social engineering kind
of change but an internal process of reduction of illusion and
emancipation. As long as knowledge is estranged from people and
seen as externally descriptive rather than constitutive of human
action, the radical reply will seem obscure in its justification and

hence appear as mere assertion. Not only this – the despairing view of Wittgenstein that science leaves the problems of life untouched will remain unchallenged.[25] For when we take the relationship of science to action to be external, the use of scientific results in practice appears to be based purely on extra-scientific principles, usually in the form of values which themselves are beyond the scope of rational evaluation. But if we recognize that 'science' itself is a practice – and one dependent on adherence to certain values – and that social objects include other knowing subjects, the emancipatory goal cannot in principle be denied without contradiction.

The qualification 'in principle' is needed because in both the rhetorical questions and the previous paragraph I abstracted from the actual concrete contexts in which social research is conducted. Although the property of being 'knowing subjects' is common to both the researchers and the researched, there are also significant differences between them. The former have a much greater freedom to change their ideas because of their position in the social division of labour which detaches them from the routinized practices and their associated ideas which form a large part of their object, and in which the researched are located. Also, in primarily leading a life of reflection, it is easy for the researchers to forget that changing people's thinking may leave the world of practice largely unchanged, although a relation of dissonance may be induced between the two where once there was harmony.

Not surprisingly, critical theorists have taken a special interest in concrete situations in which the differences between subject and object are minimized and where material circumstances pose least resistance to change. Examples of these are psychotherapy and self-reflection.[26] As the link between the quest for knowledge and emancipation is unassailable in these cases, critical theorists have sometimes tried to treat them as exemplars of what a critical social science might look like in general. Ideally this would involve an elimination of the division between the researcher and the researched and hence also the distinction between science and everyday thinking. For the time being, however, the division is deeply rooted in our society as part of the broader division between intellectual and subaltern labour, and other divisions, particularly of class, mean that interests are far from compatible. In these circumstances the development of certain types of knowledge may (and often does) have the effect of reinforcing domination and subordination and hence opposing a general emancipation. Social divisions therefore frequently override the immanent link between knowledge and emancipation.

Unfortunately, critical theorists have said little about how critical social science might be carried out in concrete terms. One possible type of research which might fit the bill in attempting both to investigate and change its object is 'action research'. For example, a few years ago, a project called 'The Workers' Enquiry into the Motor Industry' was carried out in which academics, unions and workers co-operated to investigate the latter's circumstances in a way which would simultaneously gather information and raise consciousness so that they could better defend their interests.[27] Although the intellectual–subaltern division of labour could not be removed, its boundaries were softened and its one-sidedness reduced. For example, interviews and questionnaires were not organized so that workers would simply yield up information at the bidding of external researchers who had nothing to offer in return and who would go away and analyse and publish the results in academic seclusion (the usual situation);[28] rather, the research process was kept interactive and open-ended so that workers could pose and discuss questions and hence reconsider their position. That objective conditions did not change much as a result should not surprise us: education is not a sufficient condition for social change and actions which attempt to change practice are constrained by existing structures.

One field in which critical social science of sorts has been widely practised has been development studies. While this field has provided numerous examples of ethnocentric research doing more harm than good, there are now many signs that researchers are overcoming these problems, through greater appreciation of the way in which researchers have to learn from the researched, and by paying more attention to the social and political relationships involved, both in the situation under study and in the research process itself.[29]

Critical theory's avowed intent to influence and change those whom it studies naturally raises ethical problems. But so too does the orthodox conception of social science. The detached stance of the latter may be associated with a research process which exploits those it studies, extracting information for self-advancement and giving nothing in return, failing to help even where the researched

might very easily be helped by simply providing needed information. Like any activity, research is a social process, and adopting
the traditional academic conception does not render the research
process innocent or ethically neutral; on the contrary, the belief
that it does may permit insensitivity and political naïvety. While
these general warnings about ethical problems must be heeded,
actual decisions must be made in the light of an evaluation of
the *particular* politics (including one's own 'personal politics') of
the situation under study, with all its conflicting interests and
imbalances of power.[30]

Adopting a critical theory approach also poses problems of
feasibility, particularly in attempts to use action research. This
depends heavily on the type of social practices being researched;
it is obviously more limited for phenomena such as world trade
systems (!) than it is for, say, women and gender. It cannot be
done for very disparate 'target' groups and some kind of political
understanding must be reached between the researchers and the
researched. Certainly there are many areas of social study in
which methods based on the psycho-therapeutic encounter are
not remotely possible. But note that from the point of view of
the orthodox conception of science, the absence of interaction
between subject and object in many kinds of social study is an
advantage; from the point of view of the alternative conception
it is a problem.

However, there are other ways in which the goals of a critical
social science might be approached. First, it should be noted that
critical theory does not simply *replace* research on what *is* with
criticism of what is, plus assessments of what *might be* from the
point of view of emancipation. It would be a poor critical social
science which imagined that it could dispense with abstract and
concrete knowledge of what is in society. If certain mechanisms
are to be overridden or undermined and new ones established
we need abstract knowledge of the structures of social relations
and material conditions by virtue of which the mechanisms exist.
And for some practiical purposes, such as economic planning, a
detailed concrete knowledge of the system may be needed too.

If we look at it from the opposite direction, we can also see
that it would be a poor abstract or concrete research which was
unaware of the fact that what *is* need not necessarily be, and which
failed to note that people have powers which remain unactivated in
the society in question but which *could* be activated. And if the

realist theory of causation is right, these possibilities are grounded in the nature of the present in terms of what we are now. Thus, for example, an account of women's position in society which failed to note (at least implicitly) the contingent status of their present position and their ability to change it would be deficient as an account of what is. More generally, to deny the people we study the status of subjects, however circumscribed their field of self-determination, is to fail to represent them 'objectively'. Abstract, concrete and critical social science therefore have overlapping rather than separate domains.

The unavoidability of critical social science is at last being recognized, but too often the unavoidability of understanding 'what is' and choosing appropriate methods of study is simply forgotten. The challenge of the philosophy of social science is to abandon simplistic, monistic accounts, of whatever kind, without lapsing into a feeble eclecticism. We need an integrated understanding of the differentiated character of social science – one which recognizes the interdependencies between aims, methods and objects and yet is able to distinguish those combinations of elements which are legitimate from those which are incoherent. I hope this book has made a contribution to that task.

Appendix

Notes on realism, writing and the future of method in social science

With only a few exceptions[1] social scientists have paid surprisingly little attention to the fact that their knowledge is invariably presented in the form of texts. Typically they refer to the task of 'writing up' their research, as if it were merely a bothersome conclusion to their real work. But this wholly underestimates the significance of the fact that academic knowledge takes this textual form. It is not only that language and the devices and forms we use for constructing texts have a degree of autonomy and a largely hidden influence on how we re-present knowledge and how it is read, they also influence the content of the research itself.

> Literary processes – metaphor, figuration, narrative – affect the ways . . .
> phenomena are registered, from the first jotted 'observations', to the
> completed book, to the ways these configurations 'make sense' in a
> determined reading.[2]

If these things make a difference to what social scientists produce and how they understand one another they can be regarded as relevant to method. This should not occasion surprise. What is surprising is that so little attention has been given to the language, description, rhetoric and the construction of texts. In these notes I shall indicate the kinds of issues that need to be addressed via a discussion of the narrative versus analysis debate, the neglect of description and the influence of rhetoric.

Narrative versus analysis

This debate illustrates particularly well the interaction between content and form, between representation and presentation, or between our knowledge and the way in which we communicate it.

By narrative I mean an account of some process or development in terms of a story, in which a series of events are depicted chronologically. In everyday life, narrative is the taken-for-granted, natural form of discourse, through which events 'seem to tell themselves'.[3] Its power derives from the way in which putting things in chronological order, in a story, gives the appearance of a causal chain or logic in which each event leads to the conclusion.

By analysis I mean the explanation of concrete cases by the direct application of abstractions or theoretical models of what are believed to be widely replicated structures and mechanisms. As such it tends to abstract from particular historical sequences. Analysis requires a leap across the intermediate steps between abstract and concrete in the hope that the model will still serve to identify key processes without too much distortion. When it is successful, its power lies in its potential for explaining much by little.

Let us consider an example: the explanation of the rise of Silicon Valley in California. A narrative would take us through a series of events, leading in quasi-teleological fashion to its conclusion: the chance location of Stanford University, with its strong electrical engineering interests and the presence of Frederick Terman, who made great efforts to encourage the local development of commercial applications of university electronics research; the arrival of William Shockley, the inventor of the transistor, who chose to live in Palo Alto so as to be near his ageing mother; the proliferation of new firms spinning off from existing ones, and the emergence of a localized pool of top scientific and managerial skills, and so on. On the other hand, analysis would abstract from the 'historical accidents' and apply concepts like 'agglomeration economies' and 'vertical disintegration' which purport to be applicable to a wide range of cases of industrial development.[4]

Both narrative and analysis have their dangers but from a realist point of view we should not be surprised that to some extent their value varies according to the nature of their object. In everyday life we rarely question whether the social world really presents 'itself to perception in the form of well-made stories with central subjects, proper beginnings, middles, and ends, and a coherence that permits us to see "the end" in every beginning'.[5] By contrast, the legitimacy of analysis, and the irrelevance of narrative, are taken for granted in the natural sciences (with the possible exception of evolutionary biology). Since atoms and the like do not have histories (or geographies) but change only in fixed ways we do not expect physical scientists to tell stories about their objects of interest. Meanwhile, faced with open systems and concept-dependent objects, social scientists tend to disagree over whether narrative or analysis is appropriate in their field. Those in the analysis camp worry about what Abrams terms 'the dereliction of method that results from excessive sensitivity to detail', while those in the narrative camp worry about 'the dereliction of scholarship that results from excessive attachment to theoretical generalization'.[6]

Narratives suffer from a tendency to under-specify causality in the processes they describe. They may causally explain some events – usually in everyday terms – but they are not *primarily* concerned with explaining the nature, conditions and implications of social structures. Secondly, the preoccupation with telling a story of a sequence of events tends to gloss over the difference between mere temporal succession and causality: as a result they present only implicit, under-examined, aetiologies. Storytelling pulls us along, makes us follow, but not necessarily thanks to the ability of its explanation to grasp what happens. Rather, as Abrams puts it, the principles of explanation underpinning the research are buried 'beneath the rhetoric of a story'.[7] Discussing an example of the use of narrative in history, Abrams comments:

> My own impression is that the function of narrative in this enterprise is to carry – in a highly persuasive way not accessible to intellectual scrutiny – those bits of the argument the author does not choose to make available for direct critical examination on the part of his readers.[8]

Narrative is further alleged to be hampered by its linearity, which supposedly leads to a tendency to neglect synchronic relations (or what Ricoeur terms the configurational dimension) at the expense of temporal successions (the episodic dimension).[9] Ricoeur objects to this judgement:

> . . . the activity of narrating does not consist simply in adding episodes to one another; it also constructs meaningful totalities out of scattered events. . . . The act of narrating, as well as the corresponding art of

following a story, therefore require that we are able *to extract a configuration* from a succession.[10]

Thus every narrative includes a competition between its 'episodic dimension' and its 'configurational dimension'.[11] But given the linearity of writing and speech, it is inevitably more difficult to represent the configurational dimension than the episodic.[12] For these reasons, narrative has often been seen as inherently parochial. This has become more evident as societies have stretched across wider spaces, bringing successively more people into relationships of interdependence, albeit ones of which they were often unaware, for it has become progressively harder to represent all the influences bearing upon specific people in particular places in terms of a linear narrative.[13] There are devices for dealing with the fact that many things happen and interact at once ('Meanwhile back at the ranch. . .') and many familiar terms in social science imply a configurational dimension ('system', 'structure', 'division of labour' etc.). But grasping the whole, the many things that happen at once, is harder than grasping what happens next in a story. Moreover, it is difficult to break up the narrative flow too much in order to stress this dimension without making the text appear disorganized. In such ways, the very organization of a text, the unavoidable juxtapositions and separations imposed by its linear flow, can affect the way readers interpret it in ways which were not intended by the author.[14]

Narrative is often accused of failing to problematize its categories, interpretations and explanations. The presentation of an unfolding story tends not to invite disputation or to pre-empt objections. But this problem of closure is not restricted to narrative. The form of the typical economics textbook, which presents a series of theorems and models, hardly encourages one to write 'I disagree' in the margin. Similarly, analyses of concrete systems can close off disputation equally well. Obviously, some propositions must at least be provisionally accepted if a discussion or account is even to begin, but sometimes the closure needs to be contested. Narratives can be interrupted in order to problematize some of their categories and explanations, though this is liable to disrupt their linear flow. But then reading is not wholly linear and the problem can be reduced by building redundancy into texts.

These criticisms of narrative are not intended to imply that explanations of concrete situations through analysis are *necessarily* better. A necessary condition of the effectiveness of analysis is that its referents are indeed general and pivotal. If not, the attempt to explain the concrete (the many-sided) by reference to just a small number of its elements courts the dangers of 'pseudo-concrete research' (p. 238). Thus if we try to explain the development of Silicon Valley through the application of a theoretical model of agglomeration economies we risk reductionism or identification errors, if the effects attributed to our chosen mechanisms are actually the result of other processes. For example, that the agglomeration might be largely an effect of government intervention could be overlooked. There are also risks of functionalist and structuralist errors, if, in abstracting from the origins of the conditions necessary for the central processes, we assume that whatever is functional for them was created in order to fulfil their functions, and if the contingency of the reproduction of the structures is forgotten. Nevertheless these are only hazards, not unavoidable problems of analysis.

Analysis claims the virtue of explaining 'much by little' and 'reducing the burden of fact' while proponents of narrative disparage this as 'thin description' and call for 'thick description'.[15] These are tendentious metaphors. The first plays on the appeal of simplicity and economy, but at the risk of making us forget that the simplest, most elegant explanation may not be the most practically adequate and that there may be costs in deliberately depleting our vocabularies. On the other hand, we shouldn't be cowed by the dismissive tone of 'thin description'; though analysis has arguably proved poorly suited to ethnographic work it may remain superior for the explanation of other phenomena, such as economic processes.

Any verdict on the issue of narrative versus analysis must therefore depend on the object of study and the purpose. The economizing view of theory is more appropriate to abstraction of objects (relations, mechanisms, concepts) which are stable and pervasive, while thick description is more appropriate for accounts of concrete situations in which there is considerable historical and geographical specificity and change.

The neglect of description

Those, like Geertz, who favour thick description tend not to value the density of terms graced with the label 'theoretical' (i.e. not used in everyday language)[16] which are supposed to explain much by little. Instead they admire the highly developed, multiple sensitivities of the author, the richness and subtlety of the observation, the awareness of contextuality, and the command of ordinary language, rather than of a supposedly 'theoretical' language.

In their favour, these arguments about the language of description remind us of the extraordinary neglect of language in social science methodology. To capture the subtleties of actions and actors' interpretations we need a rich vocabulary, not one purged in the interest of scientific neutrality of terms that seem either too mundane or too 'literary' – rather than 'literal'. The objects of natural science tend to be highly durable, context-independent mechanisms often capable of being studied in closed system conditions. Social phenomena have histories and geographies and their intrinsic meanings can be multiple and transient. In view of this it is hardly surprising that natural scientists can rely upon a more stable vocabulary than can social scientists.

Though having very different styles, Raymond Williams and Pierre Bourdieu are good examples of authors not only able to use mega-concepts or technical abstractions but also extraordinarily gifted in exploiting the cognitive insights of ordinary language, insights missed by those with more restricted, if also more esoteric vocabularies.[17] This should not alarm the self-appointed guardians of theory. Concepts are not the same as the technical terms which name them and their power can often be enhanced by expressing them through other terms. So the sparsity of ostentatiously 'theoretical' language (in the sense of academic technical terms) does not necessarily make accounts atheoretical: on the contrary it may enhance abstract theory by making us examine what is normally taken for granted.

Thick description need not be seen as antithetical to theory, or synonymous with narrative. It could be a product of a concrete research which combines and works up the insights of a range of theories dealing with particular aspects of the object. But the danger of thick description is that, in practice, the attempt to combine many theoretical insights can easily become unmanageable, so that we fail to examine our concepts. This tendency is common in empirical research precisely because of the immediacy of lay-knowledge and the need to engage with it. Ironically, there are therefore dangers of allowing a pluralistic view of the role of theory in concrete research to permit a retreat from theory.

Notwithstanding the value of the critique of thin description and of the neglect of descriptive language, it also contains a further danger. The call for a greater concern with the 'art' of description could signal an indulgent and amateurish celebration of 'literary' ways of writing which does not penetrate its devices. This is often associated with a slide towards a complacent advocacy of the ineffable qualities of 'craft'. Craft always eludes specification, except that it is invariably supposed to be exemplified by the work of those who have had longest to absorb it – the elders of a discipline – and it is usually invoked to deflect theoretical scrutiny. When someone says 'craft', reach for your gun.

We must obviously never return to the days when research students were told not to worry their little heads with theory but to admire craft and immerse themselves in the empirical sources. On the other hand immersion in the sources is no bad thing provided it is coupled with examination of theory, and if actors' accounts and academic accounts are brought into engagement.

The influence of rhetoric

Although 'rhetoric' has a largely pejorative sense in everyday language it is defined here as referring to the forms of persuasive argument, be they good or bad. To examine rhetoric is to explore the field constituted by the relationships between the object, the author's intentions, language and literary processes, readers' pre-understandings, moral dispositions and self-presentation.

Let us consider three examples. The first concerns an apparently mundane issue of the tense of an account. If an anthropologist writes an account of a series of events in a community in the past tense, it gives the impression that the sequence of events was contingent; it seems like a narrative description of things that could have happened differently. On the other hand an account written in the present tense tends to give the impression that this is what the people always do, what they must do. Such an account sounds more 'scientific' but it may be based on the same experience as the first rendering. In this way a simple change of tense can make a significant difference to the way in which accounts are read.[18]

The second example concerns rhetoric, self-presentation and moral persuasion. Consider the historian E. P. Thompson's statement that 'no worker ever known to historians ever had surplus

value taken out of his hide without finding some way of fighting-
back (there are plenty of ways of going *slow*)'.[19] It would be naïve
to see this simply as a description of what happened. It is also
romantic 'fighting talk', a defiant description of a defiant act of
resistance. Through such statements the author reminds us that
he is a *radical*, opposed to the soothing apologetics of bourgeois
historians; indeed it is hard to resist the conclusion that there is
an element of a moral crusade here, a reclamation of what is
rightfully ours. In so doing we are implicitly challenged to take
sides: are we not radical too? By such means we are coaxed into
accepting what is at worst a workerist romance. Perhaps, too, it
has a masculinist slant, evidenced not only by the use of 'he' to
refer to the generic worker but by the tough talk ('taken out of
his hide'). And how could a historian ever know whether the
extraction of surplus – something which is often hard to identify –
always met with resistance? Haven't there also been flag-waving,
forelock-tugging, deferential and compliant workers?[20]

The third example concerns dualistic forms of thinking and
rhetoric. At several points (pp. 22, 49), I have attacked accounts
which present their objects as split into two blocks opposing each
other across a single fault-line. By aligning dualisms or binary
oppositions in parallel it is possible to polarize whole fields of
debate or characterize historical change as the supercession of
one coherent block of characteristics by their opposites. What
impresses us about this form of rhetoric is its symmetry and
the simplicity of its basic organizational principle, rather than
its descriptive or explanatory adequacy. This temptation is evident, for example, in discussions of industrialism in terms of the
succession of Fordism by post-Fordism, in which, extraordinarily,
the future is projected as the opposite of the past.[21] While it is
quite likely that some aspects of reality are two-sided and can
reasonably be described in terms of dualisms, it is scarcely credible
that complex networks of arguments or historical change could be
resolved into neatly aligned sets of dualisms.

This is not to say that a counter-argument could evade rhetoric;
pointing out how history is always more complex is also a kind of
rhetoric, and one which can on occasion function more as an evasion of brute realities or as a way of flattering the reader's supposedly higher sensibilities, than as a better description of the world.

Such examples illustrate that we need to become more aware of
rhetoric and of the subtle interplay between object, author, reader,

language, texts and moral judgements. It is not that we could ever evade rhetoric but that we need to distinguish forms of rhetoric which are better at grasping the nature of the world from those which are inferior. As Mäki points out, there is no contradiction between realism and rhetoric here, for what is the point of all this analysis of language and discourse if not to develop a more realistic understanding of how language functions?[22] (If it is not, there is no need to pay attention.)

As such the close examination of accounts need not be merely a form of talk about talk, but a more self-aware form of talk about how we understand our world. The causes of the social phenomena we study, be they underdevelopment, violence or whatever, are what they are largely regardless of the rhetoric of academics. Yet since academic explanation and understanding always involve discourse we cannot avoid some talk about talk. Future discussions of method in social science will presumably push in this direction of the examination of rhetoric, description and language. Provided it is remembered that we need to evaluate them not just as talk but in terms of their ability to illuminate a world beyond academic discourse it should be a positive move.

Notes and references

Preface

1 For example: R. Keat and J. Urry, *Social Theory as Science*, 2nd edn. (London 1982); P. Mattick Jr., *Social Knowledge* (London 1985); W. Outhwaite, *New Philosophies of Social Science* (London 1987); R. Bhaskar, *The Possibility of Naturalism*, 2nd edn. (London 1989) and *Reclaiming Reality* (London 1989); P. Manicas, *A History and Philosophy of the Social Sciences* (Oxford 1987).

Introduction

1 R. Pawson, *A Measure for Measures* (London 1989).
2 R. Bhaskar, *Reclaiming Reality* (London 1989).
3 Some realists might argue that my failure to emphasize the similarities over the differences makes my position as much one of 'qualified anti-naturalism' as of 'qualified naturalism' à la Bhaskar's *Possibility of Naturalism*. If so, fine; impressive though the methods of natural science are, I don't think their status should tempt us to play down how far the methods of social science differ.

Chapter 1   Knowledge in context

1 L. Wittgenstein, *Tractatus Logico-Philosophocus*, 1922.
2 I say 'in abstract terms' to distinguish what follows from the more concrete concerns of the sociology of knowledge.
3 Strong cases for the practical character of knowledge of nature and society have been made by Ian Hacking with reference to natural science (*Representing and Intervening*, Cambridge 1983), and Pierre Bourdieu with reference to social knowledge (*Towards a Theory of Practice*, Cambridge 1977; *Distinction*, London, 1986). See also G. Lakoff, *Women, Fire and Dangerous Things: What Categories Reveal about the Mind* (Chicago 1987).

4 This argument is derived from the work of Habermas, particularly his *Knowledge and Human Interests* (London 1972).
5 J. Lyons, *Language, Meaning and Context* (London 1981).
6 P. Bourdieu, 'Vive la crise!: for heterodoxy in the social sciences', *Theory and Society*, **17** (1988), p. 780.
7 See A. Giddens (*Central Problems in Social Theory*, London 1979) on the distinction between discursive and practical consciousness. No one has explored the implications of the position of academics and their misrepresentation of practical knowledge as discursive knowledge more than Bourdieu, particularly in his *Outline of a Theory of Practice* (Cambridge 1977).
8 R. Williams, *Marxism and Literature* (Oxford 1977), pp. 133ff.
9 E. Fromm, *To Have or To Be* (London 1976).
10 cf. B. Barnes, *Interests and the Growth of Knowledge* (London 1977), ch. 1.
11 R. Bhaskar, *The Possibility of Naturalism* (Hassocks 1979).
12 ibid., p. 43. cf. A. Giddens, *Central Problems of Social Theory* (London 1979), on 'structuration'.
13 cf. Habermas, *Knowledge and Human Interests*, and his 'The analytical theory of science and dialectics', in T. Adorno *et al.*, *The Positivist Dispute in German Sociology* (London 1976).
14 ibid.
15 *Knowledge and Human Interest*; see also my 'Epistemology and conceptions of people and nature in geography', *Geoforum*, **10** (1979).
16 These comments on work, though less so those on communicative interaction, are derived from the work of Marx. See, for example, *Early Writings* (London 1975); *Grundrisse* (London 1973); and also A. Schmidt, *The Concept of Nature in Marx* (London 1971).
17 Hacking, *Representing and Intervening*.
18 Marx, Second thesis on Feuerbach, in C. Arthur (ed.), *The German Ideology* (London 1974), p. 121.
19 ibid.
20 K. Marx, *The Eighteenth Brumaire of Louis Bonaparte* (London 1926).
21 E. Goffman, 'The presentation of self', in D. Potter *et al.*, *Society and the Social Sciences* (London 1981).
22 Unfortunately the development of an interest in language and its effects has been accompanied in structuralist and post-structuralist writing by a bizarre and absurd abstraction of language from context, in which actors, society and the world collapse into language or discourse, and in which the status of our knowledge of the world cannot be assessed, since nothing is held to exist outside discourse. I shall suggest how these conclusions can be resisted in Chapter 2.

See T. Eagleton, *Literary Theory: An Introduction* (Oxford 1983); C. Norris, *The Contest of Faculties* (London 1985); R. Williams *Marxism and Literature*; K. Baynes *et al.*, *After Philosophy* (Cambridge, Mass. 1987).

23   cf. Marx, *Grundrisse*, p. 84.

24   Lyons, *Language, Meaning and Context*; see also Williams, *Marxism and Literature*, ch. 2.

25   cf. C. Taylor, 'Interpretation and the science of man', *Review of Metaphysics*, **25**, and reprinted in P. Connerton (ed.), *Critical Sociology* (Harmondsworth 1976).

26   Bhaskar, *The Possibility of Naturalism*, p. 31.

27   Particularly in his later work, Marx tends to collapse communicative interaction into labour. This reduction has had a detrimental effect on socialist thought and practice. See Habermas, *Knowledge and Human Interests*; A. Wellmer, *Critical Theory of Society* (Berlin 1972); and R. J. Bernstein, *The Restructuring of Social and Political Theory* (Oxford 1976).

28   Those who imagine that they are self-contained individuals, independent of society, contradict themselves every time they speak or read.

29   A. Giddens, *New Rules of Sociological Method* (London 1976).

30   B. Barnes, *Scientific Knowledge and Sociological Theory* (London 1974), p. 1.

31   Taylor, 'Interpretation and the science of man'.

32   cf. Schmidt, *The Concept of Nature*; and P. L. Berger and T. Luckmann, *The Social Construction of Reality* (London 1967).

33   L. Goldmann, *The Human Sciences and Philosophy* (London 1969).

34   Winch tends to make this reduction as in his widely-quoted claim that 'Social relations are expressions of ideas about reality'. See his *The Idea of Social Science* (London 1958), p. 23.

35   See R. Harré and P. F. Secord, *The Explanation of Social Behaviour* (Oxford 1972).

36   There is a large literature on this. Among the more accessible are B. Fay, *Social Theory and Political Practice* (London 1975); Bernstein, *The Restructuring of Social and Political Theory*; Winch, *The Idea of Social Science*; Taylor, 'Interpretation'; Giddens, *New Rules*; K.-O. Apel, 'Communication and the foundations of the humanities', in *Acta Sociologica*, **15** (1972). The term 'concept-dependent' is Bhaskar's. The following section draws extensively from their work.

37   Winch, *The Idea of Social Science*.

38   ibid.

39   Taylor, 'Interpretation'.

40   Williams, *Marxism and Literature*, ch. 2.

41 This term is due to Raymond Williams, *Communications* (Harmondsworth 1962). See also Bourdieu, *Outline of a Theory of Practice*.

42 Bourdieu, 'Vive la crise', p. 776.

43 B. Smart, *Sociology, Phenomenology and Marxian Analysis* (London 1976).

44 London 1958. See also W. E. Connolly *The Terms of Political Discourse* (Oxford 1983).

45 cf. A. Giddens, *A Contemporary Critique of Historical Materialism* (London 1981). A chronological version is to be found in Marx, in Arthur, *The German Ideology*, p. 31.

46 cf. Giddens's distinction between allocative and authoritative power in his *Central Problems of Social Theory* (London 1979).

47 Giddens, *New Rules*.

48 R. Keat, 'Positivism and statistics in social science', in J. Irvine, I. Miles and J. Evans (eds), *Demystifying Social Statistics* (London 1979).

49 Giddens, *New Rules*.

50 I am grateful to John Maclean for discussion of this point. Foucault advocates that our 'point of reference should not be to the great model of language (langue) and signs, but to that of war and battle', *Power/Knowledge* (Brighton 1980), pp. 114–15.

51 This is not to suggest that there have been no effective critiques, based on a proper understanding of hermeneutics. See, in particular, Bhaskar, *The Possibility of Naturalism*, pp. 179–95, Giddens, *New Rules of Sociological Method*, and E. Gellner, 'The new idealism – cause and meaning in the social sciences', in A. Musgrave and I. Lakatos (eds), *Problems in the Philosophy of Science* (Amsterdam 1968) and reprinted in Gellner's *Cause and Meaning in the Social Sciences* (London 1973).

52 Otto Neurath quoted in Apel, 'Communication'.

53 T. Abel, 'The operation called *Verstehen*', *American Journal of Sociology*, **54** (1948).

54 Winch appears to suggest this in *The Idea of Social Science*.

55 Taylor, 'Interpretation'.

56 E. Gellner, 'Concepts and society', reprinted in B. R. Wilson (ed.), *Rationality* (Oxford 1970).

57 Fay, *Social Theory*, provides an accessible introduction to critical theory. See also Connerton, *Critical Sociology*; and D. Held, *Introduction to Critical Theory* (London 1980).

58 P. Ricoeur, 'Restoration of meaning or reduction of illusion?' in Connerton, *Critical Sociology*.

59 Bhaskar, *The Possibility of Naturalism*, pp. 69–83.

60 The best-known exponent of radical behaviourism is B. F. Skinner;

see, for example, his *Beyond Freedom and Dignity* (London 1972).

61 Note that changes in self-understanding do not necessarily lead to material changes; slaves may come to understand fully their situation and yet be unable to do anything to escape their enslavement.

62 My argument has not been that of the 'sociology of knowledge', according to which we should evaluate knowledge by reference to the social positions and ideology of authors. As will become apparent in Chapter 2, I do not believe that recognition of this context of knowledge warrants the relativistic views associated with this school.

Chapter 2 Theory, observation and practical adequacy

1 cf. B. Barnes, *Scientific Knowledge and Sociological Theory* (London 1974), p. 21, who writes of 'disorientation and epistemological shock'.

2 W. V. O. Quine, *From a Logical Point of View* (London 1961).

3 O. Sacks, *The Man who Mistook his Wife for a Hat* (London 1986).

4 C. Taylor, 'Overcoming epistemology', in K. Baynes *et al.* (eds), *After Philosophy* (Cambridge, Mass. 1987).

5 Bhaskar, *The Possibility of Naturalism* (Hassocks 1979); *Reclaiming Reality* (London 1989).

6 Compare Raymond Williams's interesting notes on shifts in the meanings of such terms, particularly 'subjective' and 'objective', in his *Keywords* (London 1976).

7 This is perhaps most common in continental European, particularly French, marxist and marxist-influenced work.

8 M. Friedman, 'The methodology of positive economics', in his *Essays in Positive Economics* (Chicago 1953).

9 My arguments in the sections to follow, particularly those on theory and epistemology, are influenced by Mary Hesse, particularly her *The Structure of Scientific Inference* (London 1974), and *Revolutions and Reconstructions in the Philosophy of Science* (Hassocks 1980). Also R. Harré, *Theories and Things* (London 1961); W. V. O. Quine, *From a Logical Point of View* (London 1961); R. Harré, *Varieties of Realism* (Oxford 1986).

10 In Chapters 4 and 6 I shall argue that there are some restrictive conditions, generally found only in certain natural sciences, in which the ordering framework conception of theory has some rationale.

11 D. J. O. O'Connor and B. Carr, *Introduction to the Theory of Knowledge* (Brighton 1982), ch. 4. See also M. L. J. Abercrombie, *The Anatomy of Judgment* (Harmondsworth 1960).

12 ibid., p. 96.

13 ibid., p. 111–12.

14 The common expression 'data-*gathering*' should also be questioned because it suggests again that the data pre-exist their conceptualization such that they can be simply 'gathered' or 'collected'. Some writers prefer 'data production', but this can be equally misleading as it might suggest that not only the data but the objects to which the data refer are necessarily produced by us. As we will see, the conflation of statements or terms with what they refer to is a major source of epistemological confusion. cf. J. Irvine *et al.*, *Demystifying Social Statistics* (London 1979), p. 3.

15 V. Pratt, *The Philosophy of Social Science* (London 1980), p. 53.

16 E. H. Gombrich, *Art and Illusion* (London 1960), pp. 73–4.

17 Hesse, *The Structure of Scientific Inference*, pp. 22ff. See also I. Lakatos, 'Falsification and the methodology of scientific research programmes', in I. Lakatos and A. Musgrave (eds), *Criticism and the Growth of Knowledge* (Cambridge 1970), pp. 107, 129.

18 cf. Lakatos, 'Falsification', p. 107.

19 cf. Hesse, *The Structure of Scientific Inference*, p. 20 and *Revolutions and Reconstructions*, pp. 94–5. Also Pawson, *A Measure for Measures*, and Harré, *Varieties of Realism*. As Hacking and Harré have pointed out, theory-ladenness implies a very broad concept of theory which does not rest easily with more restrictive senses. These authors accept the sense in which all observation is conceptually-mediated but prefer to reserve 'theory' for these other uses (Hacking, *Representing and Intervening*).

20 Still less does it make any sense to talk of a 'knife-edge' between theory and empirics, e.g. N. Smith, 'Dangers of the empirical turn', *Antipode*, **19** no. 3, 354–63.

21 K. R. Popper, *The Logic of Scientific Disovery* (London 1959). Common though this interpretation of Popper's work is, some of his disciples have argued that he developed more sophisticated formulations later, e.g. Lakatos, 'Falsification'.

22 Gombrich, *Art and Illusion*, p. 76, and compare A. Giddens, *Central Problems in Social Theory* (London 1979), p. 12. Several philosophers have drawn upon Gombrich's work (e.g. Pratt, Barnes, Feyerabend), not always arriving at conclusions similar to mine. In some places he appears to endorse an ordering-framework model of perception, perhaps under the influence of Popper, whose work he acknowledges.

23 Giddens, *Central Problems in Social Theory*, pp. 33–4.

24 We hope that in some way these logical restrictions 'map' or 'correspond' to material restrictions (e.g. of physical possibility or impossibility) between real objects.

25 Some authors use 'denotation' in preference to 'reference', e.g. 'sense is a matter of relations that hold among linguistic expressions: that is to say, among entities all of which belong to one language or another. This distinguishes it clearly from denotation, which relates expressions to classes of entities in the world': J. Lyons, *Language, Meaning and Context* (London 1981), p. 58.

26 'Taken collectively, science has its double dependence upon language and experience; but this duality is not significantly traceable into the statements of science taken one by one': Quine, *From a Logical Point of View*, p. 42 and cf. p. 67. The same, of course, applies to non-science. Also: 'our statements about the external world face the tribunal of sense experience not individually but only as a corporate body', ibid., p. 41; and see Hesse, *The Structure of Scientific Inference*, p. 26. Nevertheless, not every part of the corporate body need be implicated in the trial.

27 cf. R. J. Bernstein, *The Restructuring of Social and Political Theory* (Oxford 1976), and R. Rorty, *Philosophy and the Mirror of Nature* (Oxford 1980), p. 273.

28 Some modern marxists, particularly (neo-) Althusserians, seem to believe that concepts can only be used when they are named. This would seem to explain the way in which the names of concepts are paraded up and down the pages, and vocabulary is deliberately restricted (i.e. impoverished) until words like 'reproduction' are used almost like incantations.

29 cf. B. Barnes, *Interests and the Growth of Knowledge* (London 1977), ch. 1.

30 Rorty, *Philosophy*. (I do not wish to endorse Rorty's refusal to consider ontology, and his consequent disinterest in the determination of the success of particular practices or ways of coping by the structure of the world. See Bhaskar, *Reclaiming Reality*.)

31 There are grounds, therefore, for allowing that some problems (or 'puzzles' as Kuhn calls them) are unsolved not because the conceptual apparatus is deficient but because their users are not sufficiently skilled. T. S. Kuhn, *The Structure of Scientific Revolutions* (Chicago 1970).

32 Maurice Bloch provides a useful critique of the tendency to overestimate context in the construction of meaning. Bloch, *Ritual History and Power* (London 1989). See also Giddens, *Social Theory and Modern Society* (Oxford 1987), p. 100.

33 J. Young commenting on the media: 'They select events which are atypical, present them in a stereotypical fashion and contrast them against a backcloth of normality which is overly typical.' Quoted in S. Cohen (ed.), *Images of Deviance* (Harmondsworth 1971).

34 See the discussions of this phenomenon in relation to 'mugging' in S. Hall *et al.*, *Policing the Crisis* (London 1978).

35 S. Cohen, *Folk Devils and Moral Panics* (London 1972).

36 M. Douglas, *Rules and Meanings* (Harmondsworth 1973), p. 13.

37 G. Lichtheim, *The Concept of Ideology* (New York 1967).

38 D. Schon, *Displacement of Concepts* (London 1963).

39 Hesse, *Revolutions and Reconstructions*; and Harré, *Theories and Things*, p. 38.

40 ibid. Against this Rorty comments, 'It is pictures rather than propositions, metaphors rather than statements, which determine most of our philosophical convictions', *Philosophy*, p. 12.

41 Friedman, 'The methodology of positive economics'.

42 See below, Chapters 5 and 6.

43 R. J. Chorley and P. Haggett, *Models in Geography* (London 1967).

44 In this way, Chorley and Haggett manage to refer at length to studies of the conceptual mediation of perception, only to ignore this in the way they interpret the relationship of 'data' to models and theories.

45 I have used the term 'naïve objectivism' in preference to the more usual 'empiricism' on the grounds that there are many variants of empiricism, not all of which are vulnerable to these criticisms. Many anti-empiricists in social science have failed to note how some of the foremost empiricist philosophers, such as Hume, attacked beliefs in the incorrigibility of observation. See O'Connor and Carr, *Introduction to the Theory of Knowledge*.

46 After Popper, these points are sometimes known as 'basic statements'.

47 R. Harré, *The Philosophies of Science* (Oxford 1972).

48 Determined idealists can always outflank such arguments by claiming that the alleged independence of the world *and* its capacity to surprise us are products of the mind. They can even refuse to accept the reality of their own practical interventions in the world too. Yet in continuing to speak and act in much the same way as believers in the existence of a real world and in still distinguishing empirically false from true propositions they retain an implicit theory of such a world even if they use elaborate contrivances for refusing to acknowledge it. cf. Bhaskar's comments on 'implicit ontologies' in his critique of Feyeraband and Bachelard, in *New Left Review*, **94** (1975).

49 cf. Barnes, *Interests and the Growth of Knowledge*, and Rorty: 'the notion of "accurate representation" is simply an automatic compliment which we pay to those beliefs which are successful in helping us do what we want to do', *Philosophy*, p. 10.

50 cf. A. Collier, 'In defence of epistemology', *Radical Philosophy*, **20** (1979), and T. Skillen, 'Discourse fever: post marxist modes of production', ibid.

51 Giddens, *Central Problems in Social Theory*, pp. 11–16, *Social Theory and Modern Society* (Oxford 1987), pp. 81ff.

52 D. Sayer, *Marx's Method: Science and Critique in Capital* (Hassocks 1979).

53 R. Bhaskar, *The Possibility of Naturalism* (Hassocks 1979), p. 31 and see note 52.

54 Layder objects to this (a) on the grounds that there are techno-logical means for spanning water (bridges, aeroplane flights, etc.) and (b) on the grounds that what is practically adequate need not be morally acceptable. But (a) is merely a change in the example – crossing a bridge or flying do not constitute walking on water! – while (b) is a red herring: no claim regarding moral acceptability was made – practical adequacy obviously need not override moral criteria. (D. Layder, *The Realist Image in Social Science*, London 1990).

55 Some 'pragmatists', such as Rorty, take the view that there is no difference between the instrumentalist and realist positions, arguing that the appeal to the nature of the world is superfluous. By default, practical adequacy appears a matter of accident or convention, as if sticks and stones could break our bones not because of their nature but because we think they can. Rorty, *Philosophy*; Bhaskar, *Reclaiming Realism* (London 1989).

56 D. Österberg, *Metasociology* (Oslo 1988), p. 78.

57 Or in Bhaskar's terms, the distinction between the transitive and the intransitive dimensions of science. See his *Realist Theory of Science* (Leeds 1975).

58 For discussions of the implications of Kuhn's work for social science, see Bernstein, *Restructuring*; A. Giddens, *Studies in Social and Political Theory* (London 1977).

59 Lakatos, 'Falsification', uses the term 'mob psychology'.

60 E. Gellner, *Culture, Identity and Politics* (Cambridge 1987), p. 156.

61 Even the arch conventionalist Feyeraband concedes that 'it is possible to refute a theory by an experience that is entirely interpreted within its own terms'. 'Consolations for the specialist', in Lakatos and Musgrave, *Criticism and the Growth of Knowledge*.

62 Pawson, *A Measure for Measure: a Manifesto for Empirical Sociology* (London 1989), p. 115. Although I would question many aspects of Pawson's view of realism and social science, I would strongly recommend his discussion of measurement in natural science as a theory-laden, material practice.

63   See the critiques of Hindness and Hirst's idealism in Collier, 'In defence of epistemology', and Skillen, 'Discourse fever'.

64   R. Norman, 'On seeing things differently', *Radical Philosophy*, I no. 1 (1972).

65   D. T. Campbell, 'Qualitative knowing in action research', in M. Brenner *et al.* (eds), *The Social Contexts of Method* (London 1978).

66   D. Shapere, 'Meaning and scientific change', in R. Colodny (ed.), *Mind and Cosmos* (Pittsburgh 1966), pp. 67–8.

67   In this context, theoretical revolutions look more modest – 'a "new theory" is simply a rather minor change in a vast network of beliefs', Rorty, *Philosophy*, p, 284.

68   Bhaskar, *The Possibility of Naturalism*, p. 189. See also R. Keat and J. Urry, *Social Theory as Science* (London 1975), p. 216; A Giddens, *New Rules of Sociological Method* (London 1976); and Bernstein, *Restructuring*, for discussions of attempts to resolve the problems of relativism by reference to hermeneutics.

69   cf. Lakatos, 'Falsification'. Hesse, *The Structure of Scientific Inference*, pp. 298ff., and *Revolutions and Reconstructions*, pp. 96ff.

70   Contrary to the naïve objectivist and conventionalist views reference need not always be an all-or-nothing affair, as it is in picking out a particular individual in a crowd, when we either get the right one or we don't. See Rorty, *Philosophy*.

71   Quine, *From a Logical Point of View*, p. 47.

72   Recently a new form of idealism, associated with 'post-structuralism', has developed. This takes language out of its practical context, denies that it can refer to something extralinguistic and focuses upon the allegedly indeterminate character of the play of difference within language as we endlessly interpret one text in the light of others. Such arguments require their proponents to deny what they must do in practice, even in the act of putting those same arguments, for without the possibility of reference and a significant degree of stability of meaning, communication is impossible. Like relativism it is self-refuting, for since it refuses authors any control and readers any authority over the interpretation of texts, consistent post-structuralists must concede readings that directly contradict post-structuralism. Notice too the emphasis on texts, reminding us of the origin of these ideas in the study of *literature*. Students of literature are quick to remind us of the common root of 'fact' and 'fiction' in the sense of something made, and that literature can claim to pursue 'truth'. But we can concede these points without having to agree that a poet and an economist or sociologist or whatever are involved in the same kind of activity and subject to the same kind of constraints and freedoms. In addition to social scientific texts,

social scientists study texts in so far as they constitute part of their object and in so far as they provide rival accounts to their own. But they also study many things which are not texts or text-like. We should therefore be wary of accepting imperialistic attempts to universalize arguments about particular and rather special kinds of knowledge. C. Norris, *The Contest of Faculties* (London 1988); A. Jefferson 'Structuralism and post-structuralism', in A. Jefferson and D. Robey (eds), *Modern Literary Theory: A Comparative Introduction* (London 1986); T. Eagleton, *Literary Theory: An Introduction* (London 1983).

73 Barnes, *Scientific Knowledge*, p. 38.

74 Cited in Quine, *From a Logical Point of View*, p. 79.

75 ibid., p. 25.

76 This danger is increased where social scientists ignore common-sense understanding. Whatever the faults of common sense, it is at least adapted to a wide range of contexts – wider, in most cases, than are scientific theories. Consequently, when social scientists, 'rediscover' formerly overlooked aspects it is sometimes found that they were recognized in everyday knowledge all along. Naturally, this hardly improves social science's reputation. If common sense is criticized for being unexamined, then we should examine it rather than ignore it or uncritically absorb it. Raymond Williams's work is interesting in this respect, for while it is usually deeply theoretical (in the sense I have suggested) it often starts from analysis of everyday concepts.

77 See, for example, Raymond Williams's meticulous explication of the changing concept of 'parliamentary democracy', in *Marxism Today*, **26** no. 6 (1982).

Chapter 3   Theory and method I: abstraction, structure and cause

1 For example, J. Elster, *Logic and Society* (London 1978), J. Roemer, *Analytical Marxism* (Cambridge 1986), Introduction.

2 My use of 'abstract' and 'concrete' is, I think, equivalent to Marx's. See, for example, the 1857 Introduction in *Grundrisse* (London 1973). Some readers may note a similarity between this initial definition of abstractions and Weberian 'ideal types'. However, the latter pay no attention to the distinctions of different types of relation introduced in this chapter. See Chapter 9 for further comments on ideal types.

3 cf. ibid. 'The concrete concept is concrete because it is a synthesis of many definitions, thus representing the unity of diverse aspects', p. 101.

4   I do not wish, however, to make any distinction between 'relations' and 'relationships', as some others have done. I will use the two terms interchangeably.

5   In case any confusion might arise from other uses of 'connection', I am restricting the term in this context to material connections and excluding logical ones in the sense of 'common factors', though conceptual connections of *dependence* (as opposed to similarity) would count as substantial.

6   Zeleny comments on a tendency to interpret all terms 'asubstantialistically' (sic!), and as purely formal. *The Logic of Marx* (Oxford 1980), p. 27.

7   cf. R. Bhaskar, *The Possibility of Naturalism* (Hassocks 1979), p. 54 and Elster, *Logic and Society*, pp. 20–5.

8   ibid. and R. Harré, *Social Being* (Oxford 1979), p. 24. I don't think the possibility of individuals internalizing such attitudes, as in 'self-respect', undermines the claim about their relational nature.

9   As we shall see, the errors also often arise because, despite their simplicity, these questions are not even *asked* in some social research, and instead analysis is restricted to the discovery of formal relations rather than these (necessary or contingent) substantial relations.

10 In view of this need to define exactly what aspects of the objects are under discussion with respect to their relata, it might be objected that it is purely a matter of definition whether we call relations internal or external. In a *limited* sense it is, but definitions which attempt to refer to real objects are not arbitrary – their applicability and practical adequacy depend on the nature of the things to which they are applied. For example, simply as a human being, I could be said to be externally related to the human beings I live with, but as personalities I have been heavily influenced by them and our actions may be internally related. The categories 'human being', 'personality' and 'action' are not arbitrarily interchangeable but refer to different aspects of the object.

11 cf. M. Barrett, *Women's Oppression Today* (London 1980) and S. Walby, *Patriarchy at Work* (Cambridge 1986). Since the term 'patriarchy' is used in many ways, we would have to clarify this too.

12 When written down, the process of abstraction may appear laborious, even ponderous – as it does in much of Marx's theoretical work – but it is an essential foundation of sound theorizing. See A. Sayer, 'Abstraction: a realist interpretation', *Radical Philosophy*, **28** (1981). As Zeleny observes, 'Marx carefully distinguishes

cases where entering into particular relations alters the substantial properties of a particular appearance, and cases where it does not alter them, where these substantial properties remain essentially unaltered by their entry into new relations.' Zeleny, *The Logic of Marx*, p. 26.

13 My definition is influenced by but not identical to Harré's in *Social Being*.

14 A. Gorz, *Farewell to the Working Class* (London 1982), p. 58.

15 Elster, *Logic and Society*, p. 97.

16 Harré, *Social Being*, p. 38.

17 Bhaskar, *The Possibility of Naturalism*, p. 44.

18 A. Giddens, *Central Problems of Social Theory*. Harré introduces the idea that concepts which are constitutive of actions can act as 'templates' and that these are necessary for the reproduction of structures: *Social Being*.

19 A. Giddens, 'Functionalism: après la lutte', in his *Studies in Social and Political Theory* (London 1977).

20 This 'structure–agency debate' has figured prominently in marxist theoretical discourse in the last twenty years – although its relevance embraces all social theory. See, for example, the Miliband–Poulantzas debate, in R. Blackburn, *Ideology and Social Science* (London 1972), and the reaction of E. P. Thompson to Althusser's structuralism, *The Poverty of Theory* (London 1979), and P. Anderson's reply to Thompson in *Arguments within English Marxism* (London 1980). Although this literature at least has the merit of discussing the problem – much of social science is simply ignorant of 'structure' – it has failed to keep abreast of the important advances made in the philosophy of social science by Giddens, Bhaskar and Bourdieu. See also the *Journal for the Theory of Social Behaviour*, **13** no. 1 (1983).

21 P. Bourdieu, *Towards a Theory of Practice* (Cambridge 1977), and also his 'Men and machines', in K. Knorr-Cetina and A. V. Cicourel, *Advances in Social Theory and Methodology: Towards an Integration of Micro- and Macro-Sociologies* (Boston 1981).

22 Williams, *Marxism and Literature*, ch. 9.

23 Cited in Bourdieu, 'Men and machines', p. 305. Strictly speaking, Marx should have said 'behaviour of things' rather than 'logic of things', but I guess that would have spoiled the effect. In this context Elster's *Logic and Society* is interesting for while it generally uses logic to great effect, it sometimes also falls foul of this trap; for example, in the treatment of causation as a question of logic.

24 cf. K. Menzies, *Sociological Theory in Use* (London 1982), pp. 127–9, and G. Kay, 'Why labour is the starting point of capital', in

D. Elson (ed.), *Value: The Representation of Labour in Capitalism* (London 1979), p. 55.

25 Giddens distinguishes between generalizations known to and applied by actors and generalizations about circumstances acting upon agents, whether they realize it or not. Each is 'unstable in respect of the other'. A. Giddens, *The Constitution of Society* (Cambridge 1984), pp. xix–xx and 343ff.

26 Harré, *Social Being*, pp. 108–9.

27 Harré, 'Men and machines', p. 147.

28 Elster, *Logic and Society*, pp. 99.

29 B. R. Berelson and G. A. Steiner, *Human Behavior: and inventory of scientific findings* (New York 1964), p. 3.

30 ibid., p. 370.

31 cf. Winch, *The Idea of Social Science* (London 1958), and A. R. Louch, *The Explanation of Human Action* (Oxford 1966), ch. 2.

32 Davis and Golden, cited in Berelson and Steiner, *Human Behavior*, p. 604.

33 M. Castells, *The Urban Question* (London 1977).

34 This is a 'generative' rather than Humean conception of cause. See Harré, *The Principles of Scientific Thinking*, p. 103; Bhaskar, *A Realist Theory of Science*. See also R. Harré and E. H. Madden, *Causal Powers* (Oxford 1975), for an exhaustive defence.

35 My elision of 'power' and 'causal power' is deliberate here, for it helps us to recognize that power need not always take the negative form of domination over others but can simply mean power to create. For an excellent realist analysis of social power, see J. Isaac, *Power and Marxist Theory: a Realist View* (Ithaca, NY 1988).

36 Bhaskar, *A Realist Theory of Science*, pp. 45ff.

37 ibid.

38 ibid., p. 238, and Harré and Madden, *Causal Powers*, p. 85.

39 But see K. Marx, *Capital*, vol. 3 (London 1963), p. 252, where he seems to *distinguish* laws from tendencies. Apart from this instance, I think Marx operates consistently with a generative concept of cause. See also Bhaskar's discussion of tendencies in *A Realist Theory of Science*, pp. 229ff.

40 The problems of testing causal claims are discussed below in Chapter 7.

41 Bhaskar, *A Realist Theory of Science*.

42 I see no reason for subscribing to the view – found in R. Keat and J. Urry, *Social Theory as Science* (London 1975), and Bhaskar – that mechanisms are always 'underlying' and unobservable. Clockwork, the ways of producing commodities, electing MPs, etc., involve mechanisms which are no less observable than the effects they produce. cf. Louch, *The Explanation of Human Action*, p. 41.

43 Harré, *The Philosophies of Science*.
44 Bhaskar, *The Possibility of Naturalism*.
45 D. B. Massey and R. A. Meegan, *The Anatomy of Job Loss* (London 1982).
46 Bhaskar, *A Realist Theory of Science*.
47 Harré, *The Philosophies of Science*, p. 117. See R. Boudon, *The Logic of Sociological Explanation* (Harmondsworth 1974), p. 53, for an example of this error. There are resemblances between the realist account and Aristotle's fourfold schema of causes – material, formal, efficient and final: material causes are the materials which constitute the thing undergoing change, such as the child undergoing socialization or the sand out of which glass is made; formal 'causes' are the forms of the things being made or resulting; the efficient cause is the thing which actually *generates* the change; and the final cause is either the state towards which the process happens to lead or towards which some agent intends it to lead. The second and fourth of these now seem redundant, and while the third seems the closest to modern conceptions it is increasingly being realized that the first cannot be ignored as they are in orthodox accounts where causation is merely presented as a relation between or succession of events.
48 My arguments are derived from Bhaskar, *The Possibility of Naturalism*, ch. 3.
49 On this example, see D. Harvey, *Social Justice and the City* (London 1973), ch. 4.
50 Research on housing has in fact been characterized by such a regress, although sometimes it has mistakenly been assumed that these 'levels' of explanation are competing rather than complementary. See K. Bassett and J. Short, *Housing and Residential Structure: Alternative Approaches* (London 1980).
51 On the relationship between explanation and evaluation, see C. Taylor, 'Neutrality in political science', in A. Ryan (ed.), *The Philosophy of Social Explanation* (Oxford 1973), and Bhaskar, *The Possibility of Naturalism*, pp. 69ff., and A. Sayer, 'Defensible values in geography', in R. J. Johnston and D. T. Herbert (eds), *Geography and the Urban Environment*, vol. 4 (London 1981).
52 See below, Chapter 7.
53 The latter are discussed in Chapter 6.
54 These methods are derived from J. S. Mill's 'Method of agreement and method of difference'. See his *A System of Logic* (London 1961), and the discussions in Harré, *The Philosophies of Science*, pp. 38ff., and D. Willer and J. Willer, *Systematic Empiricism: A Critique of Pseudoscience* (Englewood Cliffs, NJ 1973).

55   For examples, see my 'A critique of urban modelling', *Progress in Planning*, **6** part 3 (1976), pp. 187–254.

56   For example, Menzies, *Sociological Theory is Use*, p. 158, writes, 'In the light of the present development of sociology, usually the only satisfactory way of ordering the variables that can safely be used is temporal – earlier events cause later ones.' Note the significant use of 'ordering' and the substitution of studies of relationships between 'variables' for qualitative forms of analysis. Although Menzies cites realism with approval, he misses most of its useful points in assuming the search for order as the key to causal analysis.

Chapter 4   Theory and method II: types of system and their implications

1   R. Harré, *Social Being* (Oxford 1979), p. 85.
2   The following discussion is based on R. Bhaskar's *A Realist Theory of Science* (Leeds 1975), pp. 163ff., and *The Possibility of Naturalism* (Hassocks 1979), pp. 124ff. See also the discussion of emergence in A. Collier, *Scientific Realism and Socialist Thought* (Hemel Hempstead 1989).
3   ibid., ch. 2, and R. Williams, *The Long Revolution* (Harmondsworth 1961), ch. 3.
4   See K. Soper, 'Marxism, materialism and biology', in J. Mepham and D. H. Ruben (eds), *Issues in Marxist Philosophy*, vol. 2 (Hassocks 1979), for a lucid discussion of the problem.
5   Many supporters of 'socio-biology' have fallen into both traps – that is, they have ignored stratification in their analyses and traded upon the non-sequitur in their prescriptions for practice.
6   See Bhaskar, *A Reality Theory of Science*, ch. 2.
7   Other philosophers have used a concept of 'closed systems' but in different senses – usually as a totally isolated system. Such a system might not satisfy Bhaskar's criteria. See, for example, K. R. Popper, *The Poverty of Historicism* (London 1957), p. 139, or H. Blalock, *Methods of Social Research* (New York 1972). Note also that in using the word 'system' I have no intention of supporting a 'systems approach'; indeed suchlike are generally antithetical to most of what this book argues for.
8   Bhaskar, *A Realist Theory of Science*. In some cases, as we will see, regularities may help *conceal* mechanisms.
9   In comparing the 'order' of natural and social systems, some researchers have been so taken by the evidence of regularities that they have failed even to note the *intentionally-produced* character of many social 'regularities'. See, for example, R. J. Chorley and P.

Haggett (eds), *Models in Geography* (London 1967), and virtually any other text on models in geography.

10 cf. J. S. Mill, *A System of Logic* (London 1961).

11 Bhaskar, *A Realist Theory of Science*, ch. 2.

12 Those already familiar with the philosophy of science may find my use of the term 'instrumentalist' strange, for realism and instrumentalism are usually taken as opposites. As a philosophy of science having pretensions to universal applicability, instrumentalism is certainly the antithesis of realism: theories are treated as mere calculating devices which cannot claim to grasp the nature and mechanisms of their objects. Realism asserts the possibility of the latter (while accepting that the grasp is a fallible one) and dismisses the former. However, I think it has to be recognized that there are occasions when all we want is a calculating device; and, as I argue in the following section, there are conditions, albeit restricted ones, where this aim can be achieved. As long as one doesn't confuse this achievement with that of giving a causal explanation, realists can happily concede a restricted domain to instrumentalism. Indeed, if realism is characterized as a philosophy of science which tries to establish the cognitive possibilities of different types of object, it *must* make such a concession. Beliefs which are suspect as *general* beliefs often have a limited degree of practical adequacy and there is always a material basis for this adequacy.

13 *A Realist Theory of Science*, p. 95.

14 See, for example, G. G. von Wright, *Explanation and Understanding* (London 1971).

15 cf. A. R. Louch, *The Explanation of Human Action* (Oxford 1966).

16 See Bhaskar, *The Possibility of Naturalism*. Also W. Outhwaite, *New Philosophies of Social Science* (London 1987), pp. 8–10.

17 For instance, Popper's example of the physical causes of a person's death, ibid., p. 206.

18 e.g. Winch and some other advocates of hermeneutics.

19 Harré, *Social Being*, p. 129.

20 Nor can they sensibly be made objects of predictive generalizations. The example of the relationship between urbanization and industrialization discussed earlier suffered from the error of treating the processes as if they were parametric.

21 R. Harré, *The Philosophies of Science* (Oxford 1972), p. 57, cites the example of the laws of chemical combination and the theory of mechanism of chemical reactions.

22 Some philosophies of science actually eschew explanation as a goal, for example, Karl Pearson, *The Grammar of Science* (London 1892). See Chapter 4, n. 37. On the one hand the availability of closed systems in certain sciences facilitates analysis as mechanisms

and their effects stand in stable relationships; on the other, the regularities may conceal some mechanisms.

23   cf. Harré, *Principles of Scientific Thinking* (London 1970), p. 19.

24   Strictly speaking it is often not even curve fitting, because the equations are fitted to data for a single point in time rather than time series.

25   R. Keat and J. Urry, *Social Theory as Science* (London 1975), give the example of Koplik spots which precede the contraction of measles.

26   Popper, *The Poverty of Historicism*.

27   This oversight is characteristic of a social science which cannot recognize its own contribution to the development of a society in which much of what happens is beyond our control. cf. M. Horkheimer, 'Traditional and critical theory', in P. Connerton, *Critical Sociology* (Harmondsworth 1976), p. 214.

28   Some economic theories of market exchange which abstract from time have to assume such a 'pre-reconciliation' of ex ante demand and supply. See G. L. S. Shackle, *Time in Economics* (Amsterdam 1967).

29   Recall our earlier discussion of auto-pilots and our ability to respond to events whose timing is not predictable.

30   See, for example, C. Freeman, J. Clark and L. Soete, *Unemployment and Technical Innovation: a study of long waves and economic development* (London 1982).

31   Mill, *A System of Logic*, ch. 9. section 2, p. 585.

32   Marx, *Grundrisse*, p. 100.

33   For further examples from geography, see my 'Explanation in economic geography', *Progress in Human Geography*, **6** no. 1 (1982), pp. 68–88.

34   cf. A. Sohn-Rethel, *Intellectual and Manual Labour* (London 1978); L. Colletti, 'Introduction' to Marx's *Early Writings* (Harmondsworth 1975); D. Elson, *Value: the Representation of Labour in Capitalism* (London 1979), especially the essays by Elson and Kay.

35   For further discussion of abstraction and marxist theory, see my 'Abstraction: a realist interpretation'. Also B. Jessop, *The Capitalist State* (Oxford 1982), pp. 213ff.; and J. Allen, 'Property relations and landlordism: a realist approach', *Society and Space*, **1** no. 2 (1983).

36   See Chapter 5 on *a priori* elements of theories.

37   D. Sayer, *Marx's Method* (Hassocks 1979).

38   D. Harvey, 'Three myths in search of reality in urban studies', *Environment and Planning D: Society and Space*, **5** (1987), 367–76. Also, A. Warde, 'Recipes for a pudding: a comment on locality', *Antipode*, **21** (1989), 274–81.

39 J. Kornai, *Contradictions and Dilemmas: Studies on the Socialist Economy and Society* (Cambridge, Mass. 1986).

40 It is no accident that disciplines like economics which cling to conceptions of theory appropriate for closed systems should have an undersocialized conception of individuals and tend to abstract from historical change and geographical differentiation. For defences of more evolutionary, narrative approaches in economics see R. R. Nelson, 'The tension between process stories and equilibrium models', in R. Langlois (ed.), *Economics as a Process* (Cambridge 1986), pp. 135–50; M. Storper and R. A. Walker, *The Capitalist Imperative* (Oxford 1989); and P. Auerbach, *Competition: the Economics of Industrial Change* (Cambridge 1989).

41 For fuller discussions of space and social theory see: D. Gregory and J. Urry (eds), *Social Relations and Spatial Structures* (London 1985); A. Sayer, 'Space and social theory', in B. Wittrock and P. Wagner (eds), *Social Theory and Human Agency* (Stockholm 1991); N. Thrift, 'On the determination of social action in space and time', *Environment and Planning D: Society and Space*, 1 (1983); A. Giddens, *The Constitution of Society*; J. Urry, 'Society, space and locality', *Environment and Planning D: Society and Space*, 5 (1987), 4, pp. 435–44.

42 T. Hägerstrand, 'Time-geography: focus on the corporeality of man, society, and environment', *The Science and Praxis of Complexity* (London 1985).

43 J. Blaut, 'Space and process', reprinted in W. K. D. Davies (ed.), *The Conceptual Revolution in Geography* (London 1972).

44 R. D. Sack, 'A concept of physical space', *Geographical Analysis*, 5 (1973), pp. 16–34.

45 Harré, *The Principles of Scientific Thinking*.

46 Many would-be proponents of a relative concept have erred in making this deduction; see, for example, M. Castells, *The Urban Question* (London 1977). Ironically, such authors often talk uninhibitedly of developing a 'theory of space' (rather than the things which constitute space) at the same time as they castigate others for spatial fetishism.

47 See R. D. Sack, *Conceptions of Space in Social Thought* (London 1980). Although this advocates a realist approach, it is seriously flawed by a failure to appreciate the significance of closed and open systems and necessity in realist philosophy. Nevertheless, with this qualification in mind, pp. 3–19 and ch. 3 contain excellent discussions of space. See also my 'The difference that space makes', in J. Urry and D. Gregory (eds), *Social Relations and Spatial Structures* (London 1985).

48 P. Saunders, *Social Theory and the Urban Question* (London 1981).

49   It is therefore quite wrong to describe the realist conception of space as 'inherently contingent'. Cf. N. Smith 'Uneven development and location theory', in R. Peet and N. Thrift (eds.), *New Models in Geography, Vol. 1* (London 1990), pp. 142–63. Also A. Warde, 'Recipes for a pudding: a comment on locality', *Antipode*, 21 (1989), pp. 274–81.

50   It is significant that those, like Harvey and Soja, who have argued for a stronger role for space in social theory, have been unable to get beyond such vague spatial claims in their own theorizations. See D. Harvey, *The Postmodern Condition* (Oxford 1989); E. W. Soja, *Postmodern Geographies* (London 1989).

51   A. Lösch, *The Economics of Location* (New Haven, Conn. 1954).

52   Harré refers to this as the 'Principle of Spatial Indifference', *The Principles of Scientific Thinking*.

53   As I have argued elsewhere, it is important not to overstate the dangers of the abstraction from space, as some geographers have done. The fact that social scientists have got away with this abstraction for so long should not make us assume they are entirely in the right, but neither should they be dismissed in a wave of disciplinary imperialism on the part of geographers. Sayer, 'The difference that space makes', and 'Space and social theory'.

Chapter 5   Some influential misadventures in the philosophy of science

1   R. Bhaskar, *A Realist Theory of Science* (Leeds 1975), pp. 215ff.

2   R. Harré, *The Philosophies of Science* (Oxford 1972), p. 39.

3   Metaphysics concerns the meaning of the most basic categories in which we think, such as time, space, matter or relation. Despite its pejorative connotations in some circles, no system of thought can escape some or other metaphysical commitments.

4   See R. Harré and E. H. Madden, *Causal Powers* (Oxford 1975).

5   See A. R. Louch, *The Explanation of Human Action* (Oxford 1966).

6   *The Entropy Law and the Economic Process* (Cambridge, Mass. 1971), p. 64.

7   Harré and Madden, *Causal Powers*, pp. 6, 110.

8   ibid., p. 75. See also Bhaskar, *A Realist Theory of Science*, pp. 215ff.

9   ibid.

10   Harré and Madden, *Causal Powers*, p. 75.

11   These claims are, of course, fallible (or, if you will, 'vulnerable to the little problem of induction') but in this respect they are no different from observation statements or statements arrived at by

deduction, though a good deal less uncertain than claims about future contingencies.

12 Bhaskar, *A realist Theory of Science*, p. 220.

13 See A. Collier, 'In defence of epistemology', *Radical Philosophy*, **20** (1979). Recall the qualifications made in Chapter 2 about such metaphors as 'mapping'.

14 Harré and Madden, *Causal Powers*, p. 48.

15 It may help to fix this point if one imagines reactions to arbitrary claims such as 'by definition, the poor are conservative in political ideology'. Harré and Madden comment: 'Should the relation between the nature of an entity and its powers be naturally necessary, we hold this to be an *a posteriori* truth about the entity, and so it must be the case that in that world such an entity is capable of an alternative, earlier and more naïve description, under which its nature thus described is merely contingently related to those of its powers and liabilities which are later discovered to be necessary consequences of its real nature', ibid., p. 80.

16 Bhaskar, *A Realist Theory of Science*, p. 201.

17 cf. W. V. O. Quine, *From a Logical Point of View* (Cambridge, Mass. 1961).

18 I would suggest, but don't have space or energy to argue, that many philosophical puzzles such as the paradoxes of material implication, derive from sources such as this – i.e. a confusion of the relation between things with those of logic, or more generally of the objects of knowledge with knowledge itself.

19 K. R. Popper, *Conjectures and Refutations* (London 1963), p. 20.

20 K. Marx, *Capital*, vol. 1 (London 1963). Postface to the 2nd edition: 'Of course the method of presentation must differ in form from that of inquiry. The latter has to appropriate the material in detail, to analyse its different forms of development and to track down their inner connection. Only after this work has been done successfully, if the life of the subject-matter is now reflected back in the ideas, then it may appear as if we have before us an *a priori* construction.'

21 This may not matter too much as a simplifying assumption in an abstract theoretical argument but where it is applied to a concrete system (i.e. one in which we know some preferences are not revealed) then the structure of the discourse can be reasonably said to be misleading.

22 K. Marx, *Grundrisse* (Harmondsworth 1973). Attacks on theorists who are misled by the logical structure of discourse so that they confuse it with the structure of their objects are scattered throughout Marx's works, for example in his critique of Proudhon. Thanks again to modern philosophies' confusion of knowledge of objects with

objects of knowledge (what Bhaskar terms the 'epistemic fallacy') many have found Marx's criticisms difficult to understand.

23 Here I am restricting the definition to formal deductive logic, excluding other types such as the logic of norms or imperatives and informal uses such as 'the logic of the arms race'.

24 J. Elster, *Logic and Society* (London 1978), p. 2.

25 This is the main limitation of Elster's *Logic and Society* (London 1978), i.e. a tendency to ignore meaning change and historically specific forms of context dependence through a preference for more easily manipulable timeless abstractions. Elster seems to recognize the failing at one point but does nothing to remedy it.

26 R. Harré, *Social Being* (Oxford 1979), p. 160.

27 cf. Harré's definition of deductivism in his *Principles of Scientific Thinking* (London 1970).

28 Some of Popper's critics share the same problem and can only fill the gulf created by these omissions with 'values'. Given the common assumption that values are a-rational and perhaps irrational (which I do not accept), it then appears that the 'logic of science' view is to be challenged by a questioning of the *rationality* of science.

29 cf. Bhaskar, *A Realist Theory of Science*, pp. 215ff.

30 Rom Harré argues that logic is merely part of the *rhetoric* of science, and secondary to its practical and conceptual business, *Varieties. . .*, and his *The Principles of Scientific Thinking*. For a realist view of logic in social science, see J. Allen 'In search of a method: Hegel, Marx and Realism', *Radical Philosophy*, **35** (1983), pp. 26–33.

31 Both for his philosophy of science and for his critique of Marx and Freud. See, for example, *The Logic of Scientific Discovery*; *The Poverty of Historicism*; *The Open Society and its Enemies*; *Conjectures and Refutations*.

32 See above, Chapter 2.

33 The belief that it is proof is called the 'fallacy of affirming the consequent'. See below, Chapter 7.

34 *The Principles of Scientific Thinking*.

35 Bhaskar, *A Realist Theory of Science*, p. 207.

36 Authorship of this is also claimed by Carl Hempel, who has written numerous papers on the subject. See his *Aspects of Scientific Explanation* (New York 1965), for a summary. Nomological means 'involving laws'.

37 See R. Keat and J. Urry, *Social Theory as Science* (London 1975). For further criticisms of the D–N model, see T. Benton, *Philosophical Foundations of the Three Sociologies* (London 1977), chs. 2 and 3.

38 A. R. Louch, *The Explanation of Human Action* (Oxford 1966).

39 Note that both these examples, particularly the last, suggest that reasons can be causes.

40 R. G. Lipsey, *An Introduction to Positive Economics* (London 1963) (1st edn and later editions).

41 See I. Lakatos, 'Falsification and the methodology of scientific research programmes', in I. Lakatos and A. Musgrove (eds), *Criticism and the Growth of Knowledge* (Cambridge 1970). Popper's falsificationism is dealt with in more detail in Chapter 8 and some constructive suggestions on testing are offered in Chapter 7.

Chapter 6 Quantitative methods in social science

1 Quoted in B. R. Berelson and G. A. Steiner, *Human Behavior: an inventory of scientific findings* (New York 1964), p. 14.

2 Quoted in M. Dobb, *Theories of Value and Distribution since Adam Smith* (Cambridge 1973).

3 J. D. Bernal, *Science in History* (3rd edn) (Harmondsworth 1969), p. 483. But see R. Harré, *The Principles of Scientific Thinking* (London 1970), p. 9.

4 See R. J. Bernstein, *The Restructuring of Social and Political Theory* (Oxford 1976).

5 ibid.

6 See above, pp. 117–18.

7 'Cardinal measurability, therefore is not a measure just like any other, but it reflects a particular physical property of a category of things', N. Georgescu-Roegen, *Analytical Economics* (Cambridge, Mass. 1966), p. 49.

8 The error is common not only in neoclassical theory but in neo-Ricardian value theory and some interpretations of Marxian value theory. See below, section on 'the role of assumptions'.

9 See D. B. Massey and R. A. Meegan, *The Anatomy of Job Loss* (London 1982).

10 I owe this example to Doreen Massey.

11 A good illustration is provided by the economist John Roemer's use of models of economies consisting of two persons to illuminate the question of whether economic exploitation depends on the existence of classes, J. Roemer, *Free to Lose* (Cambridge 1988).

12 Input–output and many other models have a similar form.

13 *A Realist Theory of Science*, p. 77.

14 ibid.

15 D. H. Meadows *et al.*, *The Limits to Growth* (London 1972).

16 See above, Chapter 4, sections on closed systems and prediction.

17 See my 'A critique of urban modelling', *Progress in Planning*, 6 part 3 (1976), pp. 187–254.

18   These failures make a mockery of Blalock's absurd claim that
     'regression equations are the laws of science', *Causal Inferences
     in Non-experimental Research* (Chapel Hill, NC 1961), p. 384.

19   'I detect a dangerous ambiguity in our quantitative work. We do
     not distinguish carefully enough between the *testing* of hypotheses
     and the estimation of structural [*sic*] relationships. The ambigu-
     ity is rampant in economics.' P. Kenen, quoted in M. Blaug,
     The Methodology of Economics (Cambridge 1980), p. 257. (In
     our terms, 'structural' is a misnomer in the quotation.) Recall
     also the 'scrambling' effects of abstracting from space in Chapter
     4.

20   cf. J. Forrester, *Principles of Systems* (Cambridge, Mass. 1968).

21   Interestingly, many social scientists who use 'empirical models'
     believe themselves to be putting Popper's methodological prescrip-
     tions into practice! Cited in Blaug, *The Methodology of Economics*,
     p. 100. Again, the divergence from the views of economists' favoured
     philosophical mentors is striking.

22   Blaug, *The Methodology of Economics*, p. 100.

23   W. Leontief, 'Theoretical assumptions and non-observed facts',
     American Economic Review, **61** (1971), pp. 1–7.

24   See Maurice Dobb's classic critique of this inversion, 'The trend in
     modern economics', reprinted in *A Critique of Economic Theory*
     (edited by E. K. Hunt and J. G. Schwartz) (Harmondsworth 1972),
     pp. 39–82; and my 'A critique of urban modelling'.

25   ibid., pp. 256–7.

26   Perhaps the best-known discussion of this question, though hardly
     a classic, is in M. Friedman, *Essays in Positive Economics* (Chicago
     1953), but Dobb's 'The trend in modern economics' has more to
     recommend it on this subject.

27   cf. J. Robinson, *Economic Philosophy* (Harmondsworth 1962).

28   Some assumptions commonly found in praxiological models regard-
     ing time are seriously–disastrously–unrealistic. If the future were
     known so that every actor had perfect foresight, there would be
     no scope for choice!: 'if A and B have any authentic choice, then
     C and D, whose activities relate to them, cannot know *in advance*
     what they will choose, and therefore cannot know in advance
     what *they* in turn will choose to do'. A. Nove, *The Economics of
     Feasible Socialism* (London 1983), p. 39, summarizing an argument
     by Loasby.

29   Marx, *Capital*.

30   'If now our spinner, by working for one hour, can convert 1 2/3
     lbs of cotton into 1 2/3 lbs of yarn, it follows that in 6 hours he
     will convert 10 lbs of cotton into 10 lbs.', Marx, *Capital*, vol. I
     (Harmondsworth 1976), p. 297.

31   In virtue of this: 'There is, then, no necessary inner relation between the value of the total capital and the surplus value.' ibid., vol. 3, pp. 46–7.

32   Following from the confusion of derivation or calculation with explanation (see note 8), many readers of Marx have misinterpreted his value theory as an attempt to do the former rather than the latter. cf. B. Fine, *Economic Theory and Ideology* (London 1980); S. Meikle, 'Dialectical contradiction and necessity', in J. Mepham and D.-H. Ruben (eds), *Issues in Marxist Philosophy: Vol. 1, Dialectics and Method* (Hassocks 1979); and D. Elson, *Value: the Representation of Labour in Capitalism* (London 1979).

33   There are cases in physics where no non-random order has been discovered – e.g. quantum mechanics. Consequently many scientists have been tempted to suspend the usual metaphysical assumption that every event has a cause, claiming that some processes are intrinsically random. Even if this were true it would not justify a similar assumption for social processes, most of which have known causes even if in aggregate they appear random. cf. N. Georgescu-Roegen, *The Entropy Law and the Economic Process* (Cambridge, Mass. 1971).

34   That is, involving a random element.

35   See Harré's *The Principles of Scientific Thinking* for further discussions of realist views of probability.

36   'Objective' here does not mean 'true in some absolute sense' but 'pertaining to the object'. It will be recalled that the objection that knowledge of objects is 'subjective' in the sense of fallible does not mean that such objects are necessarily fictions, and hence that we cannot reasonably distinguish the existence of objects from our understanding of them.

37   Harré, *The Principles of Scientific Thinking*, p. 162.

38   Birnbaum, London 1980. Blalock comments that in statistics there is 'almost a conspiracy of silence in dealing with the problems of causality'. H. M. Blalock, *Causal Inferences in Non-experimental Research* (Chapel Hill, NC 1961), p. 38.

39   See K. Pearson, *The Grammar of Science* (London 1892).

40   Blalock, *Causal Inferences in Non-experimental Research*. At the same time, he recognizes that mathematics is acausal, e.g. p. 29.

41   In Chapter 5 I noted and inverted the orthodox view of qualitative knowledge of causal powers as a mental prop for poor logical thinkers. Here, in similar fashion, I am questioning the all-too-common use of quantitative analysis as a mental prop for poor causal thinkers.

42   cf. Harré, *The Principles of Scientific Thinking*.

43 For example, 'an experiment might consist of interviewing a housewife or recording a "yes" or "no" to a specific question'. Blalock and Blalock, *Methodology in Social Research*, p. 107n.

44 ibid. p. 56.

45 ibid. Willer and Willer's book makes some excellent criticisms of 'statistical empiricism' in social science but their arguments are unnecessarily weakened by the confused epistemology according to which theories cannot refer to real objects but merely present ways of interpreting empirical observations.

46 I suspect that texts on statistics written for natural scientists may be much better than those aimed at social scientists for showing how these questions must be considered jointly. See, for example, J. Clarke, *Statistics and Experimental Design* (London 1969), which discusses techniques in the context of types of experiment in biology. This material dimension even comes into basic definitions, e.g. distributions are defined not only mathematically but as distributively reliable (i.e. as consisting of qualitatively homogeneous individuals).

47 See R. Harré, *Social Being* (Oxford 1979), p. 133.

48 cf. P. Gould, 'Is *Statistix Inferens* the geographical name for a wild goose?', *Economic Geography*, **46** (1970), pp. 439–48, for a lively discussion of this problem in geography.

49 For further criticisms of 'variable analysis' in sociology, including the need to theorize context, see Pawson, *A Measure for Measures*. For examples of the theorization of context in industrial studies see D. B. Massey and R. A. Meegan, *Anatomy of Job Loss*, and K. Morgan and A. Sayer, *Microcircuits of Capital* (Cambridge 1988).

50 Merely noting this resonance does not, of course, amount, in itself, to a criticism. Nor am I making a *general* claim that for *any* theory (e.g. functionalism) there is a corresponding method (e.g. the survey), and vice versa. For a critique of such claims, see J. Platt, 'Functionalism and the survey: the relationship of theory and method', *Sociological Review*, **34** (1986), pp. 501–36.

51 See R. Harré and P. F. Secord, *The Explanation of Social Behaviour* (Oxford 1972).

52 This requirement, related to the principle that experiments should be replicable, makes sense as a way of reducing the risk of relying upon a single or limited number of possibly erroneous observations, but it becomes absurd when observations of distributively unreliable data are tested as replications of observations of the same phenomena. More generally, these scientific judgements appear to assume that users of qualitative methods are trying to do the same things as users of quantitative methods, i.e. estimate and generalize. See below, Chapter 9.

53 In some cases there has actually been a vogue for saying as little as possible about the objects being modelled, thereby increasing the ratio of equations to text. While some researchers may consider this practice to have a certain cachet, it might also arise from a belief in the possibility of general purpose (or 'general systems') models. See also Manicas's critical discussion of regression analyses in psychology, *A History and Philosophy of the Social Sciences*, pp. 282ff.

54 cf. note 41 above.

55 Examples from regional science are discussed in my 'A critique of urban modelling'.

56 See below, Chapter 9, on intensive research designs.

57 Compare, for instance, Paul Willis's *Learning to Labour* (Farnborough 1977), with standard 'explanations' of educational performance produced by attainment studies.

Chapter 7 Verification and falsification

1 For example, 'The building and testing of models is as important to geography as aeronautics: the test flight of a hypothesis, no less exciting, nor much less dangerous [*sic*], than a test flight of a prototype "Comet".' P. Haggett, *Locational Analysis in Human Geography* (London 1965).

2 cf. Kuhn's criticisms of the 'apodictic' view of testing reflected in the use of terms like 'mistake', 'falsification', 'refutation' (*The Structure of Scientific Revolutions* (Chicago 1970) (p. 13)). Similarly Lakatos, 'Falsification and the methodology of scientific research programmes', in I. Lakatos and A. Musgrave (eds), *Criticism and the Growth of Knowledge* (Cambridge 1970), p. 122.

3 This qualification might be made of any knowledge claim. As I argued in Chapter 2, acknowledgement of the unavoidability of this conceptual context need not lead us into a thoroughgoing relativism.

4 R. Harré, *The Principles of Scientific Thinking* (London 1970), p. 66.

5 'It is simply a mistake, arising from the preconceptions of logic and from ignorance of scientific practice, to suppose that the only knowledge sought by scientists is knowledge of regularities in observable phenomena.' ibid., p. 102.

6 ibid., p. 89.

7 A Popperian might argue that it doesn't matter if we make wildly speculative claims provided they enable testable predictions to be deduced from them. This could only be justified if we were only seeking instrumentalist theories for predicting parametric systems. If we want realist theories – i.e. ones which provide us with ways of grasping the structure of the world, the nature of its objects –

then whether new existential hypotheses contradict or comply with familiar ones matters. This is not to argue that the older existential claims are always right; indeed, sometimes they have to be changed radically and even at a metaphysical level – but hypotheses do have to be assessed in these ways if theories are to be more than mere calculating devices.

8   Harré, *The Principles of Scientific Thinking*.

9   R. Bhaaskar, *The Possibility of Naturalism* (Hassocks 1979), p. 96, n. 53.

10   Recall the example of testing the possible kinds of behaviour of building societies (p. 104).

11   The tendency to belittle the problem of conceptualization, coupled with assumptions of atomism (ontological and epistemological) and the supposition that simple statements may be tested one by one, independently of others, also support the simplistic view of testing and the commonly associated difficulty of understanding how the very ordinary activity of explanatory evaluation might be possible.

12   R. Bhaskar, *A Realist Theory of Science* (Leeds 1975), pp. 91ff.

13   W. Christaller, *Central Places in Southern Germany* (trans. C. W. Baskin) (Englewood Cliffs, NJ 1968).

14   ibid., p. 5.

15   P. Saunders, 'On the shoulders of which giant?: the case for Weberian urban political analysis', *Urban Studies Yearbook*, **1** (1983).

16   See the examples of such explanations (which would nevertheless survive a predictive test) in Chapter 5, pp. 153–5.

17   Bhaskar, *The Possibility of Naturalism*, p. 59: 'precision in meaning now assumes the place of accuracy of measurement as the *a posteriori* arbiter of theory'.

18   A. Giddens, *New Rules of Sociological Method* (London 1976), p. 59.

19   C. Geertz, *The Interpretation of Cultures* (New York 1973), p. 29.

20   See P. Willis, *Profane Culture* (London 1978): Theoretical Appendix.

21   G. E. Marcus and M. M. J. Fischer, *Anthropology as Cultural Critique* (Chicago 1986).

Chapter 8   Popper's 'falsificationism'

1   See the discussion of these versions by Lakatos, 'Falsification and the methodology of scientific research programmes', in I. Lakatos and A. Musgrave (eds), *Criticism and the Growth of Knowledge* (Cambridge 1970).

2   My criticisms of falsificationism are restricted to those interpretations which suggest the most serious consequences for realism, and vice versa.

3　Occasionally Popper acknowledges that despite the fact that this procedure of falsification is logically watertight, falsifications are often matters of degree in practice, largely because of the difficulty of identifying them.

4　'Either evidence is favourable, but useless, or evidence is unfavourable, and hence falsificatory but stultifying', R. Harré, *The Principles of Scientific Thinking* (London 1970), p. 130.

5　Popper's proposal that theories are 'prohibitions' (*Conjectures and Refutations* (London 1963), p. 36) would actually make more sense if coupled with an *acceptance* of natural necessity and allied concepts of physical possibility and impossibility.

6　Popper, ibid., p. 49: 'if we accept defeat too easily, we may prevent ourselves from finding that we were very nearly right'.

7　Personally, I think the explanatory evidence and arguments are very weak for the former, good for the latter.

8　ibid., p. 36, and see note 5, above.

9　ibid., vii.

10　See M. Blaug, *The Methodology of Economics* (Cambridge 1980).

11　J. Giedymin, 'Antipositivism in contemporary philosophy of science and humanities', *British Journal of Philosophy of Science*, **26** (1975), pp. 275–301.

12　R. Bhaskar, *The Possibility of Naturalism* (Hassocks 1979), p. 167.

Chapter 9　Problems of explanation and the aims of social science

1　H. Putnam, *Meaning and the Moral Sciences* (London 1978), p. 62.

2　'The nature of explanation depends upon the kinds of things investigated and on the exemplary cases we bring, often unconsciously, to our inquiries. Explanation, in Wittgenstein's phrase, is a family of cases, joined together only by a common aim, to make something plain or clear.' A. R. Louch, *The Explanation of Human Action* (Oxford 1966), p. 233.

3　cf. R. Bhaskar, *The Possibility of Naturalism* (Hassocks 1979), p. 167.

4　A. Giddens, *Profiles in Social Theory* (Cambridge 1982), p. 202.

5　J.-P. Sartre, *Search for a Method* (New York 1963), p. 56.

6　Williams, *Communications* (Harmondsworth 1962), p. 120. I have paraphrased Williams here in order to avoid introducing different terminology. Also I am not entirely clear that Williams would concede (at least at the time it was written) that abstract concepts can refer to real objects.

7　For critiques, see B. Jessop, *The Capitalist State* (Oxford 1982), and J. Urry, *The Anatomy of Capitalist Societies* (London 1981), and my 'Theory and empirical research in urban and regional political economy: a sympathetic critique', *University of Sussex Urban and Regional Studies Working Papers*, no. 14 (1979).

8   I owe this point to John Allen. See also the discussion below on research design.

9   This problem, coupled with the predilection for certain stereotypes of 'ordinary people', is especially common in radical interpretations of popular consciousness. It has much to do with the evident failure of the left to understand popular conservatism at the present time. 'Representativeness' *is* important: it cannot be dismissed as an 'empiricist hang-up'. See also note 23.

10 For example, Open University, DE304, *Research Methods in Social Science*. For a more balanced and thoughtful view of research design see C. Hakim, *Research Design* (London 1987).

11 R. Harré, *Social Being* (Oxford 1979), p. 132.

12 Compare S. Wallman, *Eight London Households* (London 1982).

13 Harré, *Social Being*. My account diverges from Harré's inasmuch as I do not limit intensive designs to the study of typical individuals. Harré terms studies of non-typical individuals 'ideographic'. Since the latter term was first coined (W. Windelband, 'History and natural science', *History and Theory*, **19** (1980), pp. 165–85), it has collected a number of negative associations (particularly as anti-theoretical, anti-scientific, merely intuitive and descriptive,) which I have no wish to invoke or revive.

14 R. Harré, 'Philosophical aspects of the micro-macro problem', in K. Knorr-Cetina and A. V. Cicourel (eds), *Advances in Social Theory and Methodology* (Boston 1981).

15 For fuller discussions of these arguments, see Harré, *Social Being*; M. Brenner, P. Marsh and M. Brenner (eds), *The Social Context of Method* (London 1978); A. Oakley, 'Interviewing women', in H. Roberts, *Doing Feminist Research* (London 1981); and Pawson, *A Measure for Measures*.

16 cf. P. Willis, *Profane Culture* (London 1978), Theoretical Appendix.

17 See Sack, *Conceptions of Space in Social Thought*, ch. 3.

18 A. Sayer and K. Morgan, 'A modern industry in a declining region: links between method, theory and policy', in D. Massey and R. A. Meegan (eds), *The Politics of Method* (London 1984).

19 See Morgan and Sayer, *Microcircuits of Capital*.

20 For further discussion of the question of generality see Sayer, 'Beyond the locality debate: deconstructing geography's dualisms', *Environment and Planning A*, **23** (1991), pp. 283–308.

21 In natural science, particularly where closed systems can be found or constructed, it may be possible to classify individuals taxonomically

and causally simultaneously, by reference to properties which are causally relevant in similar ways for all individuals. Statistical analysis is likely to be most effective in assisting causal explanation under such circumstances. For a research design which combines taxonomic and causal groups in social science, see J. Allen and L. McDowell's *Landlords and Property* (Cambridge 1989).

22 G. Stedman Jones, *Outcast London* (Oxford 1971).
23 I suspect that some modern historians underestimate this problem. It is one thing to rebuff criticisms which presuppose that 'objectivity' can be sought in a theory-neutral way (perhaps as 'empiricist') but quite another to disregard the problem of representativeness (or testing in the sense of replication), which has nothing to do with the issue of empiricism and theory-neutrality.
24 M. Blaug, *The Methodology of Economics* (Cambridge 1980), p. 127.
25 See heading of Chapter 1.
26 See P. Connerton (ed.), *Critical Sociology* (Harmondsworth 1976).
27 The Institute for Workers' Control Committee of Enquiry into the Motor Industry, 'A workers' enquiry into the motor industry', *Capital and Class*, 2 (1977), pp. 102–18.
28 cf. A. Oakley, 'Interviewing women'.
29 See R. Chambers's eminently readable *Rural Development: Putting the Last First* (London 1982); and J. Momsen and J. Townsend *Gender and Geography in the Third World* (London 1984). This kind of work also has the virtue of avoiding the dreadful elitism and inaccessibility of the critical theory literature.
30 A. Oakley 'Interviewing women'.

Appendix: Notes on realism, writing and the future of method in social science

1 For example, G. E. Marcus and M. M. J. Fischer, *Anthropology as Cultural Critique*; J. Clifford and G. E. Marcus (eds), *Writing Culture: The Poetics and Politics of Ethnography* (Berkeley, Calif. 1986).
2 Clifford and Marcus, ibid. p. 4.
3 H. White, *The Content of the Form* (Baltimore 1987), p. x.
4 A. J. Scott and D. P. Angel, 'The US semiconductor industry: a locational analysis', *Environment and Planning A* 19 (1987), pp. 875–912.
5 White, op. cit. p. 24.
6 P. Abrams, *Historical Sociology* (Ithaca, NY 1982), p. 162.
7 ibid. p. 196.

8   ibid. p. 307.
9   P. Ricoeur, *Hermeneutics and the Human Sciences* (Cambridge 1982).
10   ibid. p. 278.
11   ibid. p. 279.
12   H. C. Darby, 'The problem of geographical description', *Transactions of the Institute of British Geographers*, **30** (1962), pp. 1–14.
13   See Marcus and Fischer, *Anthropology as Cultural Critique*, p. 77.
14   Here I am ignoring the distinction between problems of narrative as the opposite of analysis and problems of narrative in terms of the composition of texts. See Sayer, 'The "new" regional geography and problems of narrative', *Environment and Planning: Society and Space D*, **7** (1989), pp. 253–76, for further discussion of this.
15   C. Geertz, *The Interpretation of Cultures*.
16   As we saw in Chapters 2 and 3, this is hardly a coherent use of 'theory'.
17   See especially Williams's *The Country and the City* (London 1973) and Bourdieu's *Distinction* (London 1986).
18   R. Rosaldo, 'Where objectivity lies: the rhetoric of anthropology' in J. S. Nelson *et al.* (eds), *The Rhetoric of the Human Sciences* (Madison, Wis. 1987).
19   E. P. Thompson cited in S. Cohen, *Historical Culture* (Berkeley and Los Angeles 1986).
20   The statement is all the more ironic coming from someone who regards himself as a defender of a history which is attentive to empirical evidence, against the wishful thinking of theoreticists. But then the fact that ordinary people could not get away with such a dubious assertion need not diminish the power of the rhetoric; on the contrary, it could make us trust him more – only a great historian could have a strong enough command of the facts to be able simply to assert such a thing. That he doesn't need evidence indicates its truth. Such things, written with sufficient confidence by sufficiently eminent authors, can win acceptance.
21   F. Moulaert and E. Swyngedouw, 'A regulation approach to the geography of flexible production', *Environment and Planning D: Society and Space*, **7** (1987), pp. 249–62; A. Sayer, 'Dualistic thinking and rhetoric in geography', *Area*, **21** (1989), pp. 301–5, and my 'Beyond the locality debate: deconstructing geography's dualisms', *Environment and Planning A* (1991).
22   U. Mäki, 'How to combine rhetoric and realism in the methodology of economics', *Economics and Philosophy*, **4** (1989), pp. 89–109.

Bibliography

Abel, T. (1948), 'The operation called *Verstehen*', *American Journal of Sociology*, **54**, 211–18

Abercrombie, M. L. J. (1960), *The Anatomy of Judgment*, Harmondsworth: Penguin

Abrams, P. (1982), *Historical Sociology*, Ithaca, NY: Cornell University Press

Adorno, T., *et al.* (1976), *The Positivist Dispute in German Sociology*, London: Heinemann

Allen, J. (1983), 'Property relations and landlordism: a realist approach', *Society and Space*, **1** no. 2, 191–204

Allen, J. (1983), 'In search of a method: Hegel, Marx and realism', *Radical Philosophy*, **35**, 26–33

Allen, J. and McDowell, L. (1989), *Landlords and Property*, Cambridge: Cambridge University Press

Anderson, P. (1980), *Arguments within English Marxism*, London: New Left Books

Apel, K.-O. (1972), 'Communication and the foundations of the humanities', *Acta Sociologica*, **15**, 7–27

Arthur, C. (ed.) (1974), *The German Ideology*, London: Lawrence and Wishart

Auerbach, P. (1989), *Competition: the Economics of Industrial Change*, Cambridge: Polity

Barnes, B. (1974), *Scientific Knowledge and Sociological Theory*, London: Routledge and Kegan Paul

Barnes, B. (1977), *Interests and the Growth of Knowledge*, London: Routledge and Kegan Paul

Barrett, M. (1980), *Women's Oppression Today*, London: New Left Books

Bassett, K. and Short, J. (1980), *Housing and Residential Structure: Alternative Approaches*, London: Routledge and Kegan Paul

Baynes, K., Bohman, J. and McCarthy, T. A. (eds) (1987), *After Philosophy: End or Transformation?*, Cambridge, Mass.: MIT Press

Benton, T. (1977), *Philosophical Foundations of the Three Sociologies*, London: Routledge and Kegan Paul

Berelson, B. R. and Steiner, G. A. (1964), *Human Behavior: an inventory of scientific findings*, New York: Harcourt

Berger, P. L. and Luckmann, T. (1967), *The Social Construction of Reality*, London: Allen Lane

Bernal, J. D. (1969 3rd edn), *Science in History*, Harmondsworth: Penguin

Bernstein, R. J. (1976), *The Restructuring of Social and Political Theory*, Oxford: Blackwell

Bhaskar, R. (1975), *A Realist Theory of Science*, Leeds: Leeds Books

Bhaskar, R. (1976), 'Two philosophies of science', *New Left Review*, **94**, 31–55

Bhaskar, R. (1979, 2nd edn 1989), *The Possibility of Naturalism*, Hassocks: Harvester

Bhaskar, R. (1989), *Reclaiming Reality*, London: Verso

Birnbaum, I. (1981), *An Introduction to Causal Analysis in Sociology*, London: Macmillan

Blackburn, R. (1972), *Ideology and Social Science*, London: Fontana

Blalock, H. M. (1961), *Causal Inferences in Non-experimental Research*, Chapel Hill, NC: University of North Carolina Press

Blalock, H. M. (1972), *Methods of Social Research*, New York: McGrawHill

Blalock, H. M. and Blalock, A. B. (1968), *Methodology in Social Research*, New York: McGraw-Hill

Blaug, M. (1980), *The Methodology of Economics*, Cambridge: Cambridge University Press

Blaut, J. (1972), 'Space and process', in W. K. D. Davies (ed.), *The Conceptual Revolution in Geography*, London: University of London Press, pp. 42–51

Bloch, M. (1989), *Ritual, History and Power: Selected Papers in Anthropology*, London: Athlone

Boudon, R. (1974), *The Logic of Sociological Explanation*, Harmondsworth: Penguin

Bourdieu, P. (1977), *Outline of a Theory of Practice*, Cambridge: Cambridge University Press

Bourdieu, P. (1981), 'Men and machines', in K. Knorr-Cetina and A. V. Cicourel (eds), *Advances in Social Theory and Methodology: Towards an Integration of Micro- and Macro-Sociologies*, Boston: Routledge, pp. 304–18

Bourdieu, P. (1986), *Distinction: Towards a Social Critique of the Judgement of Taste*, London: Routledge

Bourdieu, P. (1988), 'Vive la crise!: for heterodoxy in the social sciences', *Theory and Society*, **17**, 773–87

Brenner, M., Marsh, P. and Brenner, M. (1979), *The Social Context of Method*, London: Croom Helm

Campbell, D. T. (1978), 'Qualitative knowing in action research', in M. Brenner, P. Marsh and M. Brenner (eds), *The Social Context of Method*, London: Croom Helm, pp. 184–209

Castells, M. (1977), *The Urban Question*, London: Edward Arnold

Chambers, R. (1982), *Rural Development: Putting the Last First*, London: Longman

Chorley, R. J. and Haggett, P. (eds) (1967), *Models in Geography*, London: Methuen

Christaller, W. (1968), *Central Places in Southern Germany*, trans. C. W. Baskin, Englewood Cliffs, NJ: Prentice-Hall

Clarke, J. (1969), *Statistics and Experimental Design*, London: Edward Arnold

Clifford, J. and Marcus, G. E. (eds) (1986), *Writing Culture: The Poetics and Politics of Ethnography*, Berkeley, Calif.: University of California Press

Cohen, S. (ed.) (1971), *Images of Deviance*, Harmondsworth: Penguin

Cohen S. (1972), *Folk Devils and Moral Panics*, London: MacGibbon

Cohen, S. (1986), *Historical Culture*, Berkeley and Los Angeles: University of California Press

Collier, A. (1979), 'In defence of epistemology', *Radical Philosophy*, **20**, 8–21

Collier, A. (1989), *Scientific Realism and Socialist Thought*, Hemel Hempstead: Wheatsheaf

Connerton, P. (ed.) (1976), *Critical Sociology*, Harmondsworth: Penguin

Connolly, W. E. (1983), *The Terms of Political Discourse*, Oxford: Martin Robertson

Darby, H. C. (1962), 'The problem of geographical description', *Transactions of the Institute of British Geographers*, **30**, 1–14

Dobb, M. (1937), 'The trend in modern economics', reprinted in E. K. Hunt and J. G. Schwartz (eds), *A Critique of Economic Theory*, Harmondsworth: Penguin, pp. 39–82

Dobb, M. (1973), *Theories of Value and Distribution since Adam Smith*, Cambridge: Cambridge University Press

Douglas, M. (1973), *Rules and Meanings*, Harmondsworth: Penguin

Eagleton, T. (1983), *Literary Theory: An Introduction*, Oxford: Blackwell

Elson, D. (1979), *Value: the Representation of Labour in Capitalism*, London: CSE Books

Elster, J. (1978), *Logic and Society*, London: Wiley

Fay, B. (1975), *Social Theory and Political Practice*, London: George Allen and Unwin

Fine, B. (1980), *Economic Theory and Ideology*, London: Edward Arnold

Forrester, J. (1968), *Principles of Systems*, Cambridge, Mass.: Wright-Allen Press

Foucault, M. (1980), *Power/Knowledge*, Brighton: Harvester

Freeman, C., Clark, J. and Soete, L. (1982), *Unemployment and Technical Innovation: a study of long waves and economic development*, London: Frances Pinter

Friedman, M. (1953), *Essays in Positive Economics*, Chicago: University of Chicago Press

Fromm, E. (1976), *To Have or to Be*, London: Harper and Row

Geertz, C. (1973), *The Interpretation of Cultures*, New York: Basic Books

Gellner, E. (1968), 'The new idealism – cause and meaning in the social sciences', in A. Musgrave and I. Lakatos (eds), *Problems in the Philosophy of Science*, Amsterdam, and reprinted in Gellner's (1973) *Cause and Meaning in the Social Sciences* (ed. with a preface by I. C. Jarvie and J. Agassi), London: Routledge and Kegan Paul

Gellner, E. (1970), 'Concepts and Society', reprinted in B. R. Wilson (ed.), *Rationality*, Oxford: Blackwell

Gellner, E. (1987), *Culture, Identity and Politics*, Cambridge: Cambridge University Press

Georgescu-Roegen, N. (1966), *Analytical Economics*, Cambridge, Mass.: Harvard University Press

Georgescu-Roegen, N. (1971), *The Entropy Law and the Economic Process*, Cambridge, Mass.: Harvard University Press

Giddens, A. (1976), *New Rules of Sociological Method*, London: Hutchinson

Giddens, A. (1977), *Studies in Social and Political Theory*, London: Hutchinson

Giddens, A. (1979), *Central Problems in Social Theory*, London: Macmillan

Giddens, A. (1981), *A Contemporary Critique of Historical Materialism*, London: Macmillan

Giddens, A. (1982), *Profiles in Social Theory*, Cambridge: Polity

Giddens, A. (1984), *The Constitution of Society*, Cambridge: Polity

Giddens, A. (1987), *Social Theory and Modern Society*, Oxford: Blackwell

Giedymin, J. (1975), 'Antipositivism in contemporary philosophy of science and humanities', *British Journal of Philosophy of Science*, **26**, 275–301

Goffman, E. (1981), 'The presentation of self', in D. Potter *et al.*, *Society and the Social Sciences*, London: Routledge and Kegan Paul

Goldmann, L. (1969), *The Human Sciences and Philosophy*, London: Jonathan Cape

Gombrich, E. G. (1960), *Art and Illusion*, London: Phaidon

Gorz, A. (1982), *Farewell to the Working Class*, London: Pluto

Gould, P. (1970),'Is *Statistix Inferens* the geographical name for a wild goose?', *Economic Geography*, **46**, 439–48

Gregory, D. (1985), 'Suspended animation: the stasis of diffusion theory', in D. Gregory and J. Urry (eds), *Social Relations and Spatial Structure*, London: Macmillan, pp. 296–336

Gregory, D. and Urry, J. (1985), *Social Relations and Spatial Structure* London: Macmillan

Habermas, J. (1972), *Knowledge and Human Interests*, London: Heinemann

Hacking, I. (1983), *Representing and Intervening*, Cambridge: Cambridge University Press

Hägerstrand, T. (1985), 'Time-geography: focus on the corporeality of man, society, and environment', *The Science and Praxis of Complexity*, London: United Nations University

Haggett, P. (1965), *Locational Analysis in Human Geography*, London: Edward Arnold

Hakim, C. (1987), *Research Design*, London: Allen and Unwin

Hall, S. *et al.* (1978), *Policing the Crisis*, London: Macmillan

Harré, R. (1961), *Theories and Things*, London: Sheed and Ward

Harré, R. (1970), *The Principles of Scientific Thinking*, London: Macmillan

Harré, R. (1972), *The Philosophies of Science*, Oxford: Oxford University Press

Harré, R. (1979) *Social Being*, Oxford: Blackwell

Harré, R. (1981), 'Philosophical aspects of the micro–macro-problem', in K. Knorr-Cetina and A. V. Cicourel (eds), *Advances in Social Theory and Methodology: toward an integration of micro- and macro-sociologies*, Boston: Routledge pp. 139–60

Harré, R. (1986), *Varieties of Realism*, Oxford: Blackwell

Harré, R. and Madden, E. H. (1975), *Causal Powers*, Oxford: Blackwell

Harré, R. and Secord, P. F. (1972), *The Explanation of Social Behaviour*, Oxford: Blackwell

Harvey, D. (1973), *Social Justice and the City*, London: Edward Arnold

Harvey, D. (1987), 'Three myths in search of reality in urban studies', *Environment and Planning D: Society and Space*, **5**, 367–76

Harvey, D. (1989), *The Postmodern Condition*, Oxford: Blackwell

Held, D. (1980), *Introduction to Critical Theory*, London: Hutchinson

Hempel, C. (1965), *Aspects of Scientific Explanation*, New York: The Free Press

Hesse, M. (1974), *The Structure of Scientific Inference*, London: Macmillan

Hesse, M. (1980), *Revolutions and Reconstructions in the Philosophy of Science*, Hassocks: Harvester

Horkheimer, M. (1976), 'Traditional and critical theory', in P. Connerton (ed.), *Critical Sociology*, Harmondsworth: Penguin, pp. 206–24

Institute for Workers' Control (1977), 'A workers' enquiry into the motor industry', *Capital and Class*, 2, 102–18.

Irvine, J., Miles, I. and Evans, J. (eds) (1979), *Demystifying Social Statistics*, London: Pluto

Isaac, J. (1988), *Power and Marxist Theory: A Realist View*, Ithaca, NY: Cornell University Press

Jefferson, A. and Robey, D. (eds) (1986), *Modern Literary Theory: A Comparative Introduction*, London: Batsford

Jessop. B. (1982), *The Capitalist State*, Oxford: Martin Robertson

Jones, G. Stedman (1971), *Outcast London*, Oxford: Clarendon Press

Journal for the Theory of Social Behaviour (1983), **13** no. 1

Keat, R. (1979), 'Positivism and statistics in social science', in J. Irvine, I. Miles and J. Evans (eds), *Demystifying Social Statistics*, London: Pluto, pp. 75–86

Keat, R. and Urry, J. (1975, 2nd edn. 1982), *Social Theory as Science*, London: Routledge and Kegan Paul

Kornai, J. (1986), *Contradictions and Dilemmas: Studies on the Socialist Economy and Society*, Cambridge, Mass.: MIT Press

Kuhn, T. S. (1970), *The Structure of Scientific Revolutions*, Chicago: University of Chicago Press

Lackoff, G. (1987), *Women, Fire and Dangerous Things: What Categories Reveal About the Mind*, Chicago: University of Chicago Press

Lakatos, I. (1970), 'Falsification and the methodology of scientific research programmes', in I. Lakatos and A. Musgrave (eds), *Criticism and the Growth of Knowledge*, Cambridge: Cambridge University Press, pp. 91–196

Lakatos, I. and Musgrave, A. (eds) (1970), *Criticism and the Growth of Knowledge*, Cambridge: Cambridge University Press

Layder, D. (1990), *The Realist Image in Social Science*, London: Macmillan

Leontief, W. (1971), 'Theoretical assumptions and non-observed facts', *American Economic Review*, **61**, 1–7

Lichtheim, G. (1967), *The Concept of Ideology*, New York: Random House

Lipsey, R. G. (1963), *An Introduction to Positive Economics*, London: Weidenfeld and Nicolson

Lösch, A. (1954), *The Economics of Location*, New Haven, Conn.: Yale University Press

Louch, A. R. (1966), *The Explanation of Human Action*, Oxford, Blackwell

Lyons, J. (1981), *Language, Meaning and Context*, London: Fontana

Mäki, U. (1989), 'How to combine rhetoric and realism in the methodology of economics', *Economics and Philosophy*, 4, 89–109

Manicas, P. (1987), *A History and Philosophy of the Social Sciences*, Oxford: Blackwell

Marcus, G. E. and Fischer, M. M. J. (1986), *Anthropology as Cultural Critique*, Chicago: University of Chicago Press

Marx, K. (1926), *The Eighteenth Brumaire of Louis Bonaparte*, London: George Allen and Unwin

Marx, K. (1956), *The Poverty of Philosophy*, Moscow: Foreign Languages Publishing House

Marx, K. (1963), *Capital*, vols. 1, 2 and 3, London: Lawrence and Wishart

Marx, K. (1973), *Grundrisse*, Harmondsworth: Penguin

Marx, K. (1975), *Early Writings*, Harmondsworth: Penguin

Marx, K. (1976), *Capital*, vol. 1, Harmondsworth: Penguin

Massey, D. B. and Meegan, R. A. (1982), *The Anatomy of Job Loss*, London: Methuen

Mattick, P. (1986), *Social Knowledge: An Essay on the Nature and Limits of Social Science*, London: Hutchinson

Meadows, D. H. et al. (1972), *The Limits to Growth*, London: Earth Island

Meikle, S. (1979), 'Dialectical contradiction and necessity', in J. Mepham and D.-H. Ruben (eds), *Issues in Marxist Philosophy: Volume 1, Dialectics and Method*, Hassocks: Harvester

Menzies, K. (1982), *Sociological Theory in Use*, London: Routledge and Kegan Paul

Mill, J. S. (1961), *A System of Logic*, London: Longman

Momsen, J. and Townsend, J. (1984), *Gender and Geography in the Third World*, London: Hutchinson

Morgan, K. and Sayer, A. (1988), *Microcircuits of Capital: 'Sunrise' Industry and Uneven Development*, Cambridge: Polity

Moulaert, F. and Swyngedouw, E. (1989), 'A regulation approach to the geography of flexible production systems', *Environment and Planning D: Society and Space*, 7, 249–62

Nelson, J. S., Megill, A. and McCloskey, D. M. (eds) (1987), *The Rhetoric of the Human Sciences*, Madison, Wis.: University of Wisconsin Press

Nelson, R. R. (1986), 'The tension between process stories and equilibrium models: analyzing the productivity-growth slowdown of the
1970s', in R. Langlois (ed.), *Economics as a Process*, Cambridge.
Cambridge University Press, pp. 135–50.

Norman, R. (1972), 'On seeing things differently', *Radical Philosophy*,
1, 6–12

Norris, C. (1985), *The Contest of Faculties*, London: Methuen

Nove, A. (1983), *The Economics of Feasible Socialism*, London: George
Allen and Unwin

Oakley, A. (1981), 'Interviewing women: a contradiction in terms', in
H. Roberts (ed.), *Doing Feminist Research*, London: Routledge and
Kegan Paul

O'Connor, D. J. O. and Carr, B. (1982), *Introduction to the Theory of
Knowledge*, Brighton: Harvester

Open University, *DE 304 Research Methods in Social Science*, Milton
Keynes: Open University Press

Österberg, D. (1988), *Metasociology: an Inquiry into the Origins and
Validity of Social Thought*, Oslo: Norwegian University Press

Outhwaite, W. (1987), *New Philosophies of Social Science*, London:
Macmillan

Pawson, R. (1989), *A Measure for Measure: a Manifesto for Empirical
Sociology*, London: Routledge

Pearson, K. (1892), *The Grammar of Science*, London: Dent

Platt, J. (1986), 'Functionalism and the survey: the relationship of theory
and method', *Sociological Review*, **34**, 501–36

Popper, K. R. (1945), *The Open Society and its Enemies, Vols. 1 and 2*,
London: Routledge and Kegan Paul

Popper, K. R. (1957), *The Poverty of Historicism*, London: Routledge
and Kegan Paul

Popper, K. R. (1959), *The Logic of Scientific Discovery*, London:
Hutchinson

Popper, K. R. (1963), *Conjectures and Refutations*, London: Routledge
and Kegan Paul

Pratt, V. (1980), *The Philosophy of Social Science*, London: Tavistock

Putnam, H. (1978), *Meaning and the Moral Sciences*, London: Routledge
and Kegan Paul

Quine, W. V. O. (1961), *From a Logical Point of View*, Cambridge,
Mass.: Harvard University Press

Ricoeur, P. (1976), 'Restoration of meaning or reduction of illusion?',
in P. Connerton, *Critical Sociology*, Harmondsworth: Penguin, pp.
194–203

Ricoeur, P. (1982), *Hermeneutics and the Human Sciences*, Cambridge: Cambridge University Press

Robinson, J. (1962), *Economic Philosophy*, Harmondsworth: Penguin

Roemer, J. (ed.) (1986), *Analytical Marxism*, Cambridge: Cambridge University Press

Roemer, J. (1988), *Free to Lose*, London: Radius

Rorty, R. (1980), *Philosophy and the Mirror of Nature*, Oxford: Blackwell

Rosaldo, R. (1987), 'Where objectivity lies: the rhetoric of anthropology', in J. S. Nelson, A. Megill and D. M. McCloskey (eds), *The Rhetoric of the Human Sciences*, Madison, Wis.: University of Wisconsin Press, pp. 87–110

Sack. R. D. (1973), 'A concept of physical space', *Geographical Analysis*, 5, 16–34

Sack, R. D. (1980), *Conceptions of Space in Social Thought*, London: Macmillan

Sacks, O. (1986), *The Man who Mistook his Wife for a Hat*, London: Picador

Sartre, J.-P. (1963), *Search for a Method*, New York: Vintage Books

Saunders, P. (1981), *Social Theory and the Urban Question*, London: Hutchinson

Saunders, P. (1983), 'On the shoulders of which giant?: the case for Weberian urban political analysis', *Urban Studies Yearbook*, 1, 41–63

Sayer, A. (1976), 'A critique of urban modelling', *Progress in Planning*, 6 no. 3, 187–254

Sayer, A. (1979), 'Theory and empirical research in urban and regional political economy: a sympathetic critique', *University of Sussex Urban and Regional Studies Working Paper No. 14*

Sayer, A. (1979), 'Epistemology and conceptions of people and nature in geography', *Geoforum*, 10, 19–44

Sayer, A. (1981), 'Abstraction: a realist interpretation', *Radical Philosophy*, 28, 6–15

Sayer, A. (1981) 'Defensible values in geography', in R. J. Johnston and D. T. Herbert (eds), *Geography and the Urban Environment*, vol. 4, London: Wiley, pp. 29–56

Sayer, A. (1982), 'Explanation in economic geography', *Progress in Human Geography*, 6 no. 1, 68–88

Sayer, A. (1985), 'The difference that space makes', in J. Urry and D. Gregory (eds), *Social Relations and Spatial Structures*, London: Macmillan, pp. 49–66

Sayer, A. (1989), 'The "new" regional geography and problems of narrative', *Environment and Planning D: Society and Space*, 7, 253–76

Sayer, A. (1989), 'Dualistic thinking and rhetoric in geography', *Area*, 21, 301–5

Sayer, A. (1991), 'Beyond the locality debate: deconstructing geography's dualisms', *Environment and Planning A*, **23**, 283–308

Sayer, A. (1991), 'Space and social theory', in B. Wittrock and P. Wagner (eds), *Social Theory and Human Agency* Stockholm

Sayer, A. and Morgan, K. (1984), 'A modern industry in a declining region: links between method, theory and policy', in D. Massey and R. A. Meegan (eds), *The Politics of Method*, London: Methuen

Sayer, D. (1979), *Marx's Method: Science and Critique in Capital*, Hassocks: Harvester

Schmidt, A. (1971), *The Concept of Nature in Marx*, London: New Left Books

Schon, D. (1963), *Displacement of Concepts*, London: Tavistock

Scott, A. J. and Angel, D. P. (1987), 'The US semiconductor industry: a locational analysis', *Environment and Planning A*, **19**, 875–912

Shackle, G. L. S. (1967), *Time in Economics*, Amsterdam: North-Holland

Shapere, D. (1966), 'Meaning and scientific change', in R. Colodny (ed.), *Mind and Cosmos*, Pittsburgh: University of Pittsburgh Press, pp. 41–85

Skillen, T. (1979), 'Discourse fever: post marxist modes of production', *Radical Philosophy*, **20**, 3–8

Skinner, B. F. (1972), *Beyond Freedom and Dignity*, London: Jonathan Cape

Smart, B. (1976), *Sociology, Phenomenology and Marxian Analysis*, London: Routledge and Kegan Paul

Smith, N. (1987), 'Dangers of the empirical turn', *Antipode*, **19**, no. 3, 59–68

Smith, N. (1990), 'Uneven development and location theory', in R. Peet and N. Thrift (eds), *New Models in Geography, Vol. 1*, London: Allen and Unwin

Sohn-Rethel, A. (1978), *Intellectual and Manual Labour*, London: Macmillan

Soja, E. W. (1989), *Postmodern Geographies*, London: Verso

Soper, K. (1979), 'Marxism, materialism and biology', in J. Mepham and D.-H. Ruben (eds), *Issues in Marxist Philosophy*, vol. 2, Hassocks: Harvester

Storper, M. and Walker, R. A. (1989), *The Capitalist Imperative*, Oxford: Blackwell

Taylor, C. (1967), 'Neutrality in political science', in A. Ryan (ed.) (1973), *The Philosophy of Social Explanation*, Oxford: Oxford University Press, pp. 139–70

Taylor, C. (1971), 'Interpretation and the science of man', *Review of Metaphysics*, **25**, and reprinted in P. Connerton (ed.) (1976), *Critical*

Sociology, Harmondsworth: Penguin, pp. 3–51

Taylor, C. (1987), 'Overcoming epistemology', in K. Baynes, J. Bohman and P. A. McCarthy (eds), *After Philosophy: End or Transformation?*, Cambridge, Mass.: MIT Press

Thompson, E. P. (1979), *The Poverty of Theory*, London: Merlin

Thrift, N. (1983), 'On the determination of social action in space and time', *Society and Space*, **1**, 23–57

Urry, J. (1981), *The Anatomy of Capitalist Societies*, London: Macmillan

Urry, J. (1987), 'Society, space and locality', *Environment and Planning D: Society and Space*, **5**, 4, 435–44

Walby, S. (1986), *Patriarchy at Work*, Cambridge: Polity

Wallman, S. (1982), *Eight London Households*, London: Tavistock

Warde, A. (1989), 'Recipes for a pudding: a comment on locality', *Antipode*, **21**, 274–81

Wellmer, A. (1972), *Critical Theory of Society*, Berlin: Herder and Herder

White, H. (1987), *The Content of the Form*, Baltimore: Johns Hopkins University Press

Willer, D. and Willer, J. (1973), *Systematic Empiricism: a critique of pseudoscience*, Englewood Cliffs, NJ: Prentice-Hall

Williams, R. (1958), *Culture and Society*, Harmondsworth: Penguin

Williams, R. (1961), *The Long Revolution*, Harmondsworth: Penguin

Williams, R. (1962), *Communications*, Harmondsworth: Penguin

Williams, R. (1973), *The Country and the City*, London: Chatto and Windus

Williams, R. (1976), *Keywords*, London: Fontana

Williams, R. (1977), *Marxism and Literature*, Oxford: Oxford University Press

Williams, R. (1982), 'Parliamentary democracy', *Marxism Today*, **26** no. 6, 14–21

Willis, P. (1977), *Learning to Labour*, Farnborough: Gower Press

Willis, P. (1978), *Profane Culture*, London: Routledge and Kegan Paul

Winch, P. (1958), *The Idea of Social Science*, London: Routledge and Kegan Paul

Windelband, W. (1980), 'History and natural science', *History and Theory*, **19**, 165–85

Wittgenstein, L. (1922), *Tractatus Logico-Philosophocus*, London: Kegan Paul

Wright, G. H. von (1971), *Explanation and Understanding*, London: Routledge and Kegan Paul

Zeleny, J. (1980), *The Logic of Marx*, Oxford: Blackwell

Index

An environmentally friendly book printed and bound in England by www.printondemand-worldwide.com

#0006 - 280515 - C0 - 216/138/18 [20] - CB - 9780415582476